Mastering the Markets: Advanced Trading Strategies for Success and Ethical Trading Practices

Alex Thompson

Published by Side Hustle Success, 2023.

MASTERING THE MARKETS: ADVANCED TRADING STRATEGIES FOR SUCCESS AND ETHICAL TRADING PRACTICES

First edition. June 8, 2023.

ISBN: 979-8223053798

Written by Alex Thompson.

Table of Contents

Chapter 1: Stock Market Investing

Introduction: In this chapter, we will delve into the world of stock market investing. We'll explore the fundamental concepts, benefits, and risks associated with investing in the stock market. Whether you are a beginner looking to start investing or an experienced investor seeking to enhance your knowledge, this chapter will provide you with a solid foundation in stock market investing.

1.1 What is the Stock Market?

The stock market is a centralized marketplace where buyers and sellers trade financial instruments known as stocks or shares. It plays a vital role in the economy by facilitating the flow of capital between individuals, businesses, and governments. The stock market provides a platform for companies to raise funds for expansion and investment by selling shares to investors. In return, investors become partial owners of the company and have the potential to benefit from its growth and profitability.

Stock exchanges are organized platforms where the buying and selling of stocks take place. They serve as intermediaries between buyers and sellers, ensuring fair and transparent transactions. Stock exchanges provide a regulated environment where investors can trade shares of publicly listed companies. Some of the well-known stock exchanges include the New York Stock Exchange (NYSE), Nasdaq, London Stock Exchange (LSE), and Tokyo Stock Exchange (TSE).

The functions of stock exchanges include:

Listing and Delisting: Stock exchanges provide a mechanism for companies to list their shares, allowing them to become publicly traded. This process involves meeting certain regulatory requirements and complying with disclosure obligations. Stock exchanges also have the authority to delist companies that fail to meet the listing criteria.

Price Discovery: Stock exchanges facilitate price discovery by matching buyers and sellers based on their willingness to buy or sell at a particular price. Through the continuous buying and selling activity, stock prices are determined based on supply and demand dynamics.

Liquidity: Stock exchanges provide liquidity to investors by creating a marketplace where shares can be bought and sold easily. This allows investors to convert their investments into cash quickly, promoting market efficiency and reducing the risk of illiquidity.

Transparency and Regulation: Stock exchanges enforce rules and regulations to ensure fair and transparent trading practices. They monitor market activities, enforce compliance with listing standards, and investigate any irregularities or market manipulation.

Publicly traded companies are businesses that have issued shares of stock to the public and are listed on a stock exchange. By going public, these companies can access capital from a broad range of investors. When a company issues shares, it divides its ownership into smaller portions called shares or stocks. Investors who purchase these shares become shareholders and have certain rights, such as voting rights and the right to receive dividends.

Shares represent ownership in a company and can be bought and sold on the stock market. Share prices fluctuate based on factors such as company performance, industry trends, economic conditions, and investor sentiment. Investors can make profits by buying shares at a lower price and selling them at a higher price, or by receiving dividends paid by the company.

Investing in publicly traded companies offers individuals the opportunity to participate in the growth of successful businesses and potentially earn returns on their investments. It also provides companies with a means to raise capital, expand their operations, and fuel economic growth.

1.2 Why Invest in the Stock Market?

Potential for Long-Term Capital Appreciation: Investing in stocks offers the potential for long-term capital appreciation. Over time, well-performing companies can experience growth in their share prices, leading to an increase in the value of the investor's holdings. By carefully selecting stocks of companies with strong fundamentals and growth prospects, investors can benefit from the appreciation in stock prices over the long term.

Dividend Income and Reinvestment Opportunities: Many publicly traded companies distribute a portion of their profits to shareholders in the form of dividends. Dividends represent a share of the company's earnings and can provide a steady stream of income to investors. Additionally, investors have the option to reinvest the dividends by purchasing more shares, which can further enhance long-term wealth accumulation through compounding.

Benefits of Stock Ownership, including Ownership Rights and Voting Privileges: As a shareholder, owning stocks grants you certain rights and privileges. These include the right to receive company disclosures, attend shareholder meetings, and vote on important company matters such as the election of board members or approving significant corporate actions. Stock ownership provides investors with a voice and the opportunity to influence the direction of the company.

Historical Returns of the Stock Market Compared to Other Asset Classes: Historically, the stock market has demonstrated strong long-term returns compared to other asset classes like bonds or cash. While short-term fluctuations and market volatility are inevitable, investing in a diversified portfolio of stocks has the potential to generate higher returns over extended periods. It's important to note that past performance does not guarantee future results, and investors should assess their risk tolerance and investment goals before allocating funds to the stock market.

It's worth mentioning that stock market returns can vary significantly depending on factors such as the overall economic conditions, market cycles, and individual company performance. Conducting thorough research, diversifying investments, and having a long-term perspective are essential when investing in the stock market. Furthermore, seeking advice from financial professionals or conducting a comprehensive analysis of historical data can provide valuable insights into the historical performance of the stock market and its potential compared to other asset classes.

1.3 Key Participants in the Stock Market

Investors: Investors in the stock market can be individuals, institutional investors, or a combination of both. Individual investors are individuals who buy and sell stocks for their personal investment portfolios. They may range from small retail investors to high net worth individuals. Institutional investors, on the other hand, are organizations that invest on behalf of others, such as pension funds, mutual funds, insurance companies, and hedge funds. Institutional investors often have substantial financial resources and can influence market trends due to their large trading volumes.

Types of Investment Strategies: Investors employ various investment strategies when participating in the stock market. Some common strategies include:

Value Investing: Seeking undervalued stocks based on fundamental analysis, focusing on companies with solid financials and growth potential.

Growth Investing: Investing in companies with high growth potential, even if their valuations may be relatively higher compared to their current earnings.

Dividend Investing: Focusing on stocks that provide regular dividend payments, often targeting companies with stable cash flows and a track record of dividend growth.

Index Investing: Investing in index funds or exchange-traded funds (ETFs) that track a specific stock market index, aiming to replicate the performance of the overall market.

Momentum Investing: Capitalizing on short-term price trends and market momentum, buying stocks that have shown recent positive price movements and selling those with negative price movements.

Stockbrokers: Stockbrokers are intermediaries between investors and the stock market. They facilitate the buying and selling of stocks on behalf of their clients. Stockbrokers provide various services, including:

Trade Execution: Executing buy and sell orders on behalf of clients, ensuring timely and accurate transactions.

Investment Advice: Providing guidance and recommendations on investment opportunities, portfolio management, and investment strategies.

Research and Analysis: Supplying research reports, market analysis, and company-specific information to assist investors in making informed investment decisions.

Account Management: Managing client accounts, including record-keeping, handling administrative tasks, and facilitating financial transactions.

Market Makers: Market makers play a crucial role in maintaining liquidity and facilitating price discovery in the stock market. They are typically brokerage firms or financial institutions that quote both buy and sell prices for specific stocks. Market makers ensure there is a continuous supply of buy and sell orders in the market by standing ready to buy or sell shares at any time. This activity creates liquidity and helps ensure efficient trading. Market makers make money through the difference between the buying and selling prices, known as the bid-ask spread.

Regulators: Regulators oversee the operations of the stock market and enforce rules and regulations to ensure fair and orderly markets. They aim to protect investors, maintain market integrity, and promote transparency. Regulators set standards for market participants, monitor compliance with trading rules, investigate potential market abuses or manipulations, and impose penalties for violations. Examples of regulatory bodies include the Securities and Exchange Commission (SEC) in the United States, the Financial Conduct Authority (FCA) in the United Kingdom, and the Securities and Exchange Board of India (SEBI).

1.4 Types of Stocks

Common Stocks:

Ownership and Voting Rights: Common stock represents ownership in a company and grants shareholders voting rights in corporate matters. Shareholders typically have the right to elect the company's board of directors and vote on important decisions, such as mergers, acquisitions, and changes to the company's bylaws.

Dividends: Common stockholders may receive dividends, which are a portion of the company's profits distributed to shareholders. Dividends are not guaranteed and are at the discretion of the company's management and board of directors.

Capital Gains: Common stocks offer the potential for capital gains. Investors can profit from an increase in the stock's price by selling their shares at a higher price than their initial purchase price.

Preferred Stocks:

Characteristics and Benefits: Preferred stock represents ownership in a company but generally does not come with voting rights. Preferred stockholders have a higher claim on a company's assets and earnings compared to common stockholders. They are entitled to receive dividends before common stockholders and have priority in the event of liquidation. Preferred stocks often offer a fixed dividend rate, providing a steady income stream to investors.

Growth Stocks:

Companies with High Growth Potential: Growth stocks are shares of companies that are expected to experience significant growth in their earnings and revenue. These companies often operate in industries with high growth potential, such as technology, biotechnology, or emerging markets. Investors in growth stocks focus on capital appreciation, as these stocks may not pay substantial dividends. Growth stocks can be more volatile than other types of stocks due to higher expectations and market sentiment.

Value Stocks:

Undervalued Companies with Growth Potential: Value stocks are shares of companies that are considered to be trading at a lower price relative to their intrinsic value. Investors in value stocks seek opportunities where the market has undervalued a company, potentially due to temporary setbacks or market pessimism. Value stocks often have lower price-to-earnings ratios and may pay dividends. Investors in value stocks aim for capital appreciation as the market recognizes the company's true value over time.

Blue-Chip Stocks:

Well-Established, Financially Stable Companies: Blue-chip stocks are shares of large, well-established companies with a history of stable earnings, strong financials, and a solid reputation. These companies are leaders in their industries, have a track record of reliable performance, and are considered financially stable. Blue-chip stocks are often considered less volatile and are favored by conservative investors seeking more stable investment options.

Small-Cap, Mid-Cap, and Large-Cap Stocks:

Understanding Market Capitalization: Market capitalization refers to the total value of a company's outstanding shares. Stocks are typically categorized into different market capitalization segments:

Small-Cap Stocks: Companies with smaller market capitalizations, usually ranging from a few hundred million to a couple of billion dollars.

Mid-Cap Stocks: Companies with medium-sized market capitalizations, generally ranging from a few billion to tens of billions of dollars.

Large-Cap Stocks: Companies with larger market capitalizations, often exceeding tens or hundreds of billions of dollars. Market capitalization provides a way to gauge the size and relative stability of a company. Small-cap stocks are often associated with higher growth potential but higher risk, while large-cap stocks are generally considered more stable but may have slower growth prospects.

Understanding these different types of stocks allows investors to diversify their portfolios and align their investment strategies with their risk tolerance and investment objectives.

1.5 Risks Associated with Stock Market Investing

Market Risk: Market risk refers to the potential for fluctuations in stock prices due to overall market conditions. It is influenced by factors such as economic trends, interest rates, geopolitical events, and investor sentiment. Market risk affects all stocks and is often measured by the performance of broader market indices, such as the S&P 500 or the Dow Jones Industrial Average. When market conditions are unfavorable, stock prices can decline, resulting in potential losses for investors.

Company-Specific Risk: Company-specific risk, also known as unsystematic risk, pertains to risks that are specific to individual companies or industries. These risks can arise from factors such as poor management decisions, competitive pressures, technological disruptions, legal or regulatory issues, or changes in consumer demand. Unlike market risk, company-specific risk can be mitigated through diversification. By investing in a variety of stocks across different industries, investors can reduce their exposure to the risks associated with any single company.

Liquidity Risk: Liquidity risk refers to the risk of not being able to buy or sell stocks at desired prices due to a lack of market participants or trading volume. Stocks with low liquidity may have wider bid-ask spreads, making it more challenging to execute trades at favorable prices. Liquidity risk is more pronounced for small-cap stocks or stocks of companies with low trading volumes. Investors should consider liquidity risk when investing in stocks, particularly if they anticipate the need to enter or exit positions quickly.

Volatility Risk: Volatility risk is the potential for significant price swings in the stock market. Stocks with higher volatility are prone to larger price fluctuations, which can result in increased investment gains or losses. Volatility is influenced by factors such as market sentiment, economic indicators, company news, or unexpected events. Investors who are risk-averse may prefer stocks with lower volatility, while those seeking higher returns may be willing to accept higher levels of volatility.

Systemic Risk: Systemic risk refers to the risk of a broader economic or financial crisis impacting the stock market as a whole. It arises from factors that can affect multiple sectors and companies simultaneously, such as economic recessions, financial market disruptions, or geopolitical shocks. Systemic risk is difficult to diversify away since it affects the overall market. Mitigating systemic risk often requires a comprehensive understanding of macroeconomic factors and diversification across different asset classes, such as bonds, real estate, or commodities.

Investors should be aware of these different types of risks and incorporate risk management strategies into their investment approach. Diversification, careful analysis of individual companies, monitoring market conditions, and setting appropriate risk tolerance levels can help investors navigate the various risks associated with investing in the stock market.

1.6 Investment Strategies for Stock Market Investing

Long-Term Investing: Long-term investing involves holding investments for an extended period, typically several years or more, with the goal of benefiting from the potential growth and compounding of returns over time. This strategy is often associated with a buy-and-hold approach, where investors select fundamentally strong assets and maintain their positions despite short-term market fluctuations. Some benefits of long-term investing include:

Potential for Higher Returns: Long-term investing allows investors to participate in the overall growth of the market and benefit from the power of compounding. Over longer periods, stocks have historically provided higher returns compared to other asset classes, such as bonds or cash.

Reduced Transaction Costs: By holding investments for the long term, investors can minimize transaction costs associated with frequent buying and selling of securities. This can lead to greater net returns over time.

Lower Tax Impact: Long-term capital gains taxes generally have a more favorable tax rate compared to short-term capital gains. Holding investments for the long term can provide tax advantages, allowing investors to keep a larger portion of their investment gains.

Value Investing: Value investing involves seeking undervalued stocks based on fundamental analysis. Value investors look for companies that appear to be trading below their intrinsic value, often due to temporary market inefficiencies, negative sentiment, or overlooked opportunities. Key principles of value investing include:

Fundamental Analysis: Value investors analyze a company's financial statements, earnings, cash flows, and other relevant factors to determine its intrinsic value. They look for companies with strong fundamentals, such as low price-to-earnings (P/E) ratios, favorable price-to-book (P/B) ratios, and solid growth prospects.

Margin of Safety: Value investors aim to buy stocks with a margin of safety, meaning they purchase shares at prices significantly below their estimated intrinsic value. This approach seeks to protect against downside risk and provides potential for capital appreciation as the market recognizes the stock's true value.

Growth Investing: Growth investing involves identifying companies with strong growth potential. Growth investors focus on companies that demonstrate above-average earnings growth rates, innovative business models, expanding market share, and the potential for substantial future earnings. Key characteristics of growth investing include:

Focus on Future Potential: Growth investors prioritize a company's future earnings and growth prospects over its current valuation metrics. They seek out companies in industries with high growth potential, such as technology, healthcare, or emerging markets.

Higher Valuations: Growth stocks often trade at higher price-to-earnings (P/E) ratios compared to value stocks, reflecting the market's optimism about their growth potential. Investors in growth stocks expect that the company's earnings will grow at a faster rate, justifying the premium valuation.

Dividend Investing: Dividend investing involves focusing on stocks that consistently pay dividends. Dividend investors seek companies with a track record of stable or growing dividend payments. Key features of dividend investing include:

Income Generation: Dividend stocks provide investors with a regular income stream in the form of dividend payments. These dividends can be reinvested or used as a source of passive income.

Dividend Stability: Dividend investors typically look for companies with a history of consistent dividend payments and strong financials. They assess dividend payout ratios, dividend growth rates, and the company's ability to sustain and increase dividend payments over time.

Index Investing: Index investing involves investing in broad market indices, such as the S&P 500 or the Dow Jones Industrial Average, through index funds or exchange-traded funds (ETFs). Key characteristics of index investing include:

Market Diversification: Index investing provides instant diversification across a wide range of stocks within the index, reducing the impact of individual stock performance on the overall portfolio. Investors gain exposure to the overall market performance.

Cost Efficiency: Index funds and ETFs generally have lower expense ratios compared to actively managed funds. This cost advantage can help improve long-term investment returns.

Index investing can be suitable for investors seeking a passive investment approach and who believe in the long-term growth of the overall market. It offers simplicity, diversification, and the ability to capture the performance of the broader market.

1.7 Opening an Investment Account

Choosing a brokerage firm or online trading platform: When selecting a brokerage firm or online trading platform, consider the following factors:

Reputation and Reliability: Research the reputation and track record of the brokerage firm or platform. Look for well-established firms with a solid reputation for reliability, security, and customer support.

Fees and Commissions: Compare the fees and commissions charged by different brokerage firms. Consider transaction fees, account maintenance fees, and any other charges that may apply. Look for a platform that offers competitive pricing and aligns with your investment strategy.

Trading Tools and Platform Features: Evaluate the trading tools, research resources, and platform features provided by the brokerage firm. Consider whether they offer real-time market data, charting tools, educational resources, and access to various investment products and markets.

User Experience: Consider the user experience and interface of the trading platform. A user-friendly platform can make it easier to execute trades, monitor investments, and access relevant information.

Customer Support: Assess the quality and availability of customer support services offered by the brokerage firm. Look for platforms that provide prompt and reliable customer support through various channels, such as phone, email, or live chat.

Types of Investment Accounts: There are several types of investment accounts available to investors:

Individual Account: An individual account is opened and owned by a single individual. It offers flexibility and allows the account owner to make investment decisions independently.

Joint Account: A joint account is opened and owned by two or more individuals. It enables multiple account owners to invest together and share the benefits and responsibilities of the account.

Retirement Accounts:

Traditional IRA (Individual Retirement Account): Contributions to a traditional IRA may be tax-deductible, and earnings grow tax-deferred until withdrawal, at which point they are subject to taxation.

Roth IRA: Contributions to a Roth IRA are made with after-tax money, and qualified withdrawals, including earnings, are tax-free in retirement.

401(k) or Employer-Sponsored Retirement Plan: Offered by employers, these retirement accounts allow employees to contribute a portion of their salary on a pre-tax basis, and earnings grow tax-deferred until withdrawal.

Custodial Account: A custodial account is established for the benefit of a minor, with an adult acting as the custodian. The custodian manages the account until the minor reaches the age of majority.

Account Setup Process and Required Documentation: The account setup process and required documentation may vary among brokerage firms, but generally, you can expect the following steps:

Choose a brokerage firm: Research and select a brokerage firm that aligns with your needs and preferences.

Complete the application: Fill out the account application form provided by the brokerage firm. This form typically requires personal information, such as your name, address, social security number, employment details, and investment objectives.

Submit identification documents: Provide identification documents to comply with anti-money laundering and know-your-customer regulations. This may include a copy of your driver's license or passport and proof of address, such as a utility bill or bank statement.

Funding the account: Once your account is approved, you will need to fund it by depositing money or transferring assets from another account.

Review and sign agreements: Read and understand the terms and conditions, account agreements, and any other legal documents provided by the brokerage firm. Sign the necessary agreements to open the account.

It's important to note that brokerage firms may have specific requirements or additional steps, so it's advisable to consult the firm's website or contact their customer support for detailed instructions on the account setup process and documentation needed.

1.8 Developing an Investment Plan

Setting Financial Goals and Investment Objectives: Financial goals and investment objectives provide a framework for your investment strategy. Consider the following steps:

Identify Your Goals: Determine your short-term and long-term financial goals, such as saving for retirement, buying a house, funding education, or achieving financial independence. Each goal should have a specific target amount and time frame.

Quantify Your Goals: Assign a monetary value to each goal and prioritize them based on importance and urgency. This will help you determine how much you need to save and invest to reach each goal.

Define Your Investment Objectives: Based on your goals, set investment objectives that align with your risk tolerance, time horizon, and desired returns. Common investment objectives include capital preservation, income generation, capital appreciation, or a combination of these.

Determining Risk Tolerance and Time Horizon: Risk tolerance and time horizon are crucial factors in determining your investment strategy. Consider the following:

Risk Tolerance: Assess your risk tolerance by considering your ability to tolerate market fluctuations and potential investment losses. Factors such as age, financial obligations, income stability, and investment experience can influence your risk tolerance. Risk tolerance can range from conservative (preferring lower-risk investments) to aggressive (comfortable with higher-risk investments).

Time Horizon: Determine your investment time horizon, which refers to the length of time you plan to invest before needing the funds. Longer time horizons generally allow for more aggressive investment strategies and greater exposure to potential market fluctuations.

Asset Allocation: Balancing Stocks with Other Investment Classes: Asset allocation involves determining the percentage of your investment portfolio allocated to different asset classes, such as stocks, bonds, cash, and alternative investments. Here are some considerations for asset allocation:

Diversification: Allocate your investments across different asset classes to reduce risk. Stocks have historically provided higher returns but come with greater volatility, while bonds offer lower returns but are generally more stable. Consider your risk tolerance, investment objectives, and market conditions when determining the appropriate mix of asset classes.

Risk-Return Tradeoff: Generally, stocks have higher return potential but also higher volatility, while bonds offer more stability but lower returns. Adjust your asset allocation based on your risk tolerance and desired level of potential returns.

Rebalancing: Regularly review and rebalance your portfolio to maintain your desired asset allocation. Market fluctuations can cause your portfolio to deviate from your target allocation, and rebalancing ensures that your investments remain aligned with your investment objectives.

Portfolio Diversification and Risk Management Strategies: Diversification is a risk management strategy that involves spreading investments across different securities, industries, and geographic regions. Consider the following:

Spread Investments: Allocate your investments across various stocks, sectors, and geographic regions to reduce the impact of individual security or market sector performance on your portfolio. Diversification can help mitigate company-specific risks and minimize losses from underperforming assets.

Asset Class Diversification: Diversify across asset classes, including stocks, bonds, cash, and alternative investments. Each asset class behaves differently under different market conditions, which can help balance your portfolio's risk and potential return.

Risk Management: Implement risk management strategies such as setting stop-loss orders, using trailing stops, or employing hedging strategies to protect your portfolio against significant losses. Regularly monitor your portfolio and stay informed about market trends and news that may impact your investments.

Remember, asset allocation, diversification, and risk management strategies should align with your risk tolerance, investment objectives, and time horizon. It's advisable to regularly review your portfolio and consult with a financial advisor to ensure your investment strategy remains suitable for your goals and circumstances.

Chapter 2: Understanding Stock Market Basics

Introduction: In this chapter, we will build upon the foundation laid in Chapter 1 by diving deeper into the essential concepts and components of the stock market. Understanding these basics will help you navigate the stock market with confidence and make informed investment decisions.

2.1 Stock Market Indices:

Definition and Purpose of Stock Market Indices: Stock market indices are statistical measures that represent the performance of a specific group of stocks or the overall stock market. They provide a snapshot of the collective performance of the underlying stocks and serve as benchmarks for evaluating market trends, investment performance, and portfolio returns. Stock market indices are widely used by investors, financial professionals, and researchers to track and compare the performance of various market segments.

Popular Stock Market Indices:

S&P 500: The Standard & Poor's 500 Index (S&P 500) is a widely followed U.S. stock market index that tracks the performance of 500 large-cap companies listed on U.S. stock exchanges. It represents approximately 80% of the total market capitalization of U.S. equities.

Dow Jones Industrial Average (DJIA): The Dow Jones Industrial Average, often referred to as the Dow, is one of the oldest and most recognized stock market indices. It tracks the performance of 30 large, publicly traded companies across various industries, providing a snapshot of the U.S. stock market's overall health.

Nasdaq Composite: The Nasdaq Composite Index includes more than 3,000 stocks listed on the Nasdaq stock exchange. It is known for its high representation of technology and growth-oriented companies.

Calculation Methods and Weighting Schemes: Stock market indices are calculated using different methods and weighting schemes, depending on the index provider and the specific index. The two commonly used methods are:

Price-weighted Index: In a price-weighted index, the stocks are weighted based on their individual share prices. Stocks with higher share prices have a greater impact on the index's value. The Dow Jones Industrial Average is an example of a price-weighted index.

Market-cap Weighted Index: In a market-cap weighted index, the stocks are weighted based on their market capitalization, which is calculated by multiplying the stock's price by the number of shares outstanding. Stocks with higher market capitalizations have a larger influence on the index's value. The S&P 500 and Nasdaq Composite are examples of market-cap weighted indices.

Using Indices as Benchmarks: Stock market indices serve as benchmarks for evaluating the performance of investment portfolios. Investors compare the returns of their portfolios to the performance of relevant indices to assess how well their investments have performed. Key uses of indices as benchmarks include:

Performance Evaluation: Investors compare their portfolio returns against the performance of a relevant index to gauge the success of their investment strategy. Positive returns that outperform the index indicate successful performance.

Investment Strategy Assessment: Investors use indices to evaluate the effectiveness of their investment strategy. They analyze whether their portfolio's asset allocation and stock selection decisions have resulted in returns that outperform or underperform the benchmark index.

Index Fund Performance: Index funds, which aim to replicate the performance of a specific index, are evaluated based on their ability to closely match the returns of the benchmark index. Tracking error, which measures the deviation of the fund's returns from the index's returns, is commonly assessed.

It's important to note that while indices provide a useful reference for evaluating portfolio performance, individual investor goals, risk tolerance, and investment time horizons should also be considered when assessing investment outcomes.

2.2 Stock Exchanges:

Overview of Major Stock Exchanges Worldwide:

New York Stock Exchange (NYSE): The NYSE is the largest stock exchange in the world based on market capitalization. It is located on Wall Street in New York City and lists many prominent U.S. companies.

NASDAQ: NASDAQ is the world's second-largest stock exchange and is known for its high-tech and growth-oriented companies. It operates an electronic trading platform and is home to many technology giants.

London Stock Exchange (LSE): The LSE is one of the oldest and largest stock exchanges globally. It operates the Main Market for trading large-cap companies and the AIM (Alternative Investment Market) for smaller, growth-oriented companies.

Tokyo Stock Exchange (TSE): The TSE is the largest stock exchange in Japan and one of the world's largest in terms of market capitalization. It plays a significant role in the Asian financial market.

Shanghai Stock Exchange (SSE): The SSE is the largest stock exchange in China, providing a platform for trading domestic Chinese stocks. It operates the Main Board and the STAR Market for technology-oriented companies.

Listing Requirements for Companies: To be traded on an exchange, companies must meet specific listing requirements set by the exchange. The requirements generally include:

Financial Performance: Companies need to meet minimum financial criteria, such as revenue, profitability, and minimum market capitalization.

Corporate Governance: Companies must adhere to certain standards of corporate governance, including board composition, independent directors, and financial reporting practices.

Public Float: A minimum percentage of the company's shares needs to be available for trading by the public.

Regulatory Compliance: Companies must comply with the exchange's regulatory and reporting requirements, including disclosure of financial statements and timely filing of reports.

Trading Mechanisms and Trading Sessions:

Pre-Market Trading: Some exchanges offer pre-market trading sessions, allowing investors to trade stocks before the regular market opens. Pre-market trading typically occurs with lower trading volumes and limited liquidity.

Regular Market Trading: This is the main trading session during regular market hours. It is when the majority of trading activity takes place, and bid and ask prices are continuously matched to facilitate transactions.

After-Hours Trading: After-hours trading enables investors to trade stocks outside of regular market hours. It provides extended trading opportunities but typically has lower liquidity and wider bid-ask spreads compared to regular market hours.

Understanding Bid and Ask Prices, Order Types, and Order Execution:

Bid and Ask Prices: The bid price is the highest price at which buyers are willing to purchase a stock, while the ask price is the lowest price at which sellers are willing to sell the stock. The difference between the bid and ask prices is called the spread.

Order Types: Investors can place different types of orders to buy or sell stocks. Common order types include market orders, limit orders, stop orders, and stop-limit orders. Each order type has specific instructions on price execution and order duration.

Order Execution: When an investor places an order, it is executed by matching it with a counterparty's order. Exchanges use electronic trading systems to match buyers and sellers based on price and order priority. The order is executed when the bid and ask prices match, and the trade is recorded.

It's important for investors to understand the trading mechanisms, order types, and order execution process to make informed trading decisions and manage their investment strategies effectively. It's advisable to familiarize yourself with the specific rules and regulations of the exchange and consult with a financial professional if needed.

2.3 Market Orders and Limit Orders:

Difference between Market Orders and Limit Orders:

Market Order: A market order is an order to buy or sell a security at the current market price. When a market order is placed, it is executed immediately at the best available price in the market. The execution of a market order is prioritized over the price at which the trade is executed.

Limit Order: A limit order is an order to buy or sell a security at a specified price or better. When a limit order is placed, it is only executed if the market price reaches or exceeds the specified limit price. The execution of a limit order is prioritized based on the specified price, rather than immediate execution.

Benefits and Considerations of Market Orders:

Benefits: Market orders provide fast execution and ensure that the order is filled. They are suitable for highly liquid stocks or situations where immediate execution is more important than the specific price.

Considerations: Market orders may be subject to price slippage, where the execution price differs from the expected price due to market volatility or liquidity. They carry a higher risk of not getting the desired price.

Benefits and Considerations of Limit Orders:

Benefits: Limit orders provide control over the execution price. They allow investors to set specific price targets and potentially get better prices than the current market price. They are suitable for investors who prioritize price over immediate execution.

Considerations: Limit orders may not be executed if the market does not reach the specified limit price. There is a possibility of the order not being filled if the market moves away from the specified limit price. It requires monitoring of market movements to ensure timely execution.

Stop Orders and Stop-Limit Orders for Risk Management and Trade Execution:

Stop Order: A stop order becomes a market order when the market price reaches a specified stop price. It is typically used to manage potential losses or protect profits. A stop order to sell is placed below the current market price, while a stop order to buy is placed above the current market price.

Stop-Limit Order: A stop-limit order combines elements of a stop order and a limit order. It includes a stop price and a limit price. When the market price reaches the stop price, the order becomes a limit order, and it is executed at the specified limit price or better.

Benefits and Considerations of Stop Orders and Stop-Limit Orders:

Benefits: Stop orders and stop-limit orders are used for risk management and trade execution. They allow investors to set predefined exit points or entry points based on market movements. They can help protect profits or limit losses.

Considerations: Stop orders and stop-limit orders are not guaranteed to be executed at the specified price. In volatile market conditions, the execution price may deviate from the stop or limit price. It's important to consider the potential for price slippage and monitor the market closely.

Understanding the differences and considerations of market orders, limit orders, stop orders, and stop-limit orders is crucial for investors to effectively manage their trades, control risk, and achieve desired execution outcomes. The choice of order type depends on individual trading goals, market conditions, and risk tolerance.

2.4 Stock Market Data:

Types of Stock Market Data Available:

Real-time Data: Real-time data provides immediate and up-to-date information on stock prices, volume, and other market-related data. It reflects the most current market conditions and is commonly used by active traders and investors who require timely information for decision-making.

Delayed Data: Delayed data refers to stock market information that is delayed by a certain period, typically 15 to 20 minutes. It is usually available for free on financial websites or through brokerage platforms. Delayed data is used by investors who do not require real-time information or for informational purposes.

Historical Data: Historical data includes past stock market information, such as price movements, trading volume, and other relevant data over a specified period. It is used for analysis, backtesting trading strategies, and identifying patterns or trends in the market.

Sources of Market Data:

Financial News Websites: Websites such as Bloomberg, Reuters, CNBC, and Yahoo Finance provide real-time and delayed stock market data. They offer a wide range of financial news, market updates, stock quotes, charts, and other relevant information.

Brokerage Platforms: Online brokerage platforms provide access to real-time and delayed market data for the stocks and other securities they offer for trading. They often provide customizable watchlists, charts, and other tools for analyzing stock market data.

Data Providers: Data providers such as Bloomberg Terminal, Thomson Reuters Eikon, and FactSet offer comprehensive market data solutions that cater to professional investors, financial institutions, and researchers. These platforms provide extensive historical and real-time data along with advanced analytics tools.

Interpreting Stock Quotes and Key Information:

Price: The stock price represents the current trading price of a particular stock. It indicates the value at which the stock is being bought or sold in the market.

Volume: Volume refers to the total number of shares traded during a specific time period. It provides insights into the liquidity and activity level of a particular stock.

Bid/Ask Spread: The bid price represents the highest price buyers are willing to pay for a stock, while the ask price represents the lowest price sellers are willing to accept. The difference between the bid and ask prices is called the bid/ask spread, which represents the transaction cost and liquidity of the stock.

Market Cap: Market capitalization is the total value of a company's outstanding shares of stock. It is calculated by multiplying the stock's price by the number of outstanding shares. Market cap provides an indication of the company's size and is used to categorize stocks into different market cap categories (e.g., large-cap, mid-cap, small-cap).

Interpreting stock quotes and understanding key information is essential for investors to assess stock performance, make informed investment decisions, and understand the market dynamics. It is advisable to use reliable sources and platforms to access accurate and up-to-date market data.

2.5 Types of Stock Market Participants:

Individual Investors: Individual investors refer to retail traders or small investors who participate in the stock market with their personal funds. They can have a significant impact on the market in aggregate due to their collective trading activities. Although individual investors may not have the same level of financial resources or market influence as institutional investors, their participation contributes to overall market liquidity and trading volume. Individually, their impact may be limited, but their collective actions can create market trends, drive stock prices, and influence market sentiment.

Institutional Investors: Institutional investors are large financial entities that invest on behalf of others, such as mutual funds, pension funds, and hedge funds. Due to their substantial financial resources, institutional investors have the potential to significantly impact the market. They can influence stock prices through their large-scale buying or selling activities. Institutional investors often have professional fund managers who employ various investment strategies to achieve their objectives, such as generating returns, managing risks, and achieving diversification.

Mutual Funds: Mutual funds pool money from multiple investors to invest in a diversified portfolio of stocks, bonds, or other securities. They offer retail investors access to professionally managed portfolios.

Pension Funds: Pension funds manage funds on behalf of employees or beneficiaries to provide retirement benefits. They typically invest in a mix of stocks, bonds, and other assets to generate long-term returns.

Hedge Funds: Hedge funds are private investment funds that employ various investment strategies, such as long/short positions, derivatives, and leverage, to seek higher returns. They are often available only to accredited investors due to their higher risk profile.

Market Makers and Specialists: Market makers play a crucial role in facilitating liquidity and maintaining orderly markets. They are firms or individuals who provide continuous bid and ask prices for specific stocks, ensuring there is always a market for the stock. Market makers buy shares from sellers (at the bid price) and sell shares to buyers (at the ask price). By doing so, they create liquidity and narrow bid/ask spreads.

Specialists, on the other hand, are market professionals who work on the trading floor of an exchange. They are responsible for maintaining fair and orderly trading in specific listed stocks. Specialists facilitate trading, match buyers and sellers, and ensure smooth market functioning.

High-Frequency Traders and Algorithmic Trading: High-frequency traders (HFTs) are market participants who use powerful computers and sophisticated algorithms to execute trades at very high speeds. HFTs aim to profit from small price discrepancies and market inefficiencies. They employ strategies that capitalize on short-term price movements and exploit fleeting opportunities in the market.

Algorithmic trading involves using computer algorithms to automatically execute trades based on predefined rules and strategies. It eliminates the need for manual intervention and allows for rapid execution. Algorithmic trading strategies can be employed by various market participants, including both institutional and individual investors.

High-frequency traders and algorithmic trading have become increasingly prevalent in today's markets due to technological advancements. They contribute to increased trading volumes, liquidity, and market efficiency. However, their activities have also raised concerns regarding market stability, fairness, and potential disruptions.

It's important to note that the impact of each market participant can vary based on their trading volumes, strategies, and access to resources. The stock market is influenced by a complex interplay of various participants, each contributing to the overall market dynamics.

2.6 Market Order Flow:

Understanding the Concept of Market Liquidity: Market liquidity refers to the ease with which a security can be bought or sold in the market without causing significant price movements. It reflects the availability of buyers and sellers and the depth of the market. A highly liquid market has a large number of participants, high trading volumes, and tight bid-ask spreads, making it easier to enter or exit positions with minimal impact on prices. On the other hand, a less liquid market may have lower trading volumes, wider bid-ask spreads, and potential price slippage, making it more challenging to execute trades without affecting prices.

Bid-Ask Spread and its Significance in Assessing Transaction Costs: The bid-ask spread represents the difference between the highest price a buyer is willing to pay (bid price) and the lowest price a seller is willing to accept (ask price). It serves as a measure of liquidity and transaction costs. A narrow bid-ask spread indicates high liquidity, as there is a small difference between the buying and selling prices. This means that investors can buy or sell the security at a more favorable price. Conversely, a wide bid-ask spread suggests lower liquidity and higher transaction costs, as the difference between the bid and ask prices is significant.

Impact of Buy and Sell Orders on Stock Prices: Buy and sell orders can impact stock prices through their influence on supply and demand dynamics. When there are more buyers than sellers (higher demand), the increased buying pressure can push stock prices higher. Conversely, when there are more sellers than buyers (higher supply), the increased selling pressure can drive stock prices lower. The interaction between buying and selling orders creates the price discovery mechanism in the market.

Large buy orders can lead to price increases due to increased demand, especially if there are limited sellers at the current price level. Similarly, large sell orders can put downward pressure on prices due to increased supply, especially if there are limited buyers at the current price level. However, the impact of individual orders on stock prices can be short-lived, especially in highly liquid markets, as new buy and sell orders continuously flow into the market.

Order Flow Analysis as a Tool for Understanding Market Dynamics: Order flow analysis involves studying the flow of buy and sell orders in the market to gain insights into market dynamics. It focuses on understanding the volume, timing, and direction of order flow to gauge market sentiment, identify potential support or resistance levels, and assess the strength of buying or selling pressure.

By analyzing order flow, traders and investors can observe whether buy or sell orders dominate, identify patterns, and anticipate potential price movements. Order flow analysis can help uncover hidden liquidity, detect institutional buying or selling, and identify potential market turning points. It is often used in conjunction with other technical and fundamental analysis tools to make informed trading decisions.

It's important to note that market liquidity, bid-ask spreads, the impact of buy and sell orders, and order flow analysis can vary across different stocks, market conditions, and timeframes. They are key considerations for traders and investors to assess transaction costs, market dynamics, and potential price movements.

2.7 Primary Market vs. Secondary Market:

The Difference between Primary and Secondary Markets: The primary market is where newly issued securities, such as stocks or bonds, are bought and sold for the first time. In the primary market, companies raise capital by issuing securities directly to investors. This process is known as the initial offering or primary offering. The transactions in the primary market involve the company or issuer and the investors directly, and the proceeds from these transactions go to the company.

On the other hand, the secondary market is where previously issued securities are bought and sold among investors. In the secondary market, investors trade these securities with each other without involvement from the issuing company. The secondary market provides liquidity to investors who want to buy or sell their securities after the initial offering. The transactions in the secondary market do not affect the company's capital structure or finances directly.

Initial Public Offerings (IPOs) and the Process of Going Public: An Initial Public Offering (IPO) is the process by which a privately held company offers its shares to the public for the first time. Going public through an IPO allows the company to raise capital from a wide range of investors. The process typically involves hiring investment banks to underwrite the offering and help determine the offering price. The company files a registration statement with the regulatory authorities, such as the Securities and Exchange Commission (SEC) in the United States, containing information about the company, its financials, and the planned offering. After the regulatory review and approval, the company's shares are listed on a stock exchange, and the public can start trading the shares in the secondary market.

Rights Offerings and Follow-on Offerings: Rights offerings and follow-on offerings are methods through which companies raise additional capital after their initial public offering.

A rights offering allows existing shareholders to purchase additional shares of the company at a specified price and within a certain time frame. Shareholders receive subscription rights, which give them the opportunity to maintain their ownership percentage by buying more shares. This type of offering is often made at a discount to the current market price, providing an incentive for shareholders to participate.

Follow-on offerings, also known as secondary offerings or subsequent offerings, involve the sale of additional shares to the public after the initial public offering. In follow-on offerings, the company issues new shares, and the proceeds typically go to the company to fund growth initiatives, acquisitions, or other capital requirements.

Trading Stocks on the Secondary Market through Exchanges or Over-the-Counter (OTC) Markets: In the secondary market, investors can buy and sell stocks that are already issued and traded. This can be done through traditional stock exchanges, such as the New York Stock Exchange (NYSE) or the Nasdaq Stock Market, where stocks are traded on a centralized platform with specific listing requirements and regulations.

Alternatively, stocks can also be traded over-the-counter (OTC). In the OTC market, trades are conducted directly between buyers and sellers without a centralized exchange. OTC trading may include stocks of smaller companies that are not listed on major exchanges or certain types of financial instruments.

While stock exchanges provide transparency, liquidity, and regulation, the OTC market offers flexibility and accessibility to a broader range of securities. However, trading on the OTC market may involve less stringent regulatory oversight, and investors should exercise caution and conduct thorough research when trading OTC securities.

Overall, both primary and secondary markets play crucial roles in the financial markets, allowing companies to raise capital and providing investors with opportunities to buy and sell securities.

2.8 Regulatory Bodies and Investor Protection:

Securities and Exchange Commission (SEC) in the United States and other regulatory bodies worldwide: The Securities and Exchange Commission (SEC) is the primary regulatory body overseeing the securities industry in the United States. Its mission is to protect investors, maintain fair and efficient markets, and facilitate capital formation. The SEC regulates various participants in the securities markets, including issuers, brokers, dealers, and investment advisors. It enforces securities laws, such as the Securities Act of 1933 and the Securities Exchange Act of 1934, and has the authority to bring enforcement actions against those who violate these laws.

Similarly, other countries have their own regulatory bodies that oversee the securities markets. For example, the Financial Conduct Authority (FCA) in the United Kingdom, the Securities and Exchange Board of India (SEBI), and the Australian Securities and Investments Commission (ASIC) are regulatory bodies in their respective countries.

Investor Protection Measures, such as Securities Laws and Regulations: Securities laws and regulations are designed to protect investors and promote fair and transparent markets. These laws establish standards for financial reporting, disclosure requirements, and conduct of market participants. They aim to prevent fraud, manipulation, and other abuses in the securities markets.

Some common investor protection measures include:

Registration requirements: Companies offering securities to the public must register with the regulatory authorities and provide detailed information about their business, financials, and risks. This helps ensure that investors have access to relevant information before making investment decisions.

Disclosure requirements: Companies are required to disclose important information to investors on an ongoing basis. This includes periodic financial reports, such as the annual report (10-K) and quarterly report (10-Q), which provide detailed financial information about the company's operations, risks, and performance.

Prohibition of insider trading: Insider trading, which involves trading securities based on non-public, material information, is prohibited to ensure fairness and prevent unfair advantages for certain market participants.

Anti-fraud provisions: Securities laws include provisions that prohibit fraudulent activities, such as making false statements or engaging in deceptive practices in connection with the offer, sale, or purchase of securities.

Understanding Financial Disclosures and Corporate Filings (10-K, 10-Q, Annual Reports): Financial disclosures and corporate filings play a crucial role in providing transparency and information to investors. Some key filings include:

10-K: The annual report filed by public companies with the SEC in the United States. It provides a comprehensive overview of the company's financial performance, business operations, risks, and governance.

10-Q: The quarterly report filed by public companies with the SEC. It provides a snapshot of the company's financials and key updates for the quarter.

Annual Reports: In addition to the regulatory filings, companies often publish annual reports that provide a more narrative and visually appealing overview of their business, including financial highlights, strategic initiatives, and achievements.

These filings are valuable sources of information for investors to assess the financial health and performance of a company, understand its risks and opportunities, and make informed investment decisions.

It's important for investors to review these filings and understand the information presented, as it can help them evaluate the company's prospects, management's analysis of risks, and overall corporate governance practices.

Chapter 3: Types of Trading Instruments: Stocks, Options, Futures, and Cryptocurrencies

Introduction: In Chapter 3, we will explore the various trading instruments available in the financial markets. Understanding the characteristics, advantages, and risks associated with each instrument will help you make informed decisions when selecting your trading approach. We will focus on four prominent trading instruments: stocks, options, futures, and cryptocurrencies.

3.1 Stocks:

Definition and Characteristics of Stocks: Stocks, also known as shares or equities, represent ownership in a company. When an investor purchases stocks, they become shareholders, which means they hold a portion of the company's ownership. Stocks are typically issued by publicly traded companies, allowing them to raise capital from investors in exchange for a share of ownership.

Characteristics of stocks include:

Ownership: By owning stocks, investors have a claim on the company's assets and earnings proportional to their ownership stake.

Divisibility: Stocks are divided into shares, which can be bought and sold in different quantities. Investors can purchase as few or as many shares as they desire.

Transferability: Stocks can be easily bought and sold on stock exchanges or over-the-counter markets, providing liquidity to investors.

Voting Rights: Shareholders of common stocks typically have the right to vote on matters affecting the company, such as electing the board of directors and approving significant corporate actions.

Ownership Rights and Privileges Conferred to Shareholders: Shareholders enjoy various rights and privileges, including:

Voting Rights: Common stock shareholders have the right to vote on key corporate decisions, such as the election of directors and major corporate actions. The voting power is typically proportional to the number of shares owned.

Dividends: When a company generates profits, it may distribute a portion of those profits to shareholders in the form of dividends. Dividends are usually paid in cash, but can also be issued as additional shares or other forms of value.

Residual Claim: Shareholders have a claim on the company's assets and earnings after all other obligations, such as debt payments, have been fulfilled. In the event of liquidation or sale of the company, shareholders have the right to a portion of the remaining assets.

Access to Information: Shareholders have the right to receive relevant information about the company's financial performance, operations, and other material events, allowing them to make informed investment decisions.

Different Types of Stocks: The two main types of stocks are common stocks and preferred stocks.

Common Stocks: Common stocks represent the majority of stocks issued by companies. Common shareholders have voting rights and may receive dividends, but their claims on assets and earnings are subordinate to creditors and preferred shareholders. Common stocks offer the potential for capital appreciation as the company's value increases.

Preferred Stocks: Preferred stocks have characteristics of both stocks and bonds. Preferred shareholders have a higher claim on the company's assets and earnings compared to common shareholders. They receive fixed dividends, which are typically higher than what common shareholders receive, and have priority in receiving dividends and assets in the event of liquidation. However, preferred shareholders generally do not have voting rights.

Benefits of Investing in Stocks: Investing in stocks offers several benefits, including:

Potential Capital Appreciation: Stocks have the potential to increase in value over time, allowing investors to profit from capital appreciation. As a company's business grows and its profits increase, the value of its stocks may rise, providing investors with potential gains.

Dividend Income: Many companies distribute a portion of their earnings as dividends to shareholders. Dividends can provide a steady income stream for investors, especially for those seeking regular cash flow.

Diversification: Stocks offer the opportunity to diversify an investment portfolio. By investing in stocks of different companies across various industries, investors can spread their risk and reduce exposure to any single company or sector.

Ownership in Companies: Investing in stocks allows individuals to become owners in companies they believe in and support. Shareholders have the potential to benefit from the success and growth of the companies they invest in.

Liquidity: Stocks are generally highly liquid, meaning they can be easily bought and sold on stock exchanges. This liquidity provides flexibility for investors to enter or exit positions as desired.

It's important to note that investing in stocks also carries risks, such as market volatility and the potential for losses. Investors should carefully research and assess companies before investing and consider their individual risk tolerance and investment objectives.

3.2 Options:

Introduction to Options as Derivative Instruments: Options are financial derivatives that give investors the right, but not the obligation, to buy or sell an underlying asset (such as stocks, commodities, or currencies) at a predetermined price within a specific time period. They provide investors with flexibility and potential profit opportunities, based on their expectations of the underlying asset's price movements.

Call Options and Put Options:

Call Options: A call option gives the holder the right to buy the underlying asset at a specified price, known as the strike price, within a predetermined time frame. Call options are typically used when investors anticipate that the price of the underlying asset will rise.

Put Options: A put option gives the holder the right to sell the underlying asset at a specified strike price within a predetermined time frame. Put options are typically used when investors expect the price of the underlying asset to decline.

Understanding Option Contracts, Strike Prices, and Expiration Dates: An option contract specifies the terms of the option, including the underlying asset, the number of shares or units covered, the strike price, and the expiration date.

Strike Price: The strike price is the predetermined price at which the underlying asset can be bought or sold. It determines the profitability of the option contract at expiration.

Expiration Date: The expiration date is the date on which the option contract expires and becomes invalid. After the expiration date, the option can no longer be exercised.

Advantages of Options Trading:

Leverage: Options provide the opportunity for investors to control a larger amount of the underlying asset with a smaller investment. This leverage allows for potentially amplified profits if the market moves in the anticipated direction.

Risk Management: Options can be used as risk management tools to protect an investment portfolio. For example, investors can use put options to hedge against potential losses or use covered call strategies to generate income from existing stock holdings.

Flexibility: Options offer a wide range of strategies and trading opportunities. Investors can use options to speculate on price movements, generate income, protect against downside risk, or take advantage of volatility in the market.

Limited Risk: When buying options, the maximum loss is limited to the premium paid for the option contract. This predefined risk can provide investors with a level of comfort and control over their potential losses.

It's important to note that options trading involves certain complexities and risks. Options can expire worthless, leading to a complete loss of the premium paid. Investors should understand the mechanics of options, study their behavior in different market conditions, and consider their risk tolerance before engaging in options trading.

3.3 Futures:

Overview of Futures Contracts and Their Role in the Financial Markets: Futures contracts are derivative financial instruments that obligate the parties involved to buy or sell an underlying asset at a predetermined price and date in the future. They play a crucial role in the financial markets by providing a means for investors to manage risks, speculate on price movements, and establish price expectations for various assets.

Understanding the Concept of Standardized Contracts and Exchange-Traded Futures: Futures contracts are typically standardized, meaning that they have predetermined contract specifications, such as the quantity and quality of the underlying asset, delivery months, and tick sizes. This standardization ensures uniformity and facilitates trading on regulated exchanges.

Exchange-Traded Futures: Futures contracts are traded on organized exchanges, such as the Chicago Mercantile Exchange (CME) or the Intercontinental Exchange (ICE). These exchanges provide a centralized marketplace where buyers and sellers can transact futures contracts in a transparent and regulated environment.

Futures Trading Mechanics, Including Margin Requirements and Settlement Procedures:

Margin Requirements: When trading futures, participants are required to deposit an initial margin, which serves as collateral for potential losses. Margin requirements are typically set by the exchange and vary based on factors like the volatility of the underlying asset. Maintenance margin must also be maintained to ensure the account remains adequately funded.

Settlement Procedures: Futures contracts have different settlement methods, depending on the asset class. Some futures contracts result in physical delivery of the underlying asset upon expiration, while others are cash-settled, where the difference between the contract price and the market price is settled in cash.

Popular Futures Markets:

Commodities: Futures contracts are widely used in commodity markets, including energy (crude oil, natural gas), agricultural products (corn, wheat, coffee), metals (gold, silver, copper), and more. Commodity futures allow participants to hedge against price fluctuations or speculate on future price movements.

Stock Indices: Futures contracts based on stock indices, such as the S&P 500 or the Dow Jones Industrial Average, enable investors to gain exposure to the broader stock market's performance. These futures contracts are used for hedging purposes, portfolio diversification, and speculation on market trends.

Interest Rates: Futures contracts on interest rates, such as Treasury bonds or Eurodollar futures, provide a way for participants to manage interest rate risks or speculate on future changes in interest rates.

Futures trading offers advantages such as liquidity, leverage, and the ability to participate in various markets. However, it also carries risks, including the potential for substantial losses, especially when using leverage. Traders and investors interested in futures should thoroughly understand the contract specifications, market dynamics, and risk management strategies before engaging in futures trading.

3.4 Cryptocurrencies:

Introduction to Cryptocurrencies and Blockchain Technology: Cryptocurrencies are digital or virtual currencies that utilize cryptographic technology to secure transactions and control the creation of new units. They operate on decentralized networks called blockchains, which are distributed ledgers that record all transactions across a network of computers.

Key Characteristics of Cryptocurrencies:

Decentralization: Cryptocurrencies are typically decentralized, meaning they are not controlled by any central authority, such as a government or financial institution. Instead, they rely on consensus mechanisms and peer-to-peer networks to verify and validate transactions.

Security: Cryptocurrencies use cryptographic techniques to secure transactions, ensuring that they are tamper-proof and resistant to fraud. The use of blockchain technology provides transparency and immutability, making it difficult to alter or manipulate transaction records.

Digital Scarcity: Many cryptocurrencies have limited supplies, which means there is a finite number of coins or tokens that can ever be created. This feature is designed to provide scarcity and potentially increase the value of the cryptocurrency over time.

Popular Cryptocurrencies:

Bitcoin (BTC): Bitcoin is the first and most well-known cryptocurrency. It was created in 2009 and operates on a decentralized blockchain. Bitcoin is often referred to as digital gold due to its store of value properties and limited supply.

Ethereum (ETH): Ethereum is a decentralized platform that enables the creation of smart contracts and decentralized applications (DApps). The native cryptocurrency of the Ethereum network is called Ether, and it is used to facilitate transactions and incentivize participants.

Ripple (XRP): Ripple is a digital payment protocol that enables fast and low-cost international money transfers. XRP is the native cryptocurrency of the Ripple network and is used as a bridge currency for facilitating transactions.

Trading Cryptocurrencies on Cryptocurrency Exchanges and Understanding Price Volatility: Cryptocurrencies can be traded on specialized cryptocurrency exchanges, which act as platforms for buying, selling, and exchanging various cryptocurrencies. These exchanges provide order books, charts, and trading functionalities to facilitate cryptocurrency trading.

It's important to note that the cryptocurrency market is known for its high price volatility. Cryptocurrency prices can experience significant fluctuations in short periods due to various factors, including market sentiment, regulatory developments, technological advancements, and macroeconomic events. Traders and investors should be aware of the risks associated with cryptocurrency trading, including the potential for substantial gains or losses.

Due to the volatile nature of cryptocurrencies, it's recommended to conduct thorough research, understand the underlying technology, and implement appropriate risk management strategies before engaging in cryptocurrency trading.

3.5 Comparison of Trading Instruments:

Risk and Return Profiles of Stocks, Options, Futures, and Cryptocurrencies:

Stocks: Stocks are considered to have moderate to high risk, depending on the specific company and market conditions. They offer the potential for long-term capital appreciation and dividend income. The returns from stocks can be influenced by factors such as company performance, industry trends, economic conditions, and market sentiment.

Options: Options are derivative instruments that derive their value from an underlying asset, such as stocks. Options can offer both potential high returns and higher risks. The risk in options trading primarily stems from the time sensitivity of options contracts and the potential for the loss of the premium paid. Options can be used for various trading strategies, including hedging, speculation, and income generation.

Futures: Futures contracts are financial derivatives that oblige the parties involved to buy or sell an asset at a predetermined price and date in the future. Futures trading carries substantial risk due to leverage and price volatility. The potential returns from futures trading can be significant, but so can the potential losses. Futures are commonly used for speculative trading, hedging, and risk management purposes.

Cryptocurrencies: Cryptocurrencies are known for their high volatility and speculative nature, which can result in significant returns but also substantial losses. The cryptocurrency market is relatively new and less regulated compared to traditional financial markets. The risk associated with cryptocurrencies includes price volatility, cybersecurity threats, regulatory uncertainties, and market manipulation risks.

Factors to Consider When Choosing a Trading Instrument:

Investment Goals: Consider your investment objectives, such as capital appreciation, income generation, or risk hedging. Different trading instruments align with different investment goals.

Risk Tolerance: Assess your risk tolerance and determine the level of volatility and potential losses you are comfortable with. Some instruments, like stocks and cryptocurrencies, can be more volatile compared to options and futures.

Time Horizon: Determine your investment time horizon, whether it's short-term, medium-term, or long-term. Some instruments, like futures and options, are more suitable for short-term trading, while stocks and cryptocurrencies can be held for the long term.

Liquidity and Market Accessibility: Evaluate the liquidity of the trading instrument, which refers to the ease of buying and selling without significant price impact. Consider the availability of markets and exchanges where the instrument is traded and the ease of access to those markets.

Regulatory Considerations and Investor Protection Measures: Understand the regulatory environment surrounding each trading instrument. Different instruments may have varying levels of regulation and investor protection measures. For example, stocks are subject to strict regulations and oversight, while cryptocurrencies are still evolving in terms of regulation.

It's crucial to conduct thorough research, seek professional advice if needed, and consider your individual circumstances and risk tolerance when choosing a trading instrument. Diversification across multiple instruments and asset classes can also help manage risk and optimize potential returns.

3.6 Trading Strategies for Each Instrument:

Fundamental Analysis and Technical Analysis Approaches for Stocks:

Fundamental Analysis: Fundamental analysis involves evaluating the intrinsic value of a stock by analyzing various factors related to the underlying company. This includes studying financial statements, analyzing industry trends, assessing management quality, and evaluating competitive advantages. Fundamental analysis aims to determine whether a stock is undervalued or overvalued relative to its intrinsic worth, with the goal of making long-term investment decisions based on the company's fundamentals.

Technical Analysis: Technical analysis focuses on studying historical price and volume data of stocks to identify patterns, trends, and potential price movements. It involves using various tools and techniques, such as chart patterns, technical indicators, and trend lines, to make predictions about future price movements. Technical analysis assumes that historical price patterns and trends can provide insights into future price behavior. Traders who use technical analysis aim to make short-term trading decisions based on the analysis of charts and patterns.

Option Strategies:

Covered Calls: This strategy involves selling call options on stocks that an investor already owns. By selling the call options, the investor receives premium income. If the stock price remains below the strike price of the call options, the investor keeps the premium and can continue holding the stock. If the stock price rises above the strike price, the investor may have to sell the stock at the strike price but still retains the premium income.

Protective Puts: This strategy involves purchasing put options as a form of insurance to protect a stock position against potential downside risk. If the stock price declines, the put options increase in value, offsetting the losses in the stock position.

Spreads: Options spreads involve simultaneously buying and selling options contracts to create a position that can limit risk or enhance potential returns. Examples of spreads include vertical spreads (such as bull spreads and bear spreads) and horizontal spreads (such as calendar spreads).

Trading Futures Contracts:

Trend Following: This strategy involves identifying and following established trends in futures prices. Traders using this strategy aim to take long or short positions based on the direction of the trend, expecting the trend to continue.

Spread Trading: Spread trading involves simultaneously buying and selling related futures contracts to profit from price differentials between them. For example, a trader might buy a futures contract for a particular commodity and sell a related contract for a different delivery month.

Technical Analysis Techniques for Cryptocurrencies:

Chart Patterns: Traders analyze chart patterns specific to cryptocurrencies, such as support and resistance levels, trend lines, triangles, and wedges. These patterns can provide insights into potential price movements and help identify entry and exit points.

Indicators: Various technical indicators, such as moving averages, Relative Strength Index (RSI), and MACD (Moving Average Convergence Divergence), are applied to cryptocurrency price charts to identify overbought or oversold conditions, trend strength, and potential reversals.

It's important to note that these strategies and techniques are not exhaustive, and there are many other approaches and strategies available for trading stocks, options, futures, and cryptocurrencies. Traders and investors should thoroughly research and understand these strategies before implementing them and consider their own risk tolerance and investment goals.

3.7 Risk Management Considerations:

Assessing and managing risks associated with each trading instrument is crucial for successful trading. Here are some considerations for risk management:

Stocks: Risks in stock trading include market risk, company-specific risk, liquidity risk, and volatility risk. To manage these risks, you can diversify your stock portfolio, conduct thorough research on individual companies, set realistic profit targets and stop-loss levels, and stay updated with market news and trends.

Options: Options trading involves various risks, including the potential loss of the premium paid, time decay, and volatility risk. To manage risks in options trading, it's important to understand the option Greeks (such as delta, gamma, theta, and vega), use appropriate position sizing, set stop-loss orders, and consider strategies that align with your risk tolerance and investment goals.

Futures: Futures trading carries risks such as market risk, leverage risk, and margin requirements. It's important to understand the contract specifications, margin requirements, and the potential for significant losses due to price movements. Risk management techniques for futures trading include setting stop-loss orders, managing leverage carefully, and diversifying your positions across different futures contracts.

Cryptocurrencies: Trading cryptocurrencies comes with unique risks, including high volatility, regulatory uncertainty, and security risks associated with digital wallets and exchanges. To manage risks in cryptocurrency trading, consider using proper position sizing, setting stop-loss orders, conducting thorough research on individual cryptocurrencies, and diversifying your cryptocurrency holdings.

Understanding the impact of leverage and margin requirements is crucial for risk management. While leverage can amplify profits, it also magnifies losses. It's important to use leverage responsibly and consider the associated risks. Margin requirements determine the amount of capital you need to have available in your trading account to trade a certain position size. Understanding and managing margin requirements helps prevent margin calls and potential forced liquidation of positions.

Implementing risk management techniques, such as stop-loss orders and position sizing, is essential. Stop-loss orders allow you to set predetermined exit points to limit potential losses. Position sizing involves determining the appropriate allocation of capital for each trade based on your risk tolerance and the size of your trading account. By implementing proper position sizing, you can control risk and avoid excessive exposure to any single trade.

Diversification and asset allocation strategies across different trading instruments can help spread risk and reduce the impact of losses. By diversifying your investments across various trading instruments and asset classes, you can potentially mitigate the risk of significant losses in any one instrument.

It's important to note that risk management is a personal and individualized process. Every trader and investor should develop their own risk management plan based on their risk tolerance, investment goals, and trading strategies. Regular monitoring and adjustments to risk management strategies are also essential as market conditions and individual circumstances change.

Chapter 4: Fundamental Analysis: Evaluating Company Financials and Performance

Introduction: In Chapter 4, we will delve into the world of fundamental analysis—a key approach for evaluating the financial health and performance of a company. By understanding how to analyze and interpret company financials, you can make informed investment decisions based on the underlying value of a company. This chapter will equip you with the knowledge and tools to conduct fundamental analysis effectively.

4.1 What is Fundamental Analysis?

Fundamental analysis is a method used to evaluate the intrinsic value of a security, such as a stock, by analyzing various factors related to the underlying company's financials, industry, management, and economic environment. Its primary goal is to determine whether a stock is overvalued or undervalued relative to its intrinsic worth. Fundamental analysis is widely used in investment decision-making and is crucial for long-term investors who seek to make informed investment choices based on a company's fundamentals and potential for future growth.

The importance of fundamental analysis lies in its ability to provide a comprehensive understanding of a company's financial health, competitive position, and growth prospects. By analyzing financial statements, such as balance sheets, income statements, and cash flow statements, fundamental analysis helps investors assess a company's profitability, liquidity, solvency, and overall financial performance. It also involves evaluating industry dynamics, competitive advantages, market trends, and management quality to gauge a company's competitive position and growth potential.

Contrasting fundamental analysis with other forms of analysis, such as technical analysis, highlights their differences in approach and focus. While fundamental analysis relies on analyzing qualitative and quantitative data to assess a company's intrinsic value, technical analysis focuses on studying historical price and volume data to identify patterns and trends that can help predict future price movements. Fundamental analysis considers factors related to the company's business operations, financials, and industry, whereas technical analysis focuses primarily on price and volume patterns.

Fundamental analysis plays a significant role in assessing a company's intrinsic value. By analyzing financial statements, fundamental analysts can calculate various valuation metrics, such as price-to-earnings (P/E) ratio, price-to-sales (P/S) ratio, and price-to-book (P/B) ratio, to determine whether a stock is overvalued or undervalued compared to its peers or historical averages. Fundamental analysis also involves estimating future earnings growth, conducting discounted cash flow (DCF) analysis, and considering qualitative factors, such as industry trends and competitive advantages, to arrive at a fair value estimate for a stock.

In summary, fundamental analysis is a critical tool in investment decision-making. It helps investors evaluate a company's intrinsic value, assess its financial health and growth potential, and make informed investment choices based on a thorough understanding of a company's fundamentals. By considering both qualitative and quantitative factors, fundamental analysis provides a comprehensive view of a company's prospects and helps investors identify investment opportunities that align with their long-term investment goals.

4.2 Key Financial Statements:

Financial statements are essential tools for analyzing a company's financial performance and understanding its financial position. The three main financial statements are the balance sheet, income statement, and cash flow statement.

Balance Sheet: The balance sheet provides a snapshot of a company's financial position at a specific point in time. It consists of three main components:

Assets: Assets represent what the company owns, such as cash, inventory, property, equipment, and investments.

Liabilities: Liabilities represent what the company owes, such as loans, accounts payable, and accrued expenses.

Equity: Equity represents the ownership interest in the company, including retained earnings and shareholders' equity.

The balance sheet equation is Assets = Liabilities + Equity, demonstrating the relationship between these components.

Income Statement: The income statement, also known as the profit and loss statement, shows a company's revenues, expenses, and net income (or net loss) over a specific period. It includes:

Revenues: Revenues represent the income generated from the company's primary operations, such as sales of goods or services.

Expenses: Expenses include the costs incurred to generate revenue, such as salaries, rent, utilities, and marketing expenses.

Net Income: Net income is the difference between revenues and expenses, representing the company's profit or loss.

The income statement provides insights into a company's profitability and its ability to generate positive net income.

Cash Flow Statement: The cash flow statement tracks the inflow and outflow of cash over a specific period, categorizing cash flows into three main categories:

Operating Activities: Cash flows from the company's core operations, such as sales, payments to suppliers, and employee salaries.

Investing Activities: Cash flows from the buying or selling of long-term assets, such as investments, property, or equipment.

Financing Activities: Cash flows from activities related to financing the company, such as issuing or repaying debt, issuing or repurchasing stock, and paying dividends.

The cash flow statement provides insights into a company's cash-generating ability, liquidity, and cash management.

Interpreting financial ratios derived from financial statements is crucial in assessing a company's financial health and performance. Common financial ratios include:

Profitability Ratios: Examples include gross profit margin, operating profit margin, and return on equity (ROE), which measure a company's ability to generate profits relative to sales and shareholders' equity.

Liquidity Ratios: Ratios such as the current ratio and quick ratio assess a company's ability to meet its short-term obligations using its current assets.

Solvency Ratios: These ratios, including the debt-to-equity ratio and interest coverage ratio, evaluate a company's long-term financial stability and ability to meet its debt obligations.

Efficiency Ratios: Ratios like inventory turnover and accounts receivable turnover measure a company's efficiency in managing its assets and converting them into sales.

By analyzing financial statements and related ratios, investors and analysts can assess a company's financial position, profitability, cash flow, and overall financial performance. These insights aid in making informed investment decisions and evaluating a company's financial health relative to its industry peers.

4.3 Financial Ratios and Metrics:

Common financial ratios used in fundamental analysis include:

Price-to-Earnings (P/E) Ratio: The P/E ratio compares a company's stock price to its earnings per share (EPS), indicating how much investors are willing to pay for each dollar of earnings. A higher P/E ratio suggests higher investor expectations for future earnings growth.

Return on Equity (ROE): ROE measures a company's profitability by calculating the return generated on shareholders' equity. It indicates how efficiently a company uses its equity capital to generate profits.

Debt-to-Equity Ratio: The debt-to-equity ratio assesses a company's financial leverage by comparing its total debt to shareholders' equity. It indicates the proportion of a company's funding that comes from debt versus equity.

Current Ratio: The current ratio assesses a company's short-term liquidity by dividing its current assets by its current liabilities. It indicates a company's ability to meet short-term obligations.

Gross Profit Margin: The gross profit margin measures the percentage of revenue remaining after deducting the cost of goods sold. It indicates a company's ability to generate profits from its core operations.

Interpreting financial ratios involves comparing a company's ratios over time, benchmarking them against industry peers, and considering industry-specific factors. A ratio's implications depend on the context, industry dynamics, and the company's business model. For example:

A high P/E ratio may suggest market expectations of future growth, while a low P/E ratio may indicate undervaluation or growth concerns.

A high ROE indicates effective utilization of equity capital, while a low ROE may reflect poor profitability or inefficient use of capital.

A high debt-to-equity ratio may signal higher financial risk, while a low ratio suggests lower reliance on debt financing.

Industry-specific ratios and benchmarks provide additional context for comparative analysis. Different industries have unique characteristics, and ratios may vary significantly. It's essential to compare ratios within the same industry to identify outliers and evaluate a company's performance relative to its peers.

However, financial ratios have limitations and should be used with caution:

Ratios provide a snapshot of a company's financial position and performance but may not capture the full picture.

Ratios rely on accurate and reliable financial statements, so inconsistencies or errors can affect their accuracy.

Ratios may not consider qualitative factors like the competitive landscape, management quality, or industry disruptions.

Industry averages and benchmarks may not be applicable to every company within the industry, as each company has its unique circumstances.

It's important to consider financial ratios in conjunction with other qualitative and quantitative factors when conducting fundamental analysis. They serve as valuable indicators but should not be the sole basis for investment decisions.

4.4 Evaluating Company Performance:

Assessing revenue growth and earnings trends over time: Analyzing a company's revenue growth and earnings trends is crucial to understanding its financial performance. By examining the revenue and earnings figures over multiple periods, such as quarters or years, you can identify patterns and trends. Consistent revenue growth indicates a healthy and expanding business, while declining or inconsistent revenue may signal challenges. Similarly, assessing earnings trends helps evaluate a company's profitability and whether it is generating sustainable profits over time.

Analyzing profitability and margins: Profitability analysis focuses on assessing a company's ability to generate profits from its operations. Key profitability metrics include gross profit margin, operating profit margin, and net profit margin. These margins measure the percentage of revenue retained after deducting various costs, such as production expenses, operating costs, and taxes. Analyzing profitability and margins helps evaluate a company's efficiency, cost management, pricing power, and competitive advantage. Comparing a company's margins to industry peers provides insights into its relative performance.

Evaluating a company's liquidity, solvency, and financial stability: Liquidity analysis involves assessing a company's ability to meet short-term obligations. Key ratios include the current ratio and quick ratio, which measure the company's ability to cover current liabilities with its current assets. Solvency analysis focuses on a company's long-term financial stability and its ability to meet long-term obligations. The debt-to-equity ratio and interest coverage ratio are commonly used solvency ratios. Evaluating liquidity and solvency helps gauge a company's financial health and its ability to weather economic downturns or industry challenges.

Understanding the impact of industry dynamics and competitive positioning on company performance: Industry dynamics and competitive positioning significantly influence a company's performance. Analyzing industry trends, such as market growth rates, technological advancements, regulatory changes, and competitive forces, helps evaluate a company's future prospects. Assessing a company's competitive positioning involves analyzing factors like market share, product differentiation, pricing power, and barriers to entry. Understanding how these factors impact a company's performance is essential for making informed investment decisions and assessing its long-term viability.

By considering revenue growth and earnings trends, profitability and margins, liquidity and solvency, and the impact of industry dynamics and competitive positioning, investors can gain a comprehensive understanding of a company's financial performance and prospects. These factors provide insights into a company's financial health, profitability, and ability to navigate challenges and capitalize on opportunities in its operating environment.

4.5 Qualitative Factors in Fundamental Analysis:

Evaluating management quality and corporate governance practices: Assessing the quality of a company's management team and its corporate governance practices is important in understanding how well the company is managed and whether it is aligned with the interests of shareholders. Factors to consider include the experience and track record of key executives, their strategic vision, transparency in financial reporting, ethical standards, and the independence of the board of directors. Strong management and effective corporate governance can contribute to long-term success and shareholder value creation.

Analyzing a company's competitive advantages and moats: Competitive advantages and moats refer to the unique qualities or advantages that enable a company to outperform its competitors and sustain its profitability over the long term. These advantages can include strong brand recognition, proprietary technology or patents, economies of scale, network effects, switching costs for customers, or exclusive access to key resources. Analyzing a company's competitive advantages helps assess its ability to defend market share, generate consistent profits, and maintain a sustainable competitive edge.

Assessing industry and market trends: Understanding industry dynamics and market trends is crucial for evaluating a company's prospects. Factors to consider include market growth rates, customer demand trends, competitive landscape, regulatory environment, and technological advancements. Analyzing industry and market trends helps identify opportunities and risks, assess market positioning, and anticipate future challenges or disruptions.

Considering macroeconomic factors and their impact on company performance: Macroeconomic factors, such as interest rates, inflation, GDP growth, and currency exchange rates, can significantly impact a company's performance. Changes in the macroeconomic environment can affect consumer spending, business investment, borrowing costs, and overall market conditions. Evaluating the potential impact of macroeconomic factors on a company helps assess its sensitivity to economic cycles, its ability to adapt to changing conditions, and the potential risks and opportunities it may face.

By evaluating management quality and corporate governance practices, analyzing a company's competitive advantages, assessing industry and market trends, and considering macroeconomic factors, investors can gain a comprehensive view of a company's prospects and potential risks. This information provides insights into the company's ability to navigate industry challenges, capitalize on market opportunities, and adapt to changing economic conditions.

4.6 Valuation Methods:

Valuation techniques are methods used to estimate the intrinsic value of a company or an investment. Here are three common valuation techniques:

Discounted Cash Flow (DCF) Analysis: DCF analysis involves estimating the future cash flows that a company is expected to generate and discounting them back to their present value. It considers the time value of money, reflecting the idea that a dollar received in the future is worth less than a dollar received today. DCF analysis requires making assumptions about future cash flows, growth rates, and the discount rate, which represents the required rate of return. The sum of the discounted cash flows represents the estimated intrinsic value of the company.

Price-to-Earnings (P/E) Ratio: The P/E ratio compares the market price of a company's stock to its earnings per share (EPS). It is calculated by dividing the stock price by the EPS. The P/E ratio is a popular valuation metric that provides a relative measure of a company's value compared to its earnings. A higher P/E ratio indicates a higher valuation relative to earnings, suggesting the market has higher expectations for future earnings growth.

Price-to-Book (P/B) Ratio: The P/B ratio compares the market price of a company's stock to its book value per share. It is calculated by dividing the stock price by the book value per share. The book value represents the net assets of the company (total assets minus total liabilities). The P/B ratio is used to assess whether a stock is undervalued or overvalued relative to its book value. A lower P/B ratio suggests a potentially better value, as the market price is lower than the book value.

Estimating a company's intrinsic value based on fundamental analysis involves using one or more of these valuation techniques and applying them to the specific financial data and projections of the company. The goal is to determine the underlying value of the company independent of its current market price.

The concept of margin of safety is an important principle in valuation. It refers to the difference between the estimated intrinsic value of a company and its market price. A margin of safety provides a cushion against uncertainties and potential errors in the valuation process. It allows investors to purchase a stock at a price significantly below its estimated intrinsic value, providing a level of protection if the valuation turns out to be overly optimistic or if unforeseen negative events occur.

Comparing a company's intrinsic value to its market price helps identify potential investment opportunities. If the intrinsic value is higher than the market price, it suggests the stock may be undervalued and potentially a good investment. Conversely, if the market price exceeds the intrinsic value, the stock may be overvalued and may not present an attractive investment opportunity.

It's important to note that valuation is not an exact science and involves making assumptions and judgments based on available information. Different valuation methods may yield different results, and the market price of a stock is influenced by various factors beyond fundamental analysis. Therefore, it's advisable to consider multiple valuation techniques and conduct a comprehensive analysis before making investment decisions.

4.7 Company Research and Data Sources:

To gather company information for investment analysis, there are several reliable sources and tools available:

Financial Reports and Regulatory Filings: Publicly traded companies are required to file financial reports and disclosures with regulatory bodies such as the Securities and Exchange Commission (SEC) in the United States. These filings include annual reports (e.g., 10-K), quarterly reports (e.g., 10-Q), and other periodic filings. These reports provide comprehensive information about a company's financial performance, operations, risks, and management discussion and analysis (MD&A).

Company Websites: Companies often provide detailed information about their operations, financials, management team, and investor relations on their official websites. Company websites can be a valuable source for accessing annual reports, investor presentations, press releases, and other relevant information. Additionally, investor relations sections on company websites may offer conference call transcripts, event presentations, and frequently asked questions (FAQs).

Financial Databases: Subscription-based financial databases such as Bloomberg, FactSet, and Reuters Eikon provide comprehensive financial data, news, research reports, and analyst opinions. These platforms offer in-depth financial metrics, historical data, company profiles, consensus estimates, and valuation tools that can aid in conducting detailed analysis.

Research Reports and Analyst Opinions: Research reports and analyst opinions from investment banks, brokerage firms, and independent research providers can provide valuable insights into a company's prospects, industry trends, and target prices. These reports often include financial analysis, industry outlooks, and investment recommendations. It's important to consider multiple sources and evaluate the credibility and track record of the analysts or research providers.

Industry Publications and News Sources: Industry-specific publications and news sources can provide industry-specific information, trends, and news related to companies and sectors of interest. These sources may include trade journals, industry magazines, online publications, and news aggregators. Staying informed about industry developments can help assess a company's competitive position and the broader market dynamics.

When gathering company information, it's crucial to critically evaluate the reliability, credibility, and timeliness of the sources. It's also important to consider a range of perspectives and perform comprehensive due diligence before making investment decisions.

4.8 Case Studies and Practical Examples:

Let's walk through a practical example of fundamental analysis and demonstrate the application of financial ratios and metrics in making investment decisions. For this example, let's consider a fictional company called XYZ Corporation, operating in the technology sector.

Step 1: Gather Financial Statements Start by accessing XYZ Corporation's financial statements, including the balance sheet, income statement, and cash flow statement. These statements provide crucial information about the company's financial performance and position.

Step 2: Analyze Revenue Growth and Earnings Trends Examine XYZ Corporation's revenue growth over the past few years. Look for consistent revenue growth, as it indicates the company's ability to generate sales. Additionally, analyze the company's earnings trends by reviewing the net income and earnings per share (EPS) over time. Consistent growth in earnings is generally a positive sign.

Step 3: Assess Profitability and Margins Calculate and analyze profitability ratios such as gross profit margin, operating profit margin, and net profit margin. These ratios help evaluate how efficiently the company generates profits from its operations. Compare these margins with industry peers to determine XYZ Corporation's relative performance.

Step 4: Evaluate Liquidity, Solvency, and Financial Stability Examine liquidity ratios such as the current ratio and quick ratio to assess XYZ Corporation's ability to meet short-term obligations. Additionally, analyze solvency ratios like the debt-to-equity ratio to gauge the company's long-term financial stability. Low levels of debt and healthy liquidity ratios indicate a financially stable company.

Step 5: Assess Industry and Market Trends Consider industry and market trends that could impact XYZ Corporation's future prospects. Evaluate factors such as technological advancements, competitive landscape, regulatory changes, and consumer demand. Understanding industry dynamics helps assess the company's competitive positioning and growth potential.

Step 6: Estimate Intrinsic Value and Compare to Market Price Utilize valuation techniques such as discounted cash flow (DCF) analysis or price-to-earnings (P/E) ratio to estimate the intrinsic value of XYZ Corporation's stock. DCF analysis involves forecasting future cash flows and discounting them to their present value. Comparing the estimated intrinsic value to the market price can help identify whether the stock is undervalued or overvalued.

Step 7: Consider Qualitative Factors In addition to financial analysis, consider qualitative factors such as the company's management team, competitive advantages, brand reputation, and product differentiation. These factors can contribute to a company's long-term success and should be taken into account when making investment decisions.

By following these steps and analyzing the financial statements, ratios, and industry trends, you can gain a comprehensive understanding of XYZ Corporation's financial health and make informed investment decisions.

Chapter 5: Technical Analysis: Tools and Techniques for Price Prediction

Introduction: In Chapter 5, we will explore the fascinating world of technical analysis—a method of analyzing historical price and volume data to predict future price movements. Technical analysis can provide valuable insights into market trends, patterns, and potential trading opportunities. This chapter will introduce you to the tools, techniques, and concepts of technical analysis.

5.1 What is Technical Analysis?

Technical analysis is a method used in trading and investing to evaluate securities by analyzing historical price and volume data and identifying patterns and trends. It aims to predict future price movements based on the belief that market trends and patterns repeat over time. Technical analysts use various tools and techniques, such as chart patterns, indicators, and trend lines, to make trading decisions.

Contrasting Technical Analysis with Fundamental Analysis: While fundamental analysis focuses on assessing the intrinsic value of a security by analyzing financial and economic factors, technical analysis focuses solely on price and volume data. Fundamental analysis examines a company's financial statements, industry trends, competitive positioning, and other qualitative factors to determine the underlying value of a security. On the other hand, technical analysis does not consider these factors and instead relies on historical price patterns and indicators to predict future price movements.

The Role of Human Psychology and Market Behavior in Technical Analysis: Technical analysis is based on the belief that market prices reflect all available information, including the psychological factors that influence market participants. It recognizes that market participants' emotions, such as fear, greed, and optimism, can drive buying and selling decisions, leading to price patterns and trends. Technical analysts study these patterns and trends to gain insights into market psychology and behavior.

For example, support and resistance levels on a price chart are seen as areas where market participants' buying or selling pressure is likely to be significant due to psychological reasons. Breakouts from these levels can indicate shifts in market sentiment. Additionally, technical analysis recognizes that market trends can persist due to herd behavior and momentum trading, leading to self-fulfilling prophecies.

However, it's important to note that technical analysis has its limitations and critics. Critics argue that technical analysis relies on subjective interpretations of historical data and patterns, which can be open to individual biases. Additionally, the efficient market hypothesis suggests that all available information is quickly reflected in market prices, making it difficult to consistently predict future price movements based solely on historical data.

Overall, technical analysis is a tool used by traders and investors to make short-term trading decisions and identify potential entry and exit points. It complements fundamental analysis by providing insights into market sentiment and behavior. However, it should be used in conjunction with other forms of analysis and risk management techniques to make well-informed investment decisions.

5.2 Basic Principles of Technical Analysis:

Price action refers to the movement and behavior of market prices as reflected in historical price charts. It is a key concept in technical analysis as it focuses on analyzing and interpreting the patterns, trends, and formations in price data to make trading decisions. Price action analysis disregards the reasons behind price movements and instead focuses on the actual price movement itself.

Significance of Historical Price and Volume Data: Historical price data provides valuable information about the past behavior of a security's price, which can be used to identify patterns and trends. By studying historical price patterns, technical analysts aim to identify recurring patterns and trends that may provide insights into future price movements. Volume data, which represents the number of shares or contracts traded, is also important as it helps assess the level of market participation and the strength of price movements.

The Role of Supply and Demand in Driving Market Trends: Supply and demand dynamics play a crucial role in driving market trends and price action. In a simplified sense, when demand for a security exceeds supply, prices tend to rise, while when supply exceeds demand, prices tend to fall. Technical analysis seeks to identify levels of support and resistance, which represent areas where supply and demand are likely to come into play.

Support levels are price levels where buying pressure is expected to be strong enough to prevent further price declines. Traders and investors often anticipate a bounce in prices when they approach support levels. Resistance levels, on the other hand, represent price levels where selling pressure is expected to be strong enough to prevent further price increases. Traders and investors may expect prices to reverse or consolidate when they approach resistance levels.

By analyzing price action and identifying support and resistance levels, technical analysts aim to gauge the balance between supply and demand and anticipate potential shifts in market trends. This understanding of supply and demand dynamics helps traders make informed decisions about entering or exiting positions.

It's important to note that price action analysis is just one aspect of technical analysis and should be used in conjunction with other technical tools and indicators to gain a comprehensive understanding of market behavior. Additionally, it is essential to consider risk management techniques and other forms of analysis, such as fundamental analysis, when making investment decisions.

5.3 Price Charts and Chart Patterns:

Different types of price charts are used in technical analysis to visualize and analyze price movements in the financial markets. The three most common types of price charts are line charts, bar charts, and candlestick charts.

Line Charts: Line charts are the simplest type of price chart. They plot the closing prices of a security over a specified period of time and connect the data points with a line. Line charts provide a basic overview of price trends but lack the detailed information provided by other chart types.

Bar Charts: Bar charts provide more information than line charts. Each bar on the chart represents a specific time period (such as a day or an hour) and includes four key components: the high, low, opening, and closing prices of the security. The high and low prices are represented by vertical lines, while the opening and closing prices are indicated by horizontal lines (or "ticks") connected by a thicker line called the "bar." Bar charts also often include volume information, typically displayed as a histogram at the bottom of the chart.

Candlestick Charts: Candlestick charts, similar to bar charts, display the high, low, opening, and closing prices of a security for a given time period. However, candlestick charts provide more visual information and are widely used in technical analysis. Each candlestick consists of a rectangular body and two thin lines called "wicks' or "shadows." The body represents the price range between the opening and closing prices, and its color (usually green or white for price increases and red or black for price decreases) indicates whether the security closed higher or lower than its opening price. The wicks represent the range between the high and low prices.

Chart patterns are formations that appear on price charts and provide insights into potential future price movements. Here are some commonly observed chart patterns:

Trends: Trends reflect the direction in which prices are moving over an extended period. An uptrend consists of higher highs and higher lows, indicating a bullish market. A downtrend consists of lower highs and lower lows, indicating a bearish market. Identifying and trading with the trend is a fundamental concept in technical analysis.

Support and Resistance: Support levels are price levels where buying pressure is expected to emerge, preventing further price declines. Resistance levels are price levels where selling pressure is expected to emerge, preventing further price increases. These levels are formed based on previous price reactions and play a crucial role in determining potential entry and exit points.

Reversal Patterns: Reversal patterns indicate a potential change in the direction of the current trend. Examples include the double top (a peak followed by a decline and another failed attempt to reach the previous peak) and the head and shoulders pattern (a peak surrounded by two smaller peaks).

Continuation Patterns: Continuation patterns suggest that the current trend is likely to continue after a temporary consolidation. Examples include flags, pennants, and triangles.

Interpreting chart patterns involves studying the formation, duration, and volume characteristics of the patterns. Traders and analysts look for confirmation signals, such as breakouts or breakdowns, to validate the patterns and make trading decisions.

It's important to note that chart patterns should be used in conjunction with other technical tools, indicators, and risk management techniques to increase the probability of successful trades. Additionally, it's crucial to practice proper money management and consider other factors, such as fundamental analysis and market conditions, when making investment decisions.

5.4 Technical Indicators:

Technical indicators are mathematical calculations applied to price and/or volume data to analyze market trends, momentum, and potential reversals. They help traders and analysts make informed trading decisions by providing additional insights into market conditions. Here's an overview of popular technical indicators:

Moving Averages: Moving averages calculate the average price over a specified period and display it as a line on the chart. They help smooth out price fluctuations and identify the overall trend direction. Common types of moving averages include the simple moving average (SMA) and the exponential moving average (EMA). Traders use moving averages to identify support and resistance levels, spot trend changes, and generate buy or sell signals when the price crosses above or below the moving average line.

Oscillators: Oscillators are indicators that fluctuate within a specific range, indicating overbought or oversold conditions in the market. Some popular oscillators include the Relative Strength Index (RSI), Stochastic Oscillator, and Commodity Channel Index (CCI). These indicators help identify potential reversal points and generate buy or sell signals when they reach extreme levels or diverge from the price.

Momentum Indicators: Momentum indicators measure the speed and strength of price movements. They provide insights into the rate of change in prices and potential continuation or reversal of trends. Examples of momentum indicators include the Moving Average Convergence Divergence (MACD), the Average Directional Index (ADX), and the Rate of Change (ROC). Traders use these indicators to identify market trends, gauge trend strength, and spot potential trend reversals.

Volume Indicators: Volume indicators analyze the trading volume associated with price movements. They provide insights into the strength and confirmation of price trends. Popular volume indicators include the On-Balance Volume (OBV), the Chaikin Money Flow (CMF), and the Volume Weighted Average Price (VWAP). These indicators help traders identify buying or selling pressure, detect potential trend reversals, and confirm the validity of price movements.

Combining multiple indicators can help confirm trading signals and increase the reliability of analysis. For example, traders might use a combination of a moving average crossover (e.g., when the shorter-term moving average crosses above the longer-term moving average) along with an oscillator (e.g., RSI) to generate a buy or sell signal. It's important to select indicators that complement each other and avoid using too many indicators, which can lead to conflicting signals and confusion.

It's worth noting that no single indicator can guarantee accurate predictions, and indicators should be used in conjunction with other tools, such as price patterns and support/resistance levels. Traders should also consider market conditions, risk management techniques, and other factors before making trading decisions.

5.5 Trend Analysis:

Identifying and analyzing market trends is an essential aspect of technical analysis. It helps traders and investors understand the prevailing direction of price movements and make informed decisions. Here are key concepts and tools used for trend identification:

Uptrend: An uptrend occurs when prices consistently make higher highs and higher lows over an extended period. It indicates a bullish market sentiment, with buyers dominating and pushing prices upward.

Downtrend: A downtrend is characterized by prices consistently making lower lows and lower highs over an extended period. It suggests a bearish market sentiment, with sellers dominating and pushing prices downward.

Sideways Trend (Consolidation): A sideways trend occurs when prices move within a relatively narrow range without making significant higher highs or lower lows. It indicates a period of indecision and balanced buying and selling pressure.

Trendlines and trend channels are commonly used tools for identifying and confirming trends:

Trendlines: Trendlines are drawn by connecting a series of higher lows in an uptrend or lower highs in a downtrend. They provide visual representation of the trend's direction and can be used to identify potential support or resistance levels. When prices break above or below a trendline, it may signal a trend reversal or continuation.

Trend Channels: Trend channels encompass the price action within two parallel trendlines, one representing the upper resistance level and the other the lower support level. In an uptrend, prices tend to move between the two trendlines, while in a downtrend, prices generally stay within the channel. Trend channels can help traders identify potential entry and exit points within a trend.

Moving averages are another useful tool for assessing the strength and direction of trends. Here's how they can be applied:

Simple Moving Average (SMA): SMAs calculate the average price over a specified period and provide a smoothed line on the chart. By plotting different SMAs with varying timeframes (e.g., 50-day, 200-day), traders can analyze the crossovers and relationships between these moving averages. A rising or upward-sloping moving average indicates an uptrend, while a declining or downward-sloping moving average suggests a downtrend.

Moving Average Crossovers: Moving average crossovers occur when two moving averages of different timeframes intersect. The most common crossover is the 50-day moving average crossing above or below the 200-day moving average. A bullish signal is generated when the shorter-term moving average crosses above the longer-term moving average, indicating the potential start of an uptrend. Conversely, a bearish signal occurs when the shorter-term moving average crosses below the longer-term moving average, suggesting the potential start of a downtrend.

When using moving averages, it's important to consider the timeframe and the market being analyzed. Shorter-term moving averages are more sensitive to price changes and can provide timely signals, while longer-term moving averages can help identify broader trends.

Remember that trend analysis should be used in conjunction with other technical analysis tools and factors, such as support and resistance levels, chart patterns, and volume analysis, to strengthen the overall analysis and decision-making process.

5.6 Support and Resistance Levels:

Support and resistance levels are key concepts in technical analysis that help identify price levels where buying and selling pressure may be significant. Here's an explanation of support and resistance and their role in trading:

Support Levels: Support levels are price levels where demand for an asset is expected to be strong enough to prevent it from falling further. These levels act as a floor for prices, as buyers are willing to enter the market and purchase the asset, creating upward pressure. Support levels are often formed at previous troughs or consolidation zones on a price chart. Traders and investors may anticipate a potential bounce or reversal in prices when they approach a support level.

Resistance Levels: Resistance levels are price levels where selling pressure is expected to be strong enough to prevent the asset from rising further. These levels act as a ceiling for prices, as sellers are willing to enter the market and sell the asset, creating downward pressure. Resistance levels are often formed at previous peaks or consolidation zones on a price chart. Traders and investors may anticipate a potential pullback or reversal in prices when they approach a resistance level.

Role Reversal: The concept of role reversal occurs when a support level, once broken, becomes a resistance level, or when a resistance level, once broken, becomes a support level. This phenomenon is based on the idea that market participants remember these levels and view them as significant. When prices break through a support level, it may indicate a shift in market sentiment, and the previous support level may now act as a barrier for upward movement. Similarly, when prices break through a resistance level, it may suggest a change in market sentiment, and the previous resistance level may now act as a support level.

Utilizing Support and Resistance Levels: Traders and investors use support and resistance levels to make trading decisions, including entry and exit points:

Entry Points: Traders often look for buying opportunities near support levels, as there is a higher probability of a bounce or a reversal in prices. They may set buy orders or look for confirmation signals, such as bullish candlestick patterns or positive indicators, to enter a trade. By entering near support levels, traders aim to limit downside risk and capture potential upside movement.

Exit Points: Resistance levels can be used as potential exit points for traders who are holding long positions. When prices approach a resistance level, there may be increased selling pressure, making it a suitable point to take profits or tighten stop-loss orders. Exit strategies may include selling the asset or adjusting risk management parameters based on the behavior of prices near resistance levels.

It's important to note that support and resistance levels are not foolproof and should be used in conjunction with other technical analysis tools and factors to strengthen trading decisions. Traders should also consider the overall market conditions, volume analysis, and other price patterns to confirm the validity of support and resistance levels.

5.7 Japanese Candlestick Patterns:

Japanese candlestick charting techniques are a popular method used in technical analysis to analyze price patterns and trends. Candlestick charts provide valuable information about the open, high, low, and closing prices for a specific time period. Each candlestick represents a single period, such as a day, week, or hour, depending on the chosen timeframe. Here's an introduction to Japanese candlestick charting techniques and some key candlestick patterns:

Doji: A doji candlestick has a small body, indicating that the opening and closing prices are very close or almost the same. It represents indecision in the market between buyers and sellers. A doji can indicate a potential reversal or a pause in the current trend, depending on the context in which it appears.

Hammer and Hanging Man: A hammer candlestick has a small body and a long lower shadow, resembling a hammer. It suggests a potential bullish reversal when it occurs after a downtrend. On the other hand, a hanging man candlestick has a small body and a long lower shadow, occurring after an uptrend, indicating a potential bearish reversal. The length of the shadow compared to the body is important in determining the significance of these patterns.

Engulfing Patterns: Engulfing patterns consist of two candlesticks, where the body of the second candlestick engulfs or completely "engulfs' the body of the first candlestick. A bullish engulfing pattern occurs when a small bearish candlestick is followed by a larger bullish candlestick, suggesting a potential reversal from a downtrend to an uptrend. A bearish engulfing pattern is the opposite, with a small bullish candlestick followed by a larger bearish candlestick, indicating a potential reversal from an uptrend to a downtrend.

Morning Star and Evening Star: The morning star is a three-candlestick pattern that occurs during a downtrend. It starts with a large bearish candlestick, followed by a small-bodied candlestick (usually a doji or a spinning top) that shows indecision, and ends with a large bullish candlestick. This pattern suggests a potential bullish reversal. The evening star is the opposite, occurring during an uptrend and indicating a potential bearish reversal.

Shooting Star and Inverted Hammer: A shooting star candlestick has a small body and a long upper shadow, resembling an inverted hammer. It appears after an uptrend and suggests a potential bearish reversal. An inverted hammer has a small body and a long upper shadow, occurring after a downtrend, indicating a potential bullish reversal.

Using Candlestick Patterns: Traders use candlestick patterns to identify potential reversals or continuation patterns in price trends. These patterns provide visual cues about the balance between buying and selling pressure in the market. Traders may look for confirmation signals, such as increased volume or other technical indicators, to validate the significance of the candlestick patterns. By understanding the interpretation of candlestick patterns, traders can make informed decisions regarding entry and exit points, stop-loss levels, and overall trend analysis.

It's important to note that candlestick patterns should not be used in isolation and should be considered within the broader context of technical analysis, including other indicators, chart patterns, and market conditions.

5.8 Volume Analysis:

Volume plays a crucial role in technical analysis as it provides valuable information about the level of participation and intensity of trading in the market. It represents the number of shares or contracts traded during a given period, such as a day, week, or hour. Volume can help confirm price movements, identify potential trend reversals or continuations, and provide insights into market sentiment. Here's an overview of the role of volume in technical analysis and some volume indicators:

Confirmation of Price Movements: Volume can help confirm the strength and validity of price movements. In an uptrend, higher trading volume accompanying price increases indicates strong buying pressure, suggesting a healthy trend. Similarly, in a downtrend, higher trading volume during price declines suggests strong selling pressure. When volume confirms the price movements, it adds credibility to the trend.

Volume Indicators: Volume indicators are technical tools that use volume data to provide additional insights into price movements. Some popular volume indicators include:

Volume Moving Average: It calculates the average volume over a specific period, smoothening out short-term fluctuations and providing a trend of volume.

On-Balance Volume (OBV): OBV measures the cumulative volume by adding volume on up days and subtracting volume on down days. It helps identify the flow of volume and can signal potential trend reversals.

Chaikin Money Flow (CMF): CMF combines volume and price data to measure the buying and selling pressure in the market. It uses the accumulation/distribution line and can provide insights into market sentiment.

Volume Oscillators: These indicators, such as the Volume Price Trend Oscillator (VPT) or the Volume Rate of Change (VROC), measure the rate of change of volume over a specific period. They can help identify overbought or oversold conditions in the market.

Volume Patterns and Market Sentiment: Analyzing volume patterns can provide insights into market sentiment.

Increasing Volume: Rising volume during a price rally suggests bullish market sentiment, indicating strong buying interest. It indicates that more participants are entering the market and supporting the upward price movement.

Decreasing Volume: Declining volume during a price rally may signal waning interest and weaker buying pressure. It could indicate that the price increase lacks conviction and might be susceptible to a potential reversal.

Volume Spikes: Unusually high trading volume compared to the average volume can indicate significant market events or news releases. Volume spikes often accompany important price movements, and they can signal a shift in market sentiment or the start of a new trend.

Analyzing volume alongside price movements and other technical indicators can provide a more comprehensive view of market dynamics. It helps traders understand the level of participation, the strength of trends, and potential shifts in market sentiment. However, it's important to consider volume in conjunction with other technical analysis tools to validate signals and confirm the accuracy of price movements.

5.9 Moving Average Crossovers:

Moving average crossovers are a popular technical analysis technique used to identify potential trend reversals, confirm existing trends, and generate entry or exit signals. This approach involves comparing two or more moving averages of different periods and observing their crossover points on a price chart. The most common moving averages used in crossover analysis are the simple moving average (SMA) and the exponential moving average (EMA).

Here's an overview of how moving average crossovers work:

Trend Confirmation: Moving average crossovers can help confirm the direction of a trend. When a shorter-term moving average (e.g., 50-day SMA) crosses above a longer-term moving average (e.g., 200-day SMA), it is known as a bullish crossover. This crossover suggests that the trend is potentially shifting from bearish to bullish, indicating a buy signal. Conversely, when the shorter-term moving average crosses below the longer-term moving average, it is called a bearish crossover, signaling a potential shift from bullish to bearish and indicating a sell signal.

Entry and Exit Points: Moving average crossovers can be used as signals to enter or exit positions. Traders may wait for a bullish crossover to initiate a long position or buy signal, indicating that the stock price is potentially entering an uptrend. Conversely, a bearish crossover can be used as a signal to exit a long position or initiate a short position, suggesting that the stock price is potentially entering a downtrend. The timing of entry and exit may vary based on the trader's strategy and time frame.

Golden Cross and Death Cross: The golden cross and death cross are notable moving average crossover patterns:

Golden Cross: A golden cross occurs when a shorter-term moving average (e.g., 50-day SMA) crosses above a longer-term moving average (e.g., 200-day SMA). This pattern is considered a bullish signal, indicating a potential shift to a long-term uptrend. Traders often interpret the golden cross as a confirmation of a strong bullish market sentiment.

Death Cross: A death cross happens when a shorter-term moving average (e.g., 50-day SMA) crosses below a longer-term moving average (e.g., 200-day SMA). This pattern is considered a bearish signal, suggesting a potential shift to a long-term downtrend. The death cross is often interpreted as a confirmation of a strong bearish market sentiment.

It's important to note that moving average crossovers are lagging indicators, meaning they react to price movements that have already occurred. They may not always provide accurate signals, especially during choppy or sideways market conditions. Traders often use moving average crossovers in conjunction with other technical analysis tools and indicators to validate signals and make informed trading decisions.

5.10 Backtesting and Trading Systems:'

Backtesting is a crucial step in developing and implementing trading strategies based on technical analysis. It involves testing a trading strategy using historical data to evaluate its performance and potential profitability before applying it in real-time trading. Here are the key aspects and benefits of backtesting:

Strategy Development and Refinement: Backtesting allows traders to develop and refine their trading strategies by analyzing historical price data and testing various parameters, indicators, entry and exit rules, and risk management techniques. It helps in identifying patterns, trends, and signals that have worked well in the past.

Performance Evaluation: Backtesting provides a quantitative assessment of a trading strategy's performance by simulating trades on historical data. Traders can analyze key performance metrics such as profit/loss, win rate, average gain/loss, maximum drawdown, and risk-to-reward ratio. This evaluation helps in determining the strategy's potential profitability and risk-adjusted returns.

Risk Management: Backtesting helps traders assess the risk associated with their strategies. By analyzing historical drawdowns and risk metrics, traders can adjust position sizes, set appropriate stop-loss levels, and fine-tune risk management rules to achieve a balance between risk and reward.

Confidence and Discipline: Backtesting instills confidence in traders by demonstrating how a strategy has performed under various market conditions. It helps traders to understand the strengths and weaknesses of their strategies, leading to increased discipline and adherence to predetermined rules during live trading.

Strategy Optimization: Backtesting allows traders to optimize their trading strategies by testing different variations, parameters, and combinations. Traders can use optimization techniques to find the best settings for their strategies based on historical data and performance metrics.

Systematic Approach: Backtesting promotes a systematic approach to trading by removing emotions and biases from decision-making. Traders can follow predefined rules and objectively evaluate the performance of their strategies without being influenced by short-term market fluctuations.

It's important to note that backtesting has its limitations. Historical performance does not guarantee future results, and market conditions can change over time. It's crucial to regularly review and update trading strategies based on evolving market dynamics. Additionally, backtesting should be conducted using reliable and accurate historical data, accounting for factors like transaction costs, slippage, and market liquidity.

Overall, backtesting is an essential tool for traders to validate and fine-tune their trading strategies, manage risk, and gain confidence in their approach before executing trades in real-time.

Chapter 6: Chart Patterns and Trends: Identifying and Trading Profitable Patterns

Introduction: In Chapter 6, we will focus on chart patterns and trends, which are essential components of technical analysis. Chart patterns can provide valuable insights into the behavior of market participants and can be used to predict future price movements. Understanding how to identify and trade profitable patterns will enhance your trading skills and improve your decision-making process.

6.1 The Importance of Chart Patterns:

Chart patterns play a significant role in technical analysis as they provide visual representations of price movements and patterns that can help identify potential trading opportunities. Chart patterns are formed by the price action on a price chart and can reflect market psychology and investor sentiment. Here are some key aspects and advantages of trading chart patterns:

Market Psychology and Investor Sentiment: Chart patterns are a reflection of the collective psychology and sentiment of market participants. They depict the tug-of-war between buyers and sellers, showcasing periods of accumulation, distribution, or indecision in the market. By analyzing chart patterns, traders can gain insights into market sentiment and anticipate potential price movements.

Pattern Recognition: Chart patterns help traders recognize recurring price formations that have historically led to specific price outcomes. These patterns can include trends, reversal patterns, and continuation patterns. Traders who are proficient in identifying chart patterns can gain an edge in predicting price behavior and making informed trading decisions.

Entry and Exit Points: Chart patterns provide traders with potential entry and exit points for their trades. For example, a breakout from a consolidation pattern or a trendline can signal a potential entry point, while a pattern failure or a reversal pattern can indicate an exit or a change in the direction of a trade. By combining chart patterns with other technical indicators or confirmation signals, traders can enhance the timing and effectiveness of their trades.

Risk Management: Chart patterns also aid in risk management by providing reference points for placing stop-loss orders. Traders can set stop-loss levels below support levels in bullish patterns or above resistance levels in bearish patterns, helping to limit potential losses if the pattern fails to follow through. This approach allows traders to define their risk and manage it accordingly.

Scalability and Timeframes: Chart patterns can be observed across different timeframes, making them applicable to various trading styles, from day trading to long-term investing. Traders can spot patterns on intraday charts for short-term trades or on longer-term charts for position trades. This scalability allows traders to adapt chart patterns to their preferred trading timeframe and strategy.

Objective Decision-Making: Chart patterns provide traders with a visual framework that helps remove emotions and biases from decision-making. By relying on objective criteria defined by chart patterns, traders can reduce the impact of subjective factors and make more disciplined and systematic trading decisions.

It's important to note that while chart patterns can provide valuable insights and trading opportunities, they are not infallible and should be used in conjunction with other technical analysis tools and risk management techniques. Traders should consider the overall market context, news events, and fundamental factors alongside chart patterns to make well-informed trading decisions.

6.2 Uptrends and Downtrends:

IDENTIFYING AND UNDERSTANDING market trends is an essential aspect of technical analysis. By recognizing and analyzing trends, traders can align their trading strategies with the prevailing market direction. Here are the key elements of identifying and understanding market trends:

Uptrends: An uptrend is characterized by a series of higher highs and higher lows. In an uptrend, prices generally move in an upward direction, indicating a bullish market sentiment. Traders and investors often seek opportunities to buy or go long in an uptrend, anticipating further price appreciation.

Downtrends: A downtrend is marked by a sequence of lower highs and lower lows. In a downtrend, prices generally move downward, signaling a bearish market sentiment. Traders and investors may consider short-selling or selling positions in a downtrend, aiming to profit from further price declines.

Sideways Trends (Consolidation): In a sideways trend, also known as consolidation, prices move within a relatively narrow range without a clear upward or downward direction. Sideways trends indicate indecision or a lack of strong market sentiment. Traders may choose to wait for a breakout from the consolidation range before taking a position.

Trendlines: Trendlines are drawn on price charts to visually represent the direction and strength of a trend. An uptrend line is drawn by connecting the higher lows, while a downtrend line is created by connecting the lower highs. Trendlines act as dynamic levels of support and resistance and can provide insights into the potential continuation or reversal of a trend. Traders use trendlines to confirm the direction of the trend and identify potential entry and exit points.

When drawing trendlines, it is essential to connect at least two significant swing highs or swing lows to create a valid trendline. The more touches a trendline has, the stronger it becomes, indicating a more significant trend. Traders should focus on the most recent swing points for drawing trendlines, as they carry more relevance in determining the current trend.

It's important to note that trendlines are not infallible and should be used in conjunction with other technical analysis tools and indicators. They provide a visual representation of market trends, but traders should consider other factors, such as volume, price patterns, and market context, to validate their trading decisions. Additionally, trendlines are subjective and can vary slightly depending on the trader's interpretation. Therefore, it is crucial to regularly reassess and adjust trendlines as new price data emerges.

6.3 Support and Resistance Levels:

Support and resistance levels are key concepts in technical analysis that help traders identify price levels at which buying (support) or selling (resistance) pressure tends to emerge. These levels are formed based on the historical price movements and represent areas where the supply and demand dynamics of an asset are expected to exert an influence.

Horizontal Support and Resistance Levels: Horizontal support and resistance levels are price levels where the buying or selling pressure has historically caused the price to stall or reverse. These levels are typically drawn as horizontal lines on a price chart and are formed by connecting multiple swing highs or swing lows. Support levels are considered potential buying opportunities as they indicate a level where demand for an asset is expected to be strong enough to prevent further price declines. Resistance levels, on the other hand, are seen as potential selling opportunities as they represent a level where supply is expected to outweigh demand, causing price reversals or consolidations.

Dynamic Support and Resistance Levels using Trendlines: Trendlines can also act as dynamic support and resistance levels. In an uptrend, an upward sloping trendline connects the higher lows and may act as a support level, representing the bullish bias in the market. In a downtrend, a downward sloping trendline connects the lower highs and may act as a resistance level, indicating the bearish sentiment. When the price approaches these trendlines, traders often watch for potential price reactions such as bounces or breakouts.

Support and resistance levels are not precise price points but rather areas where price reactions are more likely to occur. As these levels are based on historical price data, they can be influenced by market psychology and the collective actions of market participants. When support or resistance levels are broken, they can potentially reverse their roles, with previous support becoming new resistance, and vice versa. This phenomenon is known as "role reversal" and is closely observed by traders for potential trading opportunities.

It is important to note that support and resistance levels should not be considered as standalone signals for trading decisions. Traders often combine these levels with other technical analysis tools such as trendlines, chart patterns, and indicators to validate their trading strategies and make more informed trading decisions. Additionally, support and resistance levels should be regularly reassessed and adjusted as new price data becomes available, as market conditions and dynamics can change over time.

6.4 Reversal Patterns:

Reversal patterns are chart patterns that suggest a potential change in the prevailing trend. They are important to technical analysts as they can provide early indications of trend reversals and potential trading opportunities. Here are three common reversal patterns:

Head and Shoulders Pattern: The head and shoulders pattern is a reversal pattern that typically occurs at the end of an uptrend. It consists of three peaks, with the middle peak (the head) being higher than the other two (the shoulders). The neckline connects the lows between the shoulders. When the price breaks below the neckline, it indicates a bearish reversal and a potential trend change. Traders often look for this pattern as a signal to enter short positions or exit long positions.

Double Top and Double Bottom Patterns: The double top pattern forms when the price reaches a resistance level twice, fails to break above it, and reverses downward. It signifies a potential trend reversal from bullish to bearish. Conversely, the double bottom pattern occurs when the price reaches a support level twice, fails to break below it, and reverses upward. It indicates a potential trend reversal from bearish to bullish. Traders may look for confirmation of the pattern through a neckline break or other technical indicators before entering trades.

Triple Top and Triple Bottom Patterns: The triple top pattern is similar to the double top but has three peaks at approximately the same price level. It suggests a stronger resistance level and potential trend reversal. Conversely, the triple bottom pattern has three bottoms at approximately the same price level, indicating stronger support. Traders analyze the pattern and its confirmation signals to identify potential entry or exit points.

These reversal patterns are visual representations of shifts in market sentiment and can provide valuable insights into potential trend reversals. Traders often combine these patterns with other technical indicators, such as volume analysis and momentum oscillators, to confirm the validity of the pattern and enhance their trading decisions. It's important to note that not all patterns are successful in signaling reversals, so risk management and proper trade execution are crucial when trading based on these patterns.

6.5 Continuation Patterns:

Continuation patterns are chart patterns that indicate a temporary pause or consolidation in an ongoing trend before the price continues its previous direction. These patterns suggest that the prevailing trend is likely to continue once the consolidation is complete. Here are three common continuation patterns:

Flags and Pennants: Flags and pennants are short-term continuation patterns that occur after a strong price move. A flag pattern consists of a rectangular shape, while a pennant pattern is formed by converging trendlines that resemble a small symmetrical triangle. Both patterns indicate a temporary pause in the trend before it continues. Traders often look for a breakout in the direction of the prevailing trend as a signal to enter trades.

Symmetrical Triangles: Symmetrical triangles are continuation patterns that form when the price consolidates between converging trendlines. The upper trendline connects the lower highs, while the lower trendline connects the higher lows. As the pattern develops, the range between the trendlines narrows, indicating a decrease in volatility. Traders anticipate a breakout in either direction and may enter trades when the price breaks out of the pattern with strong volume.

Ascending and Descending Triangles: Ascending triangles and descending triangles are continuation patterns that indicate a period of consolidation before the price continues its trend. In an ascending triangle, the upper trendline is flat, while the lower trendline slopes upward. In a descending triangle, the lower trendline is flat, while the upper trendline slopes downward. Traders wait for a breakout above the upper trendline in an ascending triangle or a breakout below the lower trendline in a descending triangle as potential entry signals.

When trading continuation patterns, it's important to consider other technical indicators, such as volume and momentum oscillators, to confirm the validity of the pattern and support trading decisions. Traders often set price targets based on the height of the pattern or use trailing stop-loss orders to manage risk. It's essential to wait for a confirmed breakout before entering trades and to practice proper risk management techniques.

6.6 Breakout Trading Strategies:

Trading breakouts from chart patterns involves entering a trade when the price breaks out of a well-defined chart pattern, such as a consolidation or a continuation pattern. Here are some strategies and considerations for trading breakouts:

Entry Strategy:

Identify the chart pattern: Look for chart patterns that indicate a consolidation or continuation, such as rectangles, triangles, or flags.

Determine the breakout level: Identify the key level at which the price needs to break to confirm the breakout. This could be the upper or lower trendline of the pattern or a specific price level.

Wait for confirmation: Don't enter the trade until the price convincingly breaks out of the pattern. It's important to wait for a strong breakout with a significant move in price and accompanied by increased volume.

Exit Strategy:

Set a target: Determine a target price based on the height of the pattern or previous price swings. This can help you gauge the potential profit from the breakout.

Use trailing stop-loss orders: As the price moves in your favor, trail your stop-loss order to protect your profits and manage risk. This allows you to capture as much profit as possible if the price continues to trend in your desired direction.

Consider time-based exits: If the price fails to gain momentum and stalls after the breakout, it may be prudent to exit the trade to avoid potential losses.

Confirming Breakouts with Volume Analysis: Volume analysis can provide valuable confirmation for breakout trades. Here's how you can incorporate volume analysis into your breakout trading strategy:

Increase in volume: Look for a substantial increase in volume as the price breaks out of the pattern. This indicates strong participation and conviction from traders, supporting the validity of the breakout.

Volume patterns: Analyze the volume patterns leading up to the breakout. Ideally, you want to see declining volume during the consolidation phase and a sharp increase in volume during the breakout. This suggests a potential influx of buyers or sellers driving the breakout.

It's important to note that not all breakouts are successful, and false breakouts can occur. Therefore, it's crucial to apply proper risk management techniques, such as setting appropriate stop-loss orders and position sizing, to protect against potential losses. Additionally, consider using a combination of technical indicators and other analysis techniques to increase the probability of successful breakout trades.

6.7 Trend Reversal Confirmation:

Confirming trend reversals using chart patterns can provide valuable insights for traders and investors. Here are some chart patterns that can help confirm trend reversals:

Bullish and Bearish Engulfing Patterns:

Bullish Engulfing Pattern: This pattern occurs when a small bearish candle is followed by a larger bullish candle that completely engulfs the previous candle's body. It suggests a potential reversal from a downtrend to an uptrend.

Bearish Engulfing Pattern: Conversely, a bearish engulfing pattern happens when a small bullish candle is followed by a larger bearish candle that engulfs the previous candle's body. It indicates a possible reversal from an uptrend to a downtrend.

Piercing Pattern and Dark Cloud Cover:

Piercing Pattern: The piercing pattern is a bullish reversal pattern. It occurs when a bearish candle is followed by a bullish candle that opens below the previous candle's low but closes more than halfway up the previous candle's body. It suggests a potential reversal from a downtrend to an uptrend.

Dark Cloud Cover: On the other hand, the dark cloud cover is a bearish reversal pattern. It forms when a bullish candle is followed by a bearish candle that opens above the previous candle's high but closes more than halfway down the previous candle's body. It indicates a possible reversal from an uptrend to a downtrend.

Tweezer Tops and Bottoms:

Tweezer Tops: A tweezer top pattern occurs when two consecutive candles have the same high, creating a resistance level. The first candle is typically bullish, and the second candle is bearish. It suggests a potential reversal from an uptrend to a downtrend.

Tweezer Bottoms: Conversely, a tweezer bottom pattern forms when two consecutive candles have the same low, creating a support level. The first candle is usually bearish, and the second candle is bullish. It indicates a possible reversal from a downtrend to an uptrend.

To confirm trend reversals using these chart patterns, it's important to consider the following factors:

The context: Analyze the overall trend and market conditions before relying solely on the chart pattern. The reversal pattern should align with the broader market context.

Volume: Pay attention to the volume accompanying the pattern. An increase in volume during a reversal pattern can lend more credibility to the potential trend reversal.

Confirmation: Wait for additional confirmation signals, such as a break of a trendline or the occurrence of other reversal indicators, to increase the reliability of the pattern.

As with any trading strategy, it's important to manage risk by using appropriate stop-loss orders, considering position sizing, and combining chart patterns with other technical indicators or analysis techniques for a comprehensive assessment of market conditions.

6.8 Fibonacci Retracement and Extensions:

Fibonacci retracement and extension levels are widely used in technical analysis to identify potential support and resistance levels and price targets. Here's how they can be applied:

Fibonacci Retracement Levels:

Fibonacci retracement levels are drawn on a price chart to identify potential support and resistance levels during a price correction or retracement within a larger trend. The key Fibonacci retracement levels are 23.6%, 38.2%, 50%, 61.8%, and 78.6%. These levels are derived from the Fibonacci sequence and its mathematical ratios.

To apply Fibonacci retracement levels, you identify a significant swing high and low on the price chart and then draw the retracement levels between them. Traders often look for price reactions (bounces or reversals) at these levels to indicate potential support or resistance zones.

Fibonacci Extensions:

Fibonacci extensions are used to determine potential price targets for trend continuation trades. They are drawn beyond the current price range to identify where the price may reach if the trend continues. The key Fibonacci extension levels are 127.2%, 161.8%, 200%, and 261.8%.

Traders typically apply Fibonacci extensions by identifying a significant swing high and low and then extending the Fibonacci levels beyond the swing high (for bullish trends) or swing low (for bearish trends). These levels can act as potential targets for profit-taking or the initiation of new trades.

Applying Fibonacci Tools to Chart Patterns:

Fibonacci retracement and extension levels can be applied to various chart patterns to provide additional insights and potential price levels. For example, in a bullish trend, you can apply Fibonacci retracement levels to a pullback within a bullish chart pattern (e.g., flag, pennant) to identify potential support levels for a trade entry. Similarly, Fibonacci extensions can be applied to a breakout from a bullish chart pattern to determine potential price targets for a trade.

It's important to note that Fibonacci levels are not foolproof and should be used in conjunction with other technical analysis tools and indicators to confirm potential support, resistance, and price targets. Additionally, it's essential to consider other factors such as trend direction, market conditions, and price action to increase the probability of successful trades.

6.9 Cup and Handle Pattern:

The cup and handle pattern is a bullish continuation pattern that often signals a potential trend reversal and the resumption of an upward price movement. Here's an overview of the pattern and some trading strategies associated with it:

Description of the Cup and Handle Pattern:

The cup and handle pattern consists of two main components: the cup and the handle. The cup portion resembles a rounded bottom or a "U" shape, while the handle appears as a smaller consolidation or pullback after the cup formation.

The cup and handle pattern indicates a temporary pause or consolidation in an uptrend, followed by a potential breakout to new highs. It is considered a bullish signal, suggesting that buyers are gaining strength and the stock may continue its upward movement.

Trading Strategies for the Cup and Handle Pattern:

Entry Strategy: Traders typically enter a trade on the breakout of the handle portion of the pattern. This occurs when the price breaks above the resistance level formed by the handle. The breakout is often accompanied by an increase in volume, which confirms the strength of the upward move.

Stop-Loss Strategy: Traders may place a stop-loss order below the lowest point of the handle or below the breakout level. This helps protect against potential losses if the pattern fails and the price reverses.

Price Target: To determine a price target for the cup and handle pattern, traders can measure the depth of the cup and project it upward from the breakout level. This gives an estimate of the potential price move after the breakout.

Volume Analysis in Cup and Handle Patterns: Volume analysis plays a crucial role in confirming the validity of the cup and handle pattern. Here's how volume can be analyzed in this pattern:

During the formation of the cup, volume should gradually decrease as the price reaches the bottom of the cup. This indicates a decrease in selling pressure.

When the handle is being formed, volume should contract further, signaling a reduction in trading activity and consolidation.

Upon the breakout from the handle, volume should expand, reflecting increased buying interest and confirming the strength of the breakout.

Analyzing volume helps traders gauge the participation and conviction of market participants, providing additional confirmation of the pattern's validity.

As with any trading pattern, it's essential to consider other factors such as overall market conditions, company fundamentals, and other technical indicators before making trading decisions. Additionally, risk management techniques such as proper position sizing and setting stop-loss orders are crucial to protect against potential losses.

6.10 Wedge Patterns:

Rising Wedge and Falling Wedge patterns are two common chart patterns that can provide insights into potential trend reversals. Here's an overview of these patterns, trading strategies associated with them, and the role of volume analysis:

Rising Wedge:

Rising Wedge is a bearish pattern that forms when the price is making higher highs and higher lows within a narrowing price range. It indicates a potential reversal of an uptrend.

To identify a Rising Wedge, connect the swing highs and swing lows with trendlines that converge towards each other.

Trading Strategy: Traders often take a bearish approach when trading the Rising Wedge pattern. They may look for entry opportunities when the price breaks below the lower trendline, indicating a potential trend reversal. Stop-loss orders can be placed above the upper trendline to manage risk.

Falling Wedge:

Falling Wedge is a bullish pattern that forms when the price is making lower lows and lower highs within a narrowing price range. It suggests a potential reversal of a downtrend.

To identify a Falling Wedge, connect the swing lows and swing highs with trendlines that converge towards each other.

Trading Strategy: Traders typically take a bullish stance when trading the Falling Wedge pattern. They may look for entry opportunities when the price breaks above the upper trendline, indicating a potential trend reversal. Stop-loss orders can be placed below the lower trendline to manage risk.

Volume Analysis and Confirmation in Wedge Patterns: Volume analysis can provide additional confirmation for wedge patterns. Here's how it can be applied:

During the formation of both Rising Wedge and Falling Wedge patterns, volume should generally decrease as the price range narrows. This indicates a decrease in buying or selling pressure.

When the price breaks out of the wedge pattern, volume should increase, preferably above average. This surge in volume confirms the validity of the breakout and suggests greater market participation.

Analyzing volume can help confirm the strength and sustainability of the pattern breakout.

As with any chart pattern, it's important to consider other technical indicators, market conditions, and fundamental factors before making trading decisions. Risk management techniques, such as setting stop-loss orders and managing position sizes, are also crucial to protect against potential losses.

Chapter 7: Risk Management Strategies for Stock Trading

Introduction: In Chapter 7, we will shift our focus to risk management strategies—a crucial aspect of successful stock trading. While trading offers profit potential, it also involves inherent risks. Understanding and implementing effective risk management techniques will help protect your capital and mitigate potential losses. This chapter will explore various risk management strategies that can enhance your trading performance.

7.1 Importance of Risk Management:

Risk management plays a crucial role in stock trading and investing as it aims to protect capital and minimize potential losses. Here are some key aspects to understand about risk management in stock trading:

Significance of Risk Management:

Risk management involves identifying, assessing, and controlling potential risks associated with stock trading. It helps traders and investors navigate the uncertainties of the market and make informed decisions.

By implementing risk management strategies, traders can limit their exposure to potential losses and preserve their capital over the long term.

Effective risk management allows for a more disciplined and systematic approach to trading, reducing the likelihood of emotional decision-making driven by fear or greed.

Risk-Reward Relationship:

The risk-reward relationship refers to the trade-off between the potential gains and potential losses of a trade or investment. Generally, higher potential returns are associated with higher levels of risk.

Traders need to assess the potential rewards of a trade against the potential risks involved. This evaluation helps determine whether the potential reward justifies taking on the associated risk.

Risk management involves setting appropriate risk-reward ratios, such as maintaining a favorable risk-to-reward ratio of, for example, 1:2 or 1:3, where the potential reward outweighs the potential risk.

Psychological Aspects of Risk Management:

Risk management is not only about implementing technical strategies but also understanding the psychological aspects of trading.

Emotions, such as fear and greed, can significantly impact decision-making. Traders may be tempted to take excessive risks or hold on to losing positions due to emotional attachment.

Implementing risk management techniques, such as setting stop-loss orders and adhering to predetermined risk limits, helps overcome emotional biases and allows for more objective decision-making.

Managing position sizes and diversifying portfolios also play a role in mitigating emotional stress and reducing the impact of individual trade outcomes.

In conclusion, risk management is essential in stock trading to protect capital and minimize potential losses. It involves understanding the risk-reward relationship, implementing strategies to control risks, and addressing the psychological aspects of trading. By effectively managing risks, traders can maintain a disciplined approach, make informed decisions, and increase their chances of long-term success in the market.

7.2 Setting Risk Tolerance and Objectives:

Assessing your risk tolerance and establishing risk parameters is a crucial step in developing a sound risk management strategy. Here are some considerations for defining your risk tolerance and aligning it with your trading objectives:

Self-Assessment of Risk Tolerance:

Evaluate your comfort level with taking risks by considering your past experiences, financial circumstances, and emotional disposition towards risk.

Assess how much loss you can tolerate without significant distress or negative impact on your financial goals.

Consider your investment knowledge and experience as they can influence your ability to handle different levels of risk.

Understand Your Trading Objectives:

Clearly define your trading objectives, such as capital appreciation, income generation, or wealth preservation.

Determine the time horizon for your trading activities, whether it's short-term, medium-term, or long-term.

Consider your financial goals, such as saving for retirement, funding education, or achieving specific milestones.

Align Risk Tolerance with Objectives:

Ensure that your risk tolerance aligns with your trading objectives. For example, if you have a low-risk tolerance, it may be more appropriate to focus on conservative investment strategies and longer-term trading approaches.

If your risk tolerance is higher, you might consider more aggressive trading strategies that involve higher levels of risk and potential returns.

Consider Personal Circumstances:

Take into account your current financial situation, including your income, expenses, and overall financial stability.

Evaluate any unique circumstances that may affect your risk tolerance, such as dependents, existing debt obligations, or future financial commitments.

Regular Review and Adjustment:

Your risk tolerance and financial circumstances may change over time, so it's important to regularly review and reassess them.

Adjust your risk parameters accordingly to ensure they remain aligned with your trading objectives and personal circumstances.

It's worth noting that risk tolerance is a personal decision, and there is no one-size-fits-all approach. It's important to be honest with yourself about your comfort level with risk and to seek professional advice if needed. By aligning your risk tolerance with your trading objectives and considering factors such as time horizon, financial goals, and personal circumstances, you can establish appropriate risk parameters and make informed trading decisions that suit your individual needs.

7.3 Position Sizing:

Determining the appropriate position size for each trade is a crucial aspect of risk management. Here are some considerations and techniques to help you with position sizing:

Risk-Per-Trade:

Determine the maximum amount of capital you are willing to risk on each trade. This is typically expressed as a percentage of your trading capital.

Commonly recommended risk-per-trade ranges from 1% to 5% of your trading capital, depending on your risk tolerance and trading strategy.

For example, if your trading capital is $10,000 and you decide to risk 2% per trade, your maximum risk per trade would be $200.

Risk-to-Reward Ratio:

Assess the potential reward-to-risk ratio for each trade, which compares the potential profit to the potential loss.

A favorable risk-to-reward ratio typically means the potential profit is higher than the potential loss.

For example, if you set a risk-to-reward ratio of 1:2, it means you are aiming for a potential profit that is at least twice the size of your potential loss.

Position Sizing Calculation:

Calculate the position size based on your risk-per-trade and risk-to-reward ratio.

Divide the maximum risk per trade by the difference between your entry price and stop-loss level to determine the position size.

For example, if you are risking $200 on a trade and your stop-loss is $2 below your entry price, your position size would be $200 divided by $2, resulting in a position size of 100 shares or contracts.

Percentage Allocation:

Allocate a specific percentage of your trading capital to each trade.

This approach ensures that your position sizes are proportional to your trading capital and risk tolerance.

For example, if you allocate 2% of your trading capital to each trade, you would adjust your position size accordingly.

It's important to note that position sizing techniques can vary depending on your trading strategy, risk tolerance, and preferences. It's essential to find a position sizing approach that aligns with your risk management goals and trading style. Additionally, regularly reassess your trading capital and adjust your position sizes accordingly to account for changes in your capital base.

7.4 Stop Loss Orders:

Stop loss orders are an essential risk management tool used in trading to limit potential losses on a trade. Here's an overview of their purpose, benefits, and types:

Purpose of Stop Loss Orders:

The primary purpose of a stop loss order is to protect your capital by defining a predetermined exit point for a trade if the price moves against your position.

By placing a stop loss order, you set a price level at which your position will be automatically closed, helping to minimize potential losses.

Benefits of Stop Loss Orders:

Loss Limitation: Stop loss orders help limit losses by providing a predetermined exit point, allowing you to control risk and protect your capital.

Emotional Discipline: Stop loss orders remove the emotional aspect of decision-making during market fluctuations, preventing impulsive and irrational trading decisions.

Peace of Mind: Knowing that your potential losses are limited can reduce stress and provide peace of mind, allowing you to focus on other trading opportunities.

Setting Stop Loss Levels:

Stop loss levels can be determined based on technical analysis, such as support and resistance levels, trend lines, or chart patterns.

Risk tolerance also plays a role in setting stop loss levels. A more conservative trader may choose a tighter stop loss level, while a more aggressive trader may allow for a wider stop loss.

Types of Stop Loss Orders:

Market Stop Loss: This is the most common type of stop loss order. When triggered, it becomes a market order, executing the trade at the best available price after the stop price is reached.

Limit Stop Loss: This type of stop loss order specifies a price at which the trade should be closed. It becomes a limit order when the stop price is reached, and it will be executed only if the specified limit price can be met.

Trailing Stop: A trailing stop loss order adjusts dynamically as the price moves in your favor. It trails a specified distance (e.g., a fixed amount or a percentage) below the current market price, helping to lock in profits while allowing potential upside.

It's important to note that while stop loss orders are a useful risk management tool, they are not foolproof. In certain market conditions, such as gaps or slippage, the execution price may be different from the stop price. Traders should also be aware of the potential for stop loss orders to be triggered by short-term price fluctuations before the trend resumes. Regular monitoring of trades and adjusting stop loss levels as necessary is recommended.

7.5 Take Profit Orders:

Setting profit targets and utilizing take profit orders are important aspects of trade management. Here's an overview of their purpose and how they can be used:

Purpose of Profit Targets:

Profit targets are predetermined price levels at which you intend to close a portion or all of your position to lock in profits.

They help you define your desired level of profitability for a trade and provide a clear exit strategy.

Using Technical Analysis for Price Targets:

Technical analysis tools and techniques, such as support and resistance levels, chart patterns, Fibonacci retracements/extensions, and trendlines, can help identify potential price targets.

By analyzing historical price patterns and market trends, you can estimate where the price may encounter obstacles or reach significant levels.

Adjusting Profit Targets:

Profit targets should be adjusted based on market conditions, trade management, and the overall risk-reward ratio.

If the price is showing strong momentum and potential for further gains, you may consider extending the profit target to capture more profit.

Conversely, if the price encounters resistance or shows signs of reversal, it may be prudent to take profits earlier or adjust the target to secure a satisfactory return.

Utilizing Take Profit Orders:

Take profit orders are pre-set instructions to close a position partially or entirely at a specified price level.

By placing a take profit order, you ensure that your desired profit is automatically realized when the market reaches the specified price, even if you're not actively monitoring the trade.

Take profit orders help remove emotion from decision-making and allow for a disciplined approach to locking in profits.

It's important to note that while profit targets are valuable for trade management, they should be realistic and based on a comprehensive analysis of market conditions and your trading strategy. It's also advisable to regularly monitor your trades and make adjustments to profit targets as needed to reflect changing market dynamics.

7.6 Risk-Reward Ratio:

Evaluating the risk-reward ratio of each trade is an essential step in trade analysis and selection. Here's how you can assess potential profit relative to potential loss and balance risk and reward:

Assessing Potential Profit:

Identify the potential profit by considering the price target or profit objective based on your analysis and trading strategy.

Determine the price level at which you expect the trade to reach your profit target.

Calculate the potential profit as the difference between the entry price and the profit target.

Assessing Potential Loss:

Identify the potential loss by considering the stop loss level, which is the price level at which you would exit the trade to limit your losses.

Calculate the potential loss as the difference between the entry price and the stop loss level.

Calculating Risk-Reward Ratio:

The risk-reward ratio compares the potential loss to the potential profit of a trade.

Calculate the risk-reward ratio by dividing the potential profit by the potential loss.

A risk-reward ratio of 1:1 means that the potential profit is equal to the potential loss.

A risk-reward ratio greater than 1:1 indicates that the potential profit is higher than the potential loss.

Balancing Risk and Reward:

Consider your risk tolerance and trading strategy to determine an acceptable risk-reward ratio for your trades.

A higher risk-reward ratio, such as 2:1 or 3:1, may be desirable as it allows for potentially larger profits relative to losses.

However, a higher risk-reward ratio typically comes with a lower probability of success, so it's important to find a balance that aligns with your risk tolerance and trading objectives.

Optimal Trade Selection:

Evaluate potential trades based on their risk-reward ratios and select those with favorable ratios that meet your criteria.

Aim for trades with higher potential rewards relative to their risks to increase the overall profitability of your trading strategy.

However, always consider other factors such as market conditions, trade setup, and the probability of success when making trade decisions.

Remember that risk management is crucial in trading, and assessing the risk-reward ratio helps you maintain a disciplined approach to risk management and optimize your trading outcomes over the long term.

7.7 Diversification:

Diversifying your trading portfolio is crucial for managing risk and maximizing potential returns. Here's why diversification is important:

Risk Reduction: Diversification helps reduce the impact of individual stock or sector-specific risks on your portfolio. By spreading your investments across different stocks, sectors, or asset classes, you decrease the likelihood of a significant loss from a single investment. If one investment performs poorly, the potential gains from other investments can help offset the losses.

Exposure to Different Opportunities: Diversification allows you to participate in various investment opportunities. Different stocks or sectors may perform differently based on market conditions, economic factors, or industry-specific events. By diversifying, you can capture potential gains from different areas of the market and avoid being overly reliant on a single investment.

Protection Against Volatility: Markets can be volatile, and individual stocks or sectors may experience significant price fluctuations. Diversification helps mitigate the impact of volatility by spreading your investments across different assets. When one investment experiences a downturn, others may perform better, providing a level of stability to your portfolio.

Capitalizing on Different Market Cycles: Different stocks or sectors may perform better during specific market cycles. By diversifying across different sectors or asset classes, you can position yourself to benefit from different market conditions. For example, during an economic downturn, defensive sectors like utilities or consumer staples may perform relatively better, while during an economic upswing, cyclical sectors like technology or industrials may outperform.

Long-Term Growth Potential: Diversification can contribute to the long-term growth potential of your portfolio. By avoiding over-concentration in a single stock or sector, you reduce the risk of significant losses that could hinder your overall portfolio performance. This allows you to potentially achieve more consistent and stable returns over time.

When diversifying your trading portfolio, consider allocating your investments across different stocks, sectors, or asset classes that have low correlation to each other. This means that their performance does not move in lockstep, providing a greater potential for risk reduction. However, it's important to note that diversification does not guarantee profits or protect against losses, but it is a fundamental strategy to manage risk and optimize your trading portfolio's performance.

7.8 Monitoring and Trade Management:

Regularly monitoring your trades and implementing appropriate trade management techniques are essential for successful trading. Here are some key practices to consider:

Monitoring Trades: Stay actively engaged with your trades by regularly monitoring the price action and market conditions. Keep track of any news or events that could impact your trades. This allows you to make informed decisions based on real-time information.

Adjusting Stop Loss Levels: As the market moves, consider adjusting your stop loss levels to protect your profits or limit potential losses. You can move your stop loss orders closer to your entry point or adjust them based on technical levels, such as support and resistance, trendlines, or moving averages. This helps you manage risk and lock in gains as the trade progresses.

Trailing Stops: Implement trailing stops, which automatically adjust your stop loss levels as the price moves in your favor. This allows you to capture profits while giving the trade room to develop. Trailing stops trail the price at a specified distance, such as a percentage or a fixed amount, and are triggered if the price reverses by that distance. Trailing stops help protect your profits during trending markets and can be an effective trade management tool.

Scaling In/Out: Consider scaling in or out of your trades to manage your position size. Scaling in involves gradually adding to your position as the trade progresses and shows favorable price action, allowing you to increase your exposure while managing risk. Scaling out involves partially closing your position to lock in profits while leaving a portion of the trade open to capture further gains. Scaling techniques can help optimize risk-reward ratios and adapt to changing market conditions.

Exiting Trades: Define and follow predetermined rules for exiting trades. Establish profit targets based on technical analysis, such as key support/resistance levels or chart patterns. Additionally, set rules to exit trades if the market conditions or trade thesis change. Having clear exit strategies helps you avoid emotional decision-making and ensures that you maintain discipline in your trading approach.

Remember, trade management is a dynamic process that requires ongoing assessment and adjustment. Regularly review your trades, reassess your risk-reward ratios, and adapt your strategies as needed. Implementing effective trade management techniques can help you optimize your profits, protect your capital, and improve your overall trading performance.

7.9 Risk Management Tools:

Utilizing risk management tools and software can greatly assist in effectively managing your trades and assessing risk. Here are some common tools and techniques:

Risk Calculators: Risk calculators help you determine the appropriate position size based on your risk tolerance, stop loss level, and account size. These calculators take into account factors such as the distance between your entry price and stop loss, your desired risk percentage per trade, and the size of your trading account. By inputting these variables, risk calculators provide you with the recommended position size to ensure you stay within your predefined risk parameters.

Trade Journals and Trackers: Keeping a trade journal or using a trade tracking software allows you to record and analyze your trades. This includes details such as entry and exit prices, position size, stop loss levels, and profit targets. By reviewing your trade history, you can identify patterns, assess the effectiveness of your strategies, and evaluate your risk-reward ratios. Trade tracking software often provides additional features such as risk analysis, performance metrics, and reporting capabilities.

Risk Metrics Analysis: Risk metrics such as risk-reward ratio, win rate, and average risk per trade can provide insights into the performance of your trading strategy. By analyzing these metrics, you can assess the profitability and effectiveness of your trades over time. This information helps you identify areas for improvement, refine your trading approach, and make informed decisions regarding position sizing and risk management.

Risk Management Software: There are various risk management software available that can assist you in managing your trades and assessing risk. These software packages often provide features such as position sizing calculators, risk analysis tools, performance tracking, and risk reporting capabilities. They can help automate the calculation of position sizes, track your trade performance, and generate comprehensive risk metrics reports.

When utilizing risk management tools and software, it is important to choose reputable and reliable platforms that suit your specific trading needs. These tools can streamline the process of risk assessment, position sizing, and trade analysis, helping you make informed decisions and effectively manage your trading portfolio.

7.10 Emotional Control and Discipline:

Emotions play a significant role in trading decisions, and maintaining emotional control and discipline is crucial for successful trading. Here are strategies to help manage emotions and maintain discipline:

Develop a Trading Plan: Creating a well-defined trading plan is essential for managing emotions. Your trading plan should include your trading goals, risk tolerance, entry and exit criteria, and risk management strategies. By having a clear plan in place, you can rely on predetermined rules rather than making impulsive decisions based on emotions.

Stick to Your Trading Plan: Once you have a trading plan, it is important to stick to it consistently. This helps minimize emotional decision-making and impulsive trading. Trusting your plan and following its rules can help you avoid getting swayed by fear, greed, or other emotions that can lead to poor trading decisions.

Practice Risk Management: Implementing risk management techniques, such as setting stop loss levels and position sizing based on your risk tolerance, helps control potential losses and reduces emotional stress. By defining your risk parameters and strictly adhering to them, you can limit the impact of emotional reactions to market fluctuations.

Maintain Realistic Expectations: It is important to have realistic expectations about trading outcomes. Recognize that losses are a part of trading and focus on long-term profitability rather than short-term gains. Understanding that not every trade will be profitable helps to manage emotions and avoid excessive disappointment or overconfidence.

Regularly Review and Analyze Trades: Regularly reviewing and analyzing your trades can help you learn from both successes and failures. By objectively analyzing your trades, you can identify patterns and areas for improvement. This analytical approach helps shift the focus from emotions to data-driven decision-making.

Take Breaks and Manage Stress: Trading can be demanding and stressful. It is important to take breaks and manage stress effectively. Engaging in activities outside of trading, such as exercise, hobbies, or spending time with family and friends, can help maintain a balanced mindset and reduce emotional strain.

Seek Support and Education: Surrounding yourself with a supportive trading community or seeking guidance from experienced traders can provide valuable insights and help manage emotions. Additionally, continuous learning and education about trading strategies, market dynamics, and psychology can improve your understanding and ability to control emotions.

Remember that emotions are a natural part of trading, but learning to manage them effectively is key to making rational and disciplined trading decisions. By implementing these strategies and maintaining a strong focus on risk management, you can reduce emotional biases and improve your overall trading performance.

Chapter 8: Building a Trading Plan: Setting Goals and Strategies

Introduction: In Chapter 8, we will discuss the importance of creating a trading plan—a comprehensive framework that outlines your trading goals, strategies, and rules. A well-structured trading plan helps you stay disciplined, make informed decisions, and achieve consistent results in the market. This chapter will guide you through the process of building an effective trading plan.

8.1 The Significance of a Trading Plan:

A trading plan is a written document that outlines your trading goals, strategies, risk management techniques, and other important aspects of your trading approach. It serves as a blueprint for your trading activities and provides a structured framework to guide your decision-making process. Here are the purposes and benefits of having a trading plan:

Goal Clarity: A trading plan helps you define your trading goals and objectives. It clarifies what you want to achieve as a trader, whether it's consistent profits, capital preservation, or long-term growth. Setting specific and measurable goals allows you to stay focused and motivated in your trading journey.

Strategy and Methodology: A trading plan outlines the strategies and methodologies you will employ in your trading. It helps you identify the types of trades you will take, the entry and exit criteria, and the indicators or tools you will use for analysis. Having a well-defined strategy enables you to make informed decisions based on a consistent approach.

Risk Management: A trading plan includes risk management techniques that help you control potential losses and protect your trading capital. It defines your risk tolerance, position sizing rules, stop loss levels, and profit targets. By adhering to these risk management principles, you can limit your exposure to individual trades and maintain a sound risk-reward ratio.

Consistency and Discipline: One of the key benefits of a trading plan is that it promotes consistency and discipline in your trading. By following a predetermined set of rules and guidelines, you reduce the influence of emotions and impulsive decision-making. Consistently applying your trading plan helps you stick to your strategies and avoid deviating from your intended course of action.

Decision-making Framework: A trading plan provides a decision-making framework that helps you evaluate potential trade opportunities objectively. It ensures that your trading decisions are based on logical analysis rather than emotions or random factors. Your plan acts as a reference point to assess whether a trade aligns with your predefined criteria, increasing the likelihood of making rational and well-informed decisions.

Performance Evaluation: A trading plan allows you to track and evaluate your trading performance. By recording your trades and analyzing the outcomes, you can identify strengths and weaknesses in your approach. This feedback loop helps you continuously improve your trading strategies and make necessary adjustments to enhance your overall performance.

Confidence and Trust: Having a trading plan instills confidence in your trading decisions. It provides a sense of structure and control, which can help you navigate through various market conditions and stay focused on your long-term goals. Trusting your plan and its proven track record can reduce anxiety and increase your confidence in executing trades.

In summary, a trading plan serves as a roadmap for your trading activities. It provides clarity, structure, and discipline in your decision-making process. By defining your goals, strategies, risk management techniques, and evaluation processes, a trading plan helps you maintain consistency and improve your overall trading performance.

8.2 Setting Trading Goals:

Defining your trading goals is an important step in creating a trading plan and establishing a clear direction for your trading activities. Here are some considerations when setting your trading goals:

Short-Term Goals: Short-term goals focus on specific trading objectives that can be achieved within a relatively short period, such as a few weeks or months. These goals can include achieving a certain percentage of return on your trades, maintaining a consistent win rate, or developing proficiency in a specific trading strategy. Short-term goals should be specific, measurable, attainable, relevant, and time-bound (SMART goals).

Long-Term Goals: Long-term goals encompass broader objectives that may take months or even years to achieve. These goals can include building a sustainable and profitable trading business, reaching a certain level of trading capital, or achieving financial independence through trading. Long-term goals should align with your overall financial objectives and provide a sense of purpose and direction in your trading journey.

Realistic Targets: It's essential to set realistic and achievable targets that consider your trading skills, experience, and available resources. Setting overly ambitious or unrealistic goals can lead to frustration and disappointment. Evaluate your historical trading performance, risk tolerance, and time commitment to determine what targets are attainable for you. Gradually increasing your targets as you gain experience and improve your skills can help you maintain a sense of progress and motivation.

Risk Tolerance and Financial Objectives: Your trading goals should align with your risk tolerance and financial objectives. Assess your risk tolerance by considering factors such as your financial situation, time horizon, and psychological disposition towards risk. Set goals that reflect your risk tolerance, ensuring that the potential rewards are commensurate with the risks you are willing to take. Additionally, consider your financial objectives, such as generating additional income, growing your wealth, or preserving capital, and align your trading goals accordingly.

Flexibility and Adaptability: While it's important to set specific goals, it's also crucial to remain flexible and adaptable to changing market conditions and personal circumstances. The market can be unpredictable, and adjustments to your goals may be necessary along the way. Regularly review and reassess your goals to ensure they remain relevant and realistic.

Remember that trading is a journey, and goals can evolve over time. Be open to learning, adjusting your strategies, and refining your goals as you gain experience and market knowledge. Regularly monitor your progress, evaluate your performance, and make necessary adjustments to keep your trading goals aligned with your risk tolerance, financial objectives, and evolving market conditions.

8.3 Choosing Trading Strategies:

When selecting a trading strategy, it's important to consider your trading goals, risk tolerance, time commitment, and personality. Here are some commonly used trading strategies along with considerations for their suitability:

Day Trading: Day trading involves opening and closing positions within the same trading day. It requires active monitoring of the market and making quick trading decisions. Day trading is suitable for individuals who can dedicate several hours a day to trading, have the ability to handle high-stress situations, and prefer short-term trading opportunities. It may not be suitable for those with limited time availability or who prefer a more relaxed trading approach.

Swing Trading: Swing trading involves holding positions for several days to weeks, taking advantage of short-term price fluctuations. It requires less time commitment compared to day trading and allows for more flexibility. Swing trading may be suitable for individuals who can dedicate a few hours per week to monitoring the market, prefer medium-term trading opportunities, and can handle moderate risk levels.

Trend Following: Trend following strategies aim to identify and capitalize on sustained market trends. Traders using this strategy aim to enter positions in the direction of the prevailing trend and hold them until the trend reverses. Trend following requires patience and the ability to withstand short-term price fluctuations. It may be suitable for individuals who prefer a more hands-off approach to trading, can tolerate potential drawdowns during market consolidations, and have a longer-term time horizon.

Breakout Trading: Breakout trading involves entering positions when the price breaks out of a significant support or resistance level. Traders using this strategy aim to capture price movements that follow a breakout. Breakout trading requires quick decision-making and the ability to identify key support and resistance levels. It may be suitable for individuals who can dedicate time to monitor the market during potential breakout periods and prefer trading opportunities with defined entry and exit points.

Position Trading: Position trading involves taking longer-term positions that can last from weeks to months or even years. It focuses on identifying major market trends and riding them for extended periods. Position trading requires a long-term perspective, patience, and the ability to tolerate larger price fluctuations. It may be suitable for individuals with a more passive approach to trading, a longer investment horizon, and the ability to manage potential overnight risks.

When selecting a trading strategy, consider the following factors:

Time Commitment: Assess how much time you can dedicate to trading, including research, monitoring, and executing trades. Some strategies require more active involvement and real-time decision-making, while others are more flexible and require less monitoring.

Risk Appetite: Evaluate your risk tolerance and understand the potential risks and rewards associated with each strategy. Some strategies, such as day trading, may involve higher levels of risk and volatility compared to longer-term strategies like position trading.

Market Conditions: Consider the current market conditions and whether the strategy you are considering is well-suited for those conditions. Certain strategies, such as trend following, may work better in trending markets, while others, like range trading, may be more appropriate in sideways or range-bound markets.

Personality: Select a strategy that aligns with your personality traits and preferences. Some individuals thrive in fast-paced, high-stress trading environments, while others may prefer a more relaxed and patient approach. Choose a strategy that suits your temperament and allows you to trade with discipline and confidence.

It's important to note that no single strategy guarantees success, and it's common for traders to combine elements from different strategies or develop their own unique approach. Additionally, as you gain experience and refine your trading skills, you may choose to adapt or switch strategies based on your evolving goals and market conditions.

8.4 Risk Management within the Trading Plan:

Incorporating risk management strategies into your trading plan is crucial for long-term success and capital preservation. Here are some key considerations for integrating risk management into your trading plan:

Define Risk Parameters: Set clear risk parameters that align with your trading goals and risk tolerance. This includes determining the maximum amount you are willing to risk per trade or as a percentage of your trading capital. By defining your risk parameters, you establish a framework for managing your trades and limiting potential losses.

Position Sizing: Determine the appropriate position size for each trade based on your risk parameters. Position sizing involves allocating a specific portion of your trading capital to each trade, considering factors such as the trade's risk-reward ratio, stop loss level, and overall portfolio diversification. By properly sizing your positions, you control the amount of capital at risk in each trade and maintain consistency in risk exposure.

Set Stop Loss Levels: Implement effective stop loss levels for each trade to protect against excessive losses. A stop loss order is a predefined price level at which you exit a trade to limit potential losses. Set your stop loss level based on technical analysis, support and resistance levels, or other risk management techniques. Consider the volatility of the instrument you are trading and the timeframe you are operating in when determining an appropriate stop loss level.

Adjust Risk Management Practices to Your Trading Goals: Ensure that your risk management practices are in line with your trading goals. If you are pursuing higher-risk trading strategies, such as day trading, you may need to set tighter stop loss levels and allocate smaller portions of your capital to each trade. On the other hand, if you are adopting a more conservative approach, such as position trading, you may allow for wider stop loss levels and allocate larger portions of your capital to each trade.

Regularly Review and Update Risk Management Strategies: Review and assess your risk management strategies on a regular basis to ensure they remain effective and aligned with your trading objectives. As market conditions and your trading performance evolve, you may need to adjust your risk parameters, position sizing, and stop loss levels to reflect the changing landscape.

Practice Discipline and Consistency: Adhere to your risk management strategies with discipline and consistency. Avoid deviating from your predefined risk parameters or making impulsive decisions based on emotions. Consistent application of risk management practices helps protect your trading capital and maintain a structured approach to trading.

Remember, risk management is an ongoing process that requires continuous monitoring and adjustment. By incorporating risk management strategies into your trading plan and consistently following them, you can mitigate potential losses and increase your chances of long-term trading success.

8.5 Trade Entry and Exit Rules:

Establishing specific criteria for entering and exiting trades is an essential component of a trading plan. Here are some key considerations for setting criteria and exit rules:

Entry Criteria: Define clear and specific entry criteria based on your trading strategy. This may include trigger signals based on technical indicators, chart patterns, or fundamental factors. Determine the conditions or criteria that must be met before you enter a trade. This helps you avoid impulsive or emotional trading decisions and ensures that you have a systematic approach to finding trade opportunities.

Exit Rules - Profit Targets: Set profit targets for each trade based on your trading strategy and risk-reward ratio. Profit targets are predefined price levels at which you plan to close your trade and take your profits. You can base your profit targets on technical analysis, key support/resistance levels, or other relevant factors. By setting profit targets, you establish a clear objective for capturing gains and prevent greed from influencing your decision-making.

Exit Rules - Stop Loss Levels: Implement stop loss levels for each trade to limit potential losses. Stop loss levels are predefined price levels at which you exit a trade to protect against adverse price movements. Determine your stop loss levels based on your risk tolerance, technical analysis, or other risk management techniques. It is important to set stop loss levels before entering a trade and adhere to them strictly. This helps you manage risk and protect your trading capital.

Trailing Stop Strategies: Consider incorporating trailing stop strategies into your exit rules. A trailing stop order is a type of stop loss order that automatically adjusts as the price moves in your favor. It allows you to lock in profits while still giving your trade room to potentially capture further gains. Trailing stops can be based on a fixed percentage or a specific technical indicator, such as a moving average. Trailing stops help you protect profits and let winners run in trending markets.

Adjust Exit Rules Based on Market Conditions: Be flexible in adjusting your exit rules based on changing market conditions. For example, if a trade is showing strong momentum and potential for further gains, you may choose to trail your stop loss at a wider distance to capture more upside. Conversely, if market conditions become uncertain or volatile, you might tighten your profit targets or adjust your stop loss levels to protect against sudden reversals.

Regularly Evaluate and Refine Exit Rules: Regularly review and evaluate the effectiveness of your exit rules. Keep track of your trades and analyze the outcomes to identify areas for improvement. If you consistently find that your profit targets are not being reached or your stop losses are triggered too frequently, you may need to adjust your exit rules. Refining your exit rules based on your trading performance and market observations can help optimize your trading strategy.

Remember, having well-defined and consistent criteria for entering and exiting trades is crucial for maintaining discipline and managing risk. Incorporate these criteria and exit rules into your trading plan, and regularly review and adapt them as needed to stay aligned with your trading goals and market conditions.

8.6 Trade Management and Adjustments:

Managing open trades effectively is an important aspect of trading. Here are some guidelines and strategies for managing open trades:

Stick to Your Trading Plan: Always adhere to your trading plan and follow the guidelines you have set. This includes entry criteria, exit rules, position sizing, and risk management principles. Consistently applying your trading plan helps maintain discipline and reduces the influence of emotions on your trading decisions.

Monitor Trade Progress: Regularly monitor the progress of your open trades. Stay informed about market conditions, news, and any relevant factors that may impact your trades. Use technical analysis, chart patterns, and indicators to track the price movements of the trade and assess its performance.

Adjust Stop Loss Levels: As a trade moves in your favor, consider adjusting your stop loss levels to protect profits and minimize risk. This can involve moving the stop loss to breakeven or adjusting it to a level that ensures a minimum acceptable profit. Adjusting stop loss levels helps lock in gains and reduces the risk of losing profits if the market reverses.

Scale-In or Scale-Out Strategies: Scaling into or out of positions can be an effective strategy in certain situations. Scaling in involves gradually increasing your position size as the trade moves in your favor. This can be done by adding to the position at predefined price levels or when specific technical conditions are met. Scaling in allows you to capture more profits if the trade continues in your favor.

On the other hand, scaling out involves gradually reducing your position size as the trade progresses. This can be done by taking partial profits at predetermined price targets or when certain technical signals suggest potential reversal or consolidation. Scaling out helps you secure profits while still leaving a portion of the trade open to capture further gains.

Adjust Targets Based on Market Conditions: Consider adjusting your profit targets based on changing market conditions. If the trade shows strong momentum and potential for an extended move, you may choose to adjust your profit target to capture more upside. Conversely, if the market becomes uncertain or shows signs of a reversal, you might consider adjusting your profit target to secure profits at a conservative level.

Review and Manage Risk: Continually assess the risk-reward dynamics of your open trades. If the trade has moved significantly in your favor, consider trailing your stop loss to protect profits. Similarly, if the trade is not performing as expected or shows signs of weakness, reassess the trade and consider exiting if necessary. It's important to manage risk and not let losing trades significantly impact your trading capital.

Regularly Evaluate Trade Performance: Keep a record of your trades and evaluate their performance regularly. Analyze both winning and losing trades to identify patterns, strengths, and weaknesses in your trading strategy. This evaluation helps you learn from your trades and make adjustments as needed to improve your trading approach.

Remember, managing open trades requires discipline, careful monitoring, and adherence to your trading plan. By following these guidelines and strategies, you can effectively manage your trades in line with your trading objectives and risk management principles.

8.7 Market Analysis and Research:

When conducting market analysis, it's essential to rely on reliable sources of information and establish a routine for staying informed. Here are some considerations for identifying sources of market analysis, setting a routine, and determining key factors and indicators to monitor:

Reliable Sources of Market Analysis: Choose reputable and trusted sources for market analysis and research. These can include financial news outlets, research firms, brokerage firms, and economic data providers. Consider utilizing a combination of free and paid sources to access a wide range of perspectives and insights.

Research Reports and Analyst Opinions: Research reports from reputable firms can provide valuable analysis and recommendations on specific stocks, sectors, or markets. Analyst opinions can offer insights into the future performance and potential catalysts of particular companies. Be aware of any conflicts of interest that might influence the recommendations and consider multiple opinions before making decisions.

Economic Indicators and News Releases: Stay updated on key economic indicators and news releases that can impact the markets. These can include indicators like GDP growth, inflation rates, employment data, central bank decisions, and geopolitical events. Economic calendars and news platforms are helpful resources for tracking and understanding these releases.

Technical Analysis Tools and Platforms: Utilize technical analysis tools and platforms that provide charts, indicators, and patterns to analyze price movements and trends. These tools can help identify support and resistance levels, trend lines, and chart patterns. Look for platforms that offer a wide range of indicators and customizable features.

Financial Databases: Access financial databases that provide comprehensive data on stocks, indices, financial statements, and historical prices. These databases allow you to analyze company fundamentals, financial ratios, and historical performance. They often offer screening and filtering capabilities to narrow down your search for potential investment opportunities.

Industry Publications and News Sources: Subscribe to industry-specific publications and news sources that provide in-depth analysis and insights into specific sectors or markets. These sources can help you stay informed about industry trends, regulatory changes, and competitive dynamics that may impact your investment decisions.

Setting a Routine: Establish a regular routine for conducting market analysis. Set aside dedicated time each day or week to review market news, analyze charts, and assess economic indicators. Consistency is key to staying informed and making timely trading or investment decisions.

Key Factors and Indicators: Determine the key factors and indicators that align with your trading or investment strategy. These can vary depending on your approach, but common factors include company fundamentals, industry trends, economic indicators, market sentiment, and technical analysis signals. Focus on the factors that have a significant impact on the securities or markets you are trading.

Remember, market analysis is an ongoing process, and it's important to continuously update your knowledge and adapt your strategies based on changing market conditions. Regularly review and evaluate the effectiveness of your analysis routine and adjust it as needed to stay informed and make informed trading or investment decisions.

8.8 Record Keeping and Performance Evaluation:

Implementing a system for tracking trades and analyzing performance is crucial for evaluating your trading strategies and identifying areas for improvement. Here's a guide to help you set up a trade tracking system and effectively analyze and evaluate your trade results:

Trading Journal: Maintain a trading journal where you record details of each trade, including the date, security traded, entry and exit prices, position size, and rationale for the trade. Additionally, note any relevant market conditions, technical or fundamental analysis used, and emotional factors that may have influenced the trade. The trading journal helps you review your decision-making process and identify patterns or mistakes.

Performance Metrics: Define key performance metrics that align with your trading goals. Common metrics include overall profitability, win/loss ratio, average gain/loss per trade, maximum drawdown, and risk-adjusted returns (such as the Sharpe ratio or Sortino ratio). Track these metrics for each trade and calculate them periodically to evaluate your performance.

Trade Analysis: Regularly review your trade history and analyze the results. Look for patterns or trends in your winning and losing trades. Identify the factors that contributed to successful trades and those that resulted in losses. Assess the impact of risk management techniques, such as stop losses and position sizing, on your overall performance. Use this analysis to identify strengths and weaknesses in your trading approach.

Performance Reports: Generate performance reports on a regular basis to gain a comprehensive overview of your trading results. These reports can include metrics like overall performance, portfolio growth, trade win/loss breakdown, and risk-adjusted returns. Compare your performance against relevant benchmarks or industry standards to gain further insights.

Identify Areas for Improvement: Utilize your trading journal and performance reports to identify areas where you can improve. Look for recurring mistakes or weaknesses in your trading strategy. Consider whether adjustments are needed in your risk management practices, entry/exit rules, or trade selection criteria. By identifying areas for improvement, you can refine your trading strategy and enhance your future performance.

Learn from Mistakes: Analyze losing trades to understand the reasons behind them. Assess whether any errors in analysis, timing, or execution contributed to the losses. Learning from your mistakes is crucial for growth as a trader. Use these experiences to develop strategies to avoid similar pitfalls in the future.

Adjust and Iterate: Based on your trade analysis and performance evaluation, make adjustments to your trading strategy and risk management practices. Implement changes gradually and track their impact on your performance over time. Continuously iterate and refine your approach based on ongoing analysis and evaluation.

Remember, tracking trades and analyzing performance is an ongoing process. Regularly review your trades, update your trading journal, and generate performance reports to gain valuable insights. This practice will help you identify strengths, weaknesses, and areas for improvement, leading to more informed decision-making and better trading outcomes over time.

8.9 Adapting to Changing Market Conditions:

Incorporating flexibility into your trading plan is essential to adapt to changing market conditions and optimize your trading approach. Here are strategies for maintaining flexibility and adjusting your trading plan as needed:

Market Environment Analysis: Continuously monitor and analyze the market environment to identify shifts in trends, volatility, and other key factors. Stay informed about economic indicators, news events, and market sentiment that may impact your trading. This analysis will help you recognize different market environments, such as trending, range-bound, or volatile markets.

Scenario Planning: Anticipate different scenarios that may occur in the market and develop corresponding strategies. Consider how your trading approach may need to adapt in various situations, such as a sudden market downturn, increased volatility, or a significant trend reversal. Having predefined plans for different scenarios allows you to act swiftly and make informed decisions.

Adjusting Risk Management: As market conditions change, reevaluate your risk management practices. Adjust your position sizing, stop loss levels, and profit targets based on the current volatility and market conditions. In volatile markets, you may need to tighten your risk parameters to protect capital, while in trending markets, you may consider expanding your profit targets.

Review and Update Trading Rules: Regularly review and update your trading rules based on your experiences and market observations. Identify patterns or strategies that are no longer effective and consider replacing them with more suitable approaches. Additionally, identify new strategies or indicators that align with current market conditions and incorporate them into your plan.

Backtesting and Forward Testing: Before implementing significant changes to your trading plan, backtest them using historical data to assess their performance under various market conditions. Additionally, forward test new strategies by trading them in a simulated or small-scale live environment to gain real-time feedback. This helps you assess the effectiveness of adjustments before fully integrating them into your trading plan.

Learn from Experience: Continuously learn from your trading experiences and adjust your plan accordingly. Analyze both successful and unsuccessful trades to understand the factors that contributed to the outcomes. Identify areas where you could have made better decisions or where adjustments in your plan could have improved results. Apply these lessons to refine and update your trading plan.

Regular Plan Reviews: Schedule periodic reviews of your trading plan to ensure it remains aligned with your trading goals, risk tolerance, and the current market environment. Consider conducting these reviews at least quarterly or whenever significant market shifts occur. Use these reviews as an opportunity to make any necessary updates or refinements to your plan.

By incorporating flexibility into your trading plan and regularly reviewing and adjusting it, you can adapt to changing market conditions and optimize your trading approach. Remember, flexibility does not mean constantly changing strategies but rather being open to adjustments based on market dynamics and your own trading experiences. This adaptive approach can enhance your performance and help you navigate different market environments more effectively.

8.10 Review and Refinement:

Regularly reviewing and refining your trading plan is crucial for several reasons:

Performance Evaluation: Reviewing your trading plan allows you to assess your overall performance and identify areas for improvement. By analyzing your trades and results, you can determine which strategies are working well and which ones need adjustments. This evaluation helps you identify patterns, strengths, and weaknesses in your trading approach.

Risk Assessment: A trading plan review helps you assess your risk management practices and ensure they align with your risk tolerance. You can evaluate your position sizing, stop loss levels, and overall risk exposure. By identifying any potential risks or vulnerabilities, you can make necessary adjustments to protect your capital and manage risk effectively.

Market Adaptation: The financial markets are dynamic, and conditions can change rapidly. Regularly reviewing your trading plan allows you to adapt to evolving market conditions. You can identify shifts in market trends, volatility, or other factors that may require adjustments to your strategies. Staying adaptable ensures that your trading plan remains relevant and effective in different market environments.

Identifying Areas for Improvement: By reviewing your trading plan, you can pinpoint areas that need improvement. This can include refining your entry and exit strategies, enhancing your risk management techniques, or incorporating new tools and indicators. Identifying areas for improvement helps you continuously evolve as a trader and refine your skills and knowledge.

Emotional Discipline: Regularly reviewing your trading plan can help reinforce emotional discipline. It serves as a reminder of your predefined rules and guidelines, which can help you stay focused and make rational decisions during times of market volatility or uncertainty. Following a well-defined plan helps mitigate emotional biases and impulsive trading behavior.

Goal Alignment: As your trading journey progresses, your goals and objectives may evolve. Regularly reviewing your trading plan allows you to ensure that it aligns with your current goals and aspirations. You can assess whether your trading plan is still appropriate for your financial objectives, time commitments, and risk appetite. Adjustments can be made to realign your plan with your evolving needs.

Continuous Learning: Reviewing and refining your trading plan encourages ongoing learning and development. It provides an opportunity to reflect on past trades, learn from both successes and failures, and integrate new knowledge into your trading approach. By staying curious and open to learning, you can improve your skills, expand your strategies, and adapt to new market dynamics.

Remember that trading is a dynamic and evolving endeavor. Regularly reviewing and refining your trading plan allows you to stay adaptable, improve your performance, and align your strategies with changing market conditions and personal goals. Embrace the learning process, be open to making necessary adjustments, and continuously strive to evolve as a trader.

Chapter 9: Introduction to Day Trading and Swing Trading

Introduction: In Chapter 9, we will introduce you to two popular trading styles: day trading and swing trading. Day trading involves opening and closing trades within the same trading day, aiming to profit from short-term price fluctuations. Swing trading, on the other hand, focuses on capturing larger price moves over a few days to several weeks. This chapter will provide an overview of these trading styles, their characteristics, and key considerations for successful implementation.

9.1 Understanding Day Trading:

Day trading is a trading style that involves the buying and selling of financial instruments within the same trading day. Day traders aim to take advantage of short-term price fluctuations and capitalize on intraday market movements. They typically close all their positions by the end of the trading day and do not hold any overnight positions.

Key characteristics of day trading include:

Short-Term Timeframe: Day traders focus on short-term price movements, typically trading on intraday charts such as 1-minute, 5-minute, or 15-minute intervals. They aim to profit from short-term volatility and price fluctuations.

High Trading Frequency: Day traders execute multiple trades throughout the day, seeking to take advantage of small price movements. They may enter and exit positions within minutes or hours.

Leverage and Margin: Day traders often utilize leverage to amplify their trading positions. This allows them to control larger positions with a smaller amount of capital. Margin accounts are commonly used to access leverage, but it also increases the risk of losses.

Technical Analysis: Day traders heavily rely on technical analysis to identify short-term trading opportunities. They use various indicators, chart patterns, and price action analysis to make trading decisions.

Differences between day trading and other trading styles:

Holding Period: Day trading involves closing all positions before the end of the trading day, while other trading styles, such as swing trading or position trading, involve holding positions for longer periods, ranging from a few days to several weeks or months.

Time Commitment: Day trading requires continuous monitoring of the markets throughout the trading day. It demands significant time and attention, as trades need to be executed promptly and adjustments made as per market conditions. Other trading styles may require less time commitment as trades are held for longer durations.

Advantages of day trading:

Quick Profits: Day trading provides the potential for quick profits by capitalizing on intraday price movements. Successful day traders can take advantage of short-term market fluctuations and generate consistent profits.

Reduced Overnight Risk: By closing all positions before the end of the trading day, day traders eliminate the risk of overnight market events and news that could adversely impact their positions.

Increased Liquidity: Day trading focuses on highly liquid markets and instruments, enabling traders to enter and exit positions with ease. This liquidity allows for efficient execution of trades and minimal slippage.

Challenges of day trading:

High Risk and Volatility: Day trading involves rapid decision-making and executing trades in a short time frame, increasing the risk of errors and losses. The volatility of intraday price movements can also lead to substantial losses if trades go against the trader.

Emotional and Psychological Stress: The fast-paced nature of day trading can be emotionally and psychologically demanding. Traders need to manage their emotions, avoid impulsive decisions, and maintain discipline in executing their trading plan.

Capital Requirements: Day trading often requires a significant amount of capital due to the use of leverage and the need for sufficient buying power to take advantage of intraday opportunities. Meeting the minimum capital requirements can be a challenge for some traders.

It's important to note that day trading is not suitable for everyone. It requires a certain level of experience, knowledge, and risk tolerance. Traders considering day trading should thoroughly understand the risks involved and consider practicing with a demo account or engaging in paper trading before committing real capital.

9.2 Day Trading Strategies:

Scalping, momentum trading, breakout trading, and range trading are all trading strategies used by traders to profit from different market conditions. Here's an overview of each strategy:

Scalping: Scalping is a short-term trading strategy that aims to profit from small price movements. Scalpers typically enter and exit trades within seconds or minutes, capturing small price fluctuations. They rely on high trading volume and liquidity to execute multiple trades quickly. Scalping requires fast decision-making, precision, and the ability to manage risk effectively.

Momentum Trading: Momentum trading involves capitalizing on strong price trends and riding the momentum of the market. Traders identify assets that are exhibiting significant price movements and look for opportunities to join the trend and profit from continued price momentum. Momentum traders often use technical indicators and chart patterns to identify potential entry and exit points. This strategy requires monitoring market conditions and making timely trading decisions.

Breakout Trading: Breakout trading focuses on identifying and capitalizing on price breakouts from established support or resistance levels. Traders look for instances when the price breaks above resistance or below support, indicating a potential change in the direction of the trend. Breakout traders aim to enter trades early in the breakout and ride the subsequent price movement. They often use technical indicators, such as moving averages or oscillators, to confirm breakouts and manage risk.

Range Trading: Range trading involves trading within defined support and resistance levels. Traders identify price ranges where the price tends to oscillate between support and resistance without establishing a clear trend. Range traders aim to buy at support levels and sell at resistance levels, taking advantage of the repetitive price movements within the range. They use technical indicators, such as oscillators or trendlines, to identify potential entry and exit points.

Each trading strategy requires a different approach, skill set, and risk management techniques. Traders should carefully consider their trading goals, risk tolerance, and market conditions when choosing a strategy. It's also important to backtest and practice the chosen strategy before applying it with real capital. Additionally, traders may combine multiple strategies or adjust their approach based on evolving market conditions.

9.3 Day Trading Tools and Techniques:

Level 2 quotes and time and sales data are tools used in intraday trading to gain more detailed information about the current market depth and transaction data.

Level 2 quotes provide real-time information about the bid and ask prices at different price levels beyond the best bid and ask. It shows the market depth and the number of shares available at each price level. Traders use this information to assess the liquidity and demand for a particular stock, as well as to identify support and resistance levels.

Time and sales data, also known as the tape, provides a record of each individual trade that occurs in the market, including the price, volume, and timestamp. Traders analyze time and sales data to understand the trading activity and market dynamics, such as the speed and size of trades, and to identify potential buying or selling pressure.

Technical indicators are widely used in intraday analysis to identify patterns, trends, and potential entry and exit points. Popular intraday indicators include moving averages, oscillators (such as the relative strength index or stochastic oscillator), volume-based indicators (such as on-balance volume or volume-weighted average price), and trendlines. Traders apply these indicators to intraday charts to generate trading signals and make informed trading decisions.

High-volume and low-latency trading platforms are essential for intraday trading. These platforms provide real-time market data, order execution, advanced charting tools, and customizable trading interfaces. Traders can efficiently analyze market data, execute trades quickly, and manage their positions effectively using such platforms. They often offer features like hotkeys, advanced order types, and real-time market scanning to support intraday trading strategies.

Risk management is crucial in intraday trading due to the short time frames and higher volatility. Traders employ effective position sizing techniques to limit their exposure to individual trades and overall portfolio risk. They may use fixed dollar amounts or a percentage of their trading capital to determine the appropriate position size. Additionally, setting stop loss orders to protect against significant losses and having a well-defined risk-reward ratio for each trade are important risk management practices.

Overall, intraday trading requires access to real-time market data, the use of technical indicators for analysis, a robust trading platform, and disciplined risk management strategies to navigate the fast-paced and volatile nature of intraday markets.

9.4 Understanding Swing Trading:

Swing trading is a trading style that aims to capture short-to-medium-term price swings within a larger trend. It typically involves holding positions for a few days to several weeks, taking advantage of price fluctuations during that time frame.

Characteristics of swing trading include:

Time Horizon: Swing traders hold positions longer than day traders but shorter than long-term investors. They aim to capture shorter-term price movements within a trend.

Trend-Following: Swing traders focus on trading in the direction of the prevailing trend. They look for entry points when the price retraces within the larger trend, aiming to capture the next swing in the direction of the trend.

Technical Analysis: Swing traders heavily rely on technical analysis to identify potential entry and exit points. They use indicators, chart patterns, trendlines, and other technical tools to analyze price action and make trading decisions.

Position Sizing: Swing traders typically employ a position sizing strategy that allows them to manage risk and maximize potential profits. They may allocate a certain percentage of their trading capital to each trade based on their risk tolerance and the distance to the stop loss level.

Flexibility: Swing traders can adapt to different market conditions and trade various financial instruments, including stocks, commodities, forex, and indices. They can switch between long and short positions depending on the direction of the swing.

Comparing swing trading with other trading styles:

Day Trading: Swing trading has a longer time horizon compared to day trading, which involves opening and closing positions within the same trading day. Swing traders aim to capture larger price movements and are not as concerned with intraday fluctuations.

Position Trading: Swing trading falls between day trading and position trading. While position traders hold positions for months to years, swing traders hold positions for days to weeks. Swing trading focuses on shorter-term trends within a larger market trend, while position trading aims to capture the primary trend.

Advantages of swing trading:

Potential for larger profits: Swing trading allows traders to capture larger price moves compared to day trading. By holding positions for a few days to weeks, swing traders can potentially benefit from significant price swings.

Reduced time commitment: Swing trading does not require constant monitoring of the market throughout the day, making it more suitable for traders who have other commitments or prefer a less time-intensive trading approach.

Opportunity to ride trends: By trading in the direction of the prevailing trend, swing traders have the potential to profit from sustained price moves. They can take advantage of both upward and downward trends.

Challenges of swing trading:

Overnight risks: Holding positions overnight exposes swing traders to the risk of market gaps or unexpected news events that can impact the price of their positions. Proper risk management, including the use of stop loss orders, is essential to mitigate these risks.

Emotional discipline: Swing trading requires discipline and the ability to stick to the trading plan. Traders need to avoid emotional decision-making, such as exiting a trade prematurely or holding onto a losing position for too long.

Market timing: Identifying the optimal entry and exit points for swing trades can be challenging. Traders need to accurately time their entries and exits to maximize profits and minimize losses.

In summary, swing trading is a trading style that aims to capture shorter-term price swings within a larger trend. It offers the potential for larger profits compared to day trading, while requiring less time commitment than day trading. However, it also comes with challenges such as overnight risks and the need for disciplined decision-making.

9.5 Swing Trading Strategies:

Trend Following: Trend following is a trading strategy where traders aim to identify and ride medium-term price trends. Traders who follow this strategy seek to enter positions in the direction of the prevailing trend and hold them until the trend shows signs of reversing. They use technical analysis tools such as moving averages, trendlines, and price patterns to identify trends and make trading decisions.

Retracement Trading: Retracement trading involves taking advantage of temporary price pullbacks within an established trend. In an uptrend, traders look for opportunities to buy when the price retraces or pulls back from recent highs. In a downtrend, traders may look for opportunities to sell or short the market when the price rallies or bounces from recent lows. The idea is to enter positions at favorable prices during the temporary price retracements before the trend resumes.

Breakout Trading: Breakout trading involves identifying and capitalizing on significant price breakouts. Traders look for instances where the price breaks above a key resistance level in an uptrend or below a key support level in a downtrend. Breakout traders aim to enter positions early in the breakout move, expecting the price to continue in the direction of the breakout with momentum.

Support and Resistance Trading: Support and resistance trading focuses on trading bounces or breakouts at key support and resistance levels on price charts. Support levels represent areas where buying interest is expected to be strong, causing the price to bounce higher. Resistance levels represent areas where selling pressure is expected to be strong, causing the price to bounce lower. Traders who follow this strategy aim to enter positions when the price reacts to these levels, either by bouncing off them or breaking through them.

Each of these trading styles has its own advantages and challenges. Trend following can potentially lead to significant profits during sustained trends but requires the ability to identify and stay in trends for extended periods. Retracement trading allows traders to enter positions at more favorable prices within an established trend but requires skill in identifying the optimal points to enter. Breakout trading offers the potential for capturing strong price moves but requires careful analysis to distinguish between genuine breakouts and false ones. Support and resistance trading provides opportunities to trade off key levels but requires accurate identification of these levels and consideration of price behavior around them.

Traders should choose a trading style that aligns with their trading goals, risk tolerance, and personality. It is common for traders to combine different trading styles or adapt their approach depending on market conditions and the specific opportunities they encounter.

9.6 Swing Trading Tools and Techniques:

Using Technical Analysis to Identify Trends and Patterns: Technical analysis involves analyzing historical price and volume data to identify trends and patterns in the market. Traders use various tools and techniques, such as moving averages, trendlines, and chart patterns, to identify the direction and strength of trends. By analyzing trends, traders can determine whether to enter long (buy) or short (sell) positions.

Applying Indicators for Swing Trading Signals: Swing traders often use technical indicators to generate trading signals. Popular indicators for swing trading include the Relative Strength Index (RSI), Moving Average Convergence Divergence (MACD), and Stochastic Oscillator. These indicators help identify overbought and oversold conditions, potential trend reversals, and the strength of price movements. Traders use these signals to time their entries and exits in swing trades.

Utilizing Candlestick Patterns for Entry and Exit Points: Candlestick patterns provide valuable information about market sentiment and potential price reversals. Patterns such as doji, hammer, engulfing patterns, and shooting star can indicate trend exhaustion or reversal. Traders often use these patterns in combination with other technical analysis tools to determine entry and exit points. For example, a bullish engulfing pattern near a support level might signal a potential entry point for a long trade.

Employing Trailing Stops and Profit Targets for Trade Management: Traders use trailing stops and profit targets to manage their trades and protect their profits. A trailing stop is an order that adjusts the stop loss level as the price moves in the trader's favor. It allows traders to capture more profits if the price continues to move in their desired direction. Profit targets are predetermined price levels at which traders aim to exit their trades to lock in profits. Traders may use technical analysis tools, such as key support or resistance levels or Fibonacci extensions, to set profit targets.

By combining technical analysis techniques, indicators, candlestick patterns, and trade management tools like trailing stops and profit targets, swing traders can develop a systematic approach to identify entry and exit points and manage their trades effectively. It is important to remember that no trading strategy is foolproof, and proper risk management is essential to protect capital and achieve long-term success.

9.7 Risk Management in Day Trading and Swing Trading:

Position Sizing Strategies for Managing Risk: Position sizing refers to determining the appropriate size of a trade relative to your trading capital. It is an important aspect of risk management. Different position sizing strategies can be used, such as fixed dollar amount, fixed percentage of capital, or risk-based position sizing. The goal is to limit the potential loss on any single trade and manage overall portfolio risk.

Setting Stop Loss Levels Based on Volatility and Market Structure: Stop loss orders are used to limit potential losses on a trade. When setting stop loss levels, traders often consider the volatility of the instrument being traded and the structure of the market. Volatile instruments may require wider stop loss levels to account for price fluctuations, while less volatile instruments may have tighter stop loss levels. Traders may also consider key support or resistance levels, trendlines, or technical indicators as reference points for placing stop loss orders.

Applying Risk-Reward Ratios for Trade Evaluation: The risk-reward ratio is a key factor in trade evaluation. It compares the potential profit of a trade to the potential loss. By assessing the risk-reward ratio, traders can determine whether a trade is worth taking. A favorable risk-reward ratio typically involves seeking trades with higher potential rewards relative to the potential risk. For example, a trader may aim for a risk-reward ratio of 1:2, meaning they are willing to risk $1 to potentially make $2.

Diversification and Portfolio Management for Risk Mitigation: Diversification involves spreading investments across different instruments, sectors, or asset classes to reduce the impact of any single investment on the overall portfolio. By diversifying, traders can mitigate risk and potentially improve overall portfolio performance. Effective portfolio management also involves monitoring and rebalancing the portfolio regularly to maintain desired risk levels and capitalize on potential opportunities.

It is important to note that risk management is a critical aspect of trading and investing. Traders should always assess and manage risk according to their risk tolerance, trading style, and individual circumstances. Strategies such as position sizing, setting stop loss levels, evaluating risk-reward ratios, and diversification can help traders effectively manage risk and protect their capital.

9.8 Time Commitment and Lifestyle Considerations:

The time requirements of day trading and swing trading differ significantly, and it's essential to consider your personal circumstances and commitments when choosing a trading style.

Day trading typically requires more time and attention as it involves actively monitoring the markets and making quick trading decisions within a single trading day. Day traders need to dedicate several hours during market hours to actively analyze charts, execute trades, and manage positions. It requires a high level of focus and dedication throughout the trading day.

On the other hand, swing trading involves holding positions for a few days to weeks, taking advantage of medium-term price swings. Swing traders typically analyze charts and identify potential trade setups after market hours. Once a trade is entered, they monitor the position intermittently, typically spending a few hours each week on trade management and analysis.

When considering the time requirements, it's important to assess your availability and ability to dedicate uninterrupted time to trading. Day trading may be more suitable for individuals who can commit several hours each day to actively monitor the markets. Swing trading allows for more flexibility, as it requires less real-time monitoring during market hours.

Balancing trading activities with other commitments is crucial. Consider your work schedule, family obligations, and other responsibilities. It's important to ensure that trading activities do not interfere with your other commitments and that you have sufficient time and mental focus to dedicate to trading.

Assessing the suitability of each trading style is subjective and depends on your personal circumstances, preferences, and trading goals. Consider factors such as your risk tolerance, capital availability, psychological temperament, and preferred trading timeframes. Evaluate the time you can realistically allocate to trading and select a trading style that aligns with your lifestyle and objectives.

Remember, trading styles can be adapted and adjusted over time. It's important to start with a realistic assessment of your time availability and gradually increase your involvement as you gain experience and confidence in your trading abilities.

9.9 Choosing the Right Trading Style:

When deciding between day trading and swing trading, there are several factors to consider. Here are some key factors:

Personality: Different trading styles align with different personalities. Day trading requires quick decision-making, a high tolerance for stress, and the ability to make split-second judgments. Swing trading allows for more patience, as trades are held for longer periods. Consider which style suits your personality and trading preferences.

Risk Tolerance: Evaluate your risk tolerance level. Day trading often involves more frequent trades and shorter holding periods, which can lead to increased volatility and higher risk. Swing trading may involve holding positions for several days or weeks, potentially reducing the impact of short-term market fluctuations.

Goals and Time Commitment: Clarify your trading goals and the amount of time you can dedicate to trading. Day trading requires more active involvement during market hours, while swing trading allows for more flexibility and can be conducted with less time commitment.

Market Conditions: Assess the current market conditions and volatility. Day trading thrives in highly liquid and volatile markets, whereas swing trading can be more adaptable to different market conditions. Consider whether the market conditions align with your chosen trading style.

Learning Curve: Recognize the learning curve associated with each trading style. Day trading often requires a more in-depth understanding of technical analysis, chart patterns, and intraday price movements. Swing trading may involve a broader analysis of trends, support and resistance levels, and market sentiment. Consider your willingness to learn and develop the necessary skills for your chosen trading style.

Transitioning between trading styles based on market conditions is a valid approach. As market conditions change, certain trading styles may be more favorable than others. Some traders may choose to incorporate elements of both day trading and swing trading, adjusting their strategies based on the prevailing market environment.

Ultimately, the decision between day trading and swing trading should align with your personality, risk tolerance, goals, and available time commitment. It's important to choose a trading style that suits you best and allows you to effectively manage risk while pursuing your trading objectives. Regular self-assessment and ongoing evaluation of market conditions can help you make informed decisions and potentially explore new trading styles when appropriate.

9.10 Developing Trading Plans for Day Trading and Swing Trading:

Building a trading plan specific to day trading or swing trading involves defining trading goals, strategies, and rules that align with the chosen style. Here are some key considerations for each trading style:

Day Trading Plan:

Trading Goals: Clearly define your daily and weekly trading goals, such as the desired number of trades, profit targets, and risk tolerance levels.

Strategy Selection: Determine the specific day trading strategies you will focus on, such as breakout trading, scalping, or momentum trading. Choose strategies that are suitable for short-term price movements and align with your skills and preferences.

Technical Analysis: Identify the key technical indicators, chart patterns, and timeframes that are most effective for your day trading style. Focus on short-term trends, support and resistance levels, and volume analysis.

Entry and Exit Rules: Establish clear rules for entering and exiting trades based on your selected strategies and technical analysis. Define specific trigger points, confirmation signals, and profit targets. Consider using stop loss orders to manage risk.

Risk Management: Implement risk management techniques tailored to day trading. Determine the maximum amount of capital you are willing to risk per trade and establish position sizing rules. Use stop loss orders to limit potential losses.

Swing Trading Plan:

Trading Goals: Set your desired holding period for swing trades, such as days or weeks, and define your overall profit targets and risk tolerance for swing trading.

Strategy Selection: Identify the swing trading strategies that best suit your trading style, such as trend following, breakout trading, or mean reversion. Choose strategies that align with your preferred timeframe and market conditions.

Technical Analysis: Focus on longer-term trends, support and resistance levels, and chart patterns that are relevant to swing trading. Use technical indicators and oscillators to identify entry and exit points.

Entry and Exit Rules: Define specific criteria for entering swing trades, such as breakouts from key levels or confirmation of trend reversals. Determine exit rules based on profit targets or technical indicators indicating potential trend exhaustion.

Risk Management: Develop risk management strategies for swing trading, including position sizing based on risk-per-trade or percentage of capital. Set stop loss levels based on market structure and volatility. Consider trailing stops to protect profits.

In both trading plans, it is crucial to regularly review and adjust your strategies and rules based on your trading performance and evolving market conditions. Additionally, incorporate record-keeping and journaling to track your trades and evaluate your performance against your trading plan. Effective risk management, adherence to rules, and continuous improvement are essential components of successful day trading and swing trading.

Chapter 10: Trend Trading Strategies: Riding Market Momentum

Introduction: In Chapter 10, we will explore trend trading strategies, which aim to capitalize on sustained price movements in the market. Trend trading is based on the premise that markets tend to move in persistent directions for extended periods. By identifying and riding market momentum, trend traders seek to capture significant profit potential. This chapter will introduce you to various trend trading strategies and techniques to help you effectively trade with the trend.

10.1 Understanding Market Trends:

Market trends play a crucial role in trading as they provide a framework for making trading decisions and capturing potential profit opportunities. Understanding different types of trends and their characteristics is essential for successful trading. Here's an overview:

Uptrend: An uptrend occurs when the price of an asset consistently moves higher over a period of time. In an uptrend, higher highs and higher lows are formed, indicating a bullish bias in the market. Buyers dominate, and prices generally rise as demand outweighs supply.

Key characteristics of an uptrend:

Higher Highs: Each peak in the price chart is higher than the previous peak.

Higher Lows: Each trough in the price chart is higher than the previous trough.

Steady Buying Pressure: Demand exceeds supply, leading to continuous price advancement.

Bullish Sentiment: Traders and investors are optimistic about the asset's prospects.

Downtrend: A downtrend occurs when the price of an asset consistently moves lower over a period of time. In a downtrend, lower lows and lower highs are formed, indicating a bearish bias in the market. Sellers dominate, and prices generally decline as supply exceeds demand.

Key characteristics of a downtrend:

Lower Lows: Each trough in the price chart is lower than the previous trough.

Lower Highs: Each peak in the price chart is lower than the previous peak.

Steady Selling Pressure: Supply exceeds demand, leading to continuous price decline.

Bearish Sentiment: Traders and investors are pessimistic about the asset's prospects.

Sideways Market (Consolidation): A sideways market occurs when the price of an asset moves within a relatively narrow range, without showing a clear trend in either direction. In a sideways market, the price tends to oscillate between support and resistance levels.

Key characteristics of a sideways market:

Range-bound Price Movement: The price moves horizontally, often between well-defined support and resistance levels.

Lack of Clear Trend: There is no consistent higher high or lower low formation.

Indecision: Traders and investors are unsure about the asset's direction, leading to reduced buying or selling pressure.

Contraction in Volatility: Volatility tends to decrease as the market consolidates.

Identifying market trends is an essential part of technical analysis. Traders use trend analysis to determine the overall direction of the market and align their trading strategies accordingly. Uptrends are typically favored for long positions or buying opportunities, while downtrends are preferred for short positions or selling opportunities. Sideways markets can present range trading or breakout trading opportunities, depending on the trader's approach.

It's important to note that trends can occur in different timeframes, such as short-term, medium-term, or long-term. Traders should consider the relevant timeframe based on their trading style and goals. Additionally, it's crucial to combine trend analysis with other technical indicators and price patterns to confirm the strength and sustainability of a trend before making trading decisions.

10.2 Trend Identification:

Recognizing trend direction is a fundamental aspect of technical analysis, and price action analysis is a powerful tool for identifying trends. Here are a few techniques commonly used:

Price Action Analysis: Price action analysis involves studying the movement and behavior of price itself without relying heavily on indicators. Traders analyze patterns, formations, and key levels on the price chart to determine trend direction. Uptrends are characterized by higher highs and higher lows, while downtrends exhibit lower lows and lower highs. By observing the price action and its structure, traders can gain insights into the prevailing trend.

Moving Averages: Moving averages are popular technical indicators that can help identify and confirm trends. A moving average is calculated by averaging the price over a specific period, smoothing out short-term fluctuations. The most commonly used moving averages are the simple moving average (SMA) and the exponential moving average (EMA). When the price is above a rising moving average, it suggests an uptrend, while a declining moving average below the price indicates a downtrend. Traders often use multiple moving averages with different timeframes to confirm trend direction.

Trendlines: Trendlines are lines drawn on a price chart to connect swing highs or swing lows. An uptrend is confirmed when an ascending trendline connects consecutive higher lows, while a downtrend is confirmed when a descending trendline connects lower highs. Trendlines provide visual representation of trend direction and can act as dynamic support or resistance levels. Traders look for price bounces or breaks of trendlines to confirm trend continuation or potential reversals.

Trend Channels: Trend channels are created by drawing parallel lines along the trendlines to form a channel. The upper line connects the swing highs, while the lower line connects the swing lows. Trend channels provide a visual framework for trend confirmation and can help identify potential support and resistance levels within the trend. Traders look for price bounces or breaks at the boundaries of the trend channel for trading opportunities.

When utilizing these techniques, it's important to consider the timeframe of the chart being analyzed. Trends can vary across different timeframes, and what appears as an uptrend on a short-term chart may be part of a larger downtrend on a higher timeframe. Traders should align their analysis with their trading timeframe and consider multiple timeframes for a comprehensive view of the trend.

It's worth noting that no single indicator or technique guarantees accurate trend identification. Traders often combine multiple tools, such as price action analysis, moving averages, trendlines, and trend channels, to increase the probability of correctly identifying and confirming trend direction.

10.3 Trend Following Strategies:

Trend following is a popular trading approach that aims to identify and profit from sustained price movements in the direction of a prevailing trend. It is based on the belief that markets tend to exhibit trends and that these trends can persist for extended periods.

Key characteristics of trend following include:

Trend Identification: Trend following strategies focus on identifying and following the direction of a market trend. This can be done using various technical analysis tools such as moving averages, trendlines, and price patterns.

Long and Short Positions: Trend following strategies are not limited to buying or going long on an asset. They can also take short positions to profit from downward trends.

Patience and Discipline: Trend following requires patience as trends can take time to develop and unfold. Traders following this approach often wait for confirmation of a trend before entering a trade and maintain positions until there is evidence of a trend reversal.

Breakout strategies play an important role in trend following. Breakouts occur when the price of an asset breaks through a significant support or resistance level, signaling the potential beginning or continuation of a trend. Trend followers often enter trades when breakouts occur, aiming to capture the momentum of the emerging trend.

Moving average crossover strategies are another common technique used in trend following. A moving average crossover occurs when a shorter-term moving average (e.g., 50-day) crosses above or below a longer-term moving average (e.g., 200-day). A bullish crossover (shorter-term moving average crossing above longer-term moving average) is seen as a potential signal to enter a long position, indicating the start of an uptrend. Conversely, a bearish crossover (shorter-term moving average crossing below longer-term moving average) may signal a potential short position, indicating the start of a downtrend. Moving average crossovers can also be used as exit signals when the opposite crossover occurs.

It's important to note that trend following strategies are not foolproof and can experience periods of drawdowns when trends fail to materialize or reverse unexpectedly. Risk management, including the use of stop-loss orders and position sizing techniques, is crucial when employing trend following strategies to protect against potential losses and manage overall portfolio risk.

Overall, trend following strategies aim to capitalize on the momentum of established trends and can be applied to various financial markets and timeframes. Traders using this approach seek to profit from the potential continuation of trends rather than predicting market reversals or short-term price fluctuations.

10.4 The Importance of Pullbacks and Retracements:

Pullbacks and retracements are temporary price movements against the prevailing trend within a larger trend. They provide opportunities for traders to enter trades at more favorable prices in the direction of the overall trend.

During an uptrend, a pullback occurs when prices temporarily decline before resuming their upward movement. Similarly, during a downtrend, a pullback refers to a temporary upward movement before the downward trend resumes. Pullbacks are considered normal and healthy within a trend, providing traders with potential entry opportunities.

Strategies for entering trades during pullbacks include:

Trendline Breakout: Draw trendlines connecting the higher lows in an uptrend or lower highs in a downtrend. Enter a trade when the price breaks above the trendline during an uptrend or below the trendline during a downtrend.

Fibonacci Retracement Levels: Use Fibonacci retracement levels to identify potential support areas during an uptrend or resistance areas during a downtrend. Common retracement levels are 38.2%, 50%, and 61.8%. Look for price reactions and potential reversal signals near these levels to enter trades.

Candlestick Patterns: Look for bullish candlestick patterns, such as hammer, bullish engulfing, or morning star patterns, during an uptrend to enter long positions. For downtrends, look for bearish candlestick patterns, such as shooting star, bearish engulfing, or evening star patterns, to enter short positions.

Moving Average Bounces: Monitor the price's interaction with moving averages. During an uptrend, look for pullbacks that bounce off a rising moving average (such as the 50-day or 200-day moving average) as potential entry points. In a downtrend, look for pullbacks that fail to break above a declining moving average as opportunities to enter short positions.

Utilizing Fibonacci retracement levels can be particularly useful in identifying potential entry points during pullbacks. Fibonacci retracement levels are based on mathematical ratios derived from the Fibonacci sequence and are used to identify potential support and resistance levels. Traders often look for price reactions or reversal signals near these levels to enter trades.

To apply Fibonacci retracement levels, identify a significant swing high and low within the trend. Then, draw Fibonacci retracement lines from the low to the high in an uptrend or from the high to the low in a downtrend. The retracement levels will appear as horizontal lines on the chart. Traders watch for price to bounce off or reverse near these levels as potential entry points.

It's important to note that no trading strategy guarantees success, and proper risk management is essential. Setting stop-loss orders to limit potential losses and managing position sizing based on risk tolerance are crucial when trading pullbacks or any other strategy. Additionally, combining pullback entry strategies with other technical analysis tools and indicators can help confirm potential trade opportunities.

10.5 Riding Trends with Moving Averages:

Moving averages are commonly used in trend-following strategies to help traders stay aligned with the trend and identify potential entry and exit points. The two main types of moving average crossovers used for trade entry are the "Golden Cross" and the "Death Cross."

Golden Cross: The Golden Cross occurs when a shorter-term moving average, such as the 50-day moving average, crosses above a longer-term moving average, such as the 200-day moving average. This crossover suggests a bullish signal and indicates a potential uptrend. Traders may consider entering a long trade when the Golden Cross occurs, as it confirms the upward momentum.

Death Cross: The Death Cross is the opposite of the Golden Cross. It occurs when the shorter-term moving average crosses below the longer-term moving average. For example, when the 50-day moving average crosses below the 200-day moving average. This crossover suggests a bearish signal and indicates a potential downtrend. Traders may consider entering a short trade when the Death Cross occurs, as it confirms the downward momentum.

While moving average crossovers can be useful for trade entry signals, it's important to consider other factors, such as market conditions and confirmation from other indicators or chart patterns, before entering a trade. False crossovers can occur, resulting in whipsaw trades, so it's important to analyze the overall context of the market.

Moving averages can also be used to manage trade exits. Traders may consider exiting a long position when the price crosses below a shorter-term moving average or when the shorter-term moving average crosses below the longer-term moving average (Death Cross). This exit signal suggests a potential loss of upward momentum. Conversely, traders may consider exiting a short position when the price crosses above a shorter-term moving average or when the shorter-term moving average crosses above the longer-term moving average (Golden Cross). This exit signal indicates a potential loss of downward momentum.

However, it's worth noting that moving averages are lagging indicators, meaning they are based on past price data. Therefore, it's important to use them in conjunction with other technical analysis tools and indicators to confirm trade signals and avoid false signals. Traders may also consider using trailing stops or combining moving averages with other exit strategies, such as price targets or chart pattern breakouts, to manage trade exits effectively.

10.6 Trend Indicators:

Trend indicators are technical analysis tools that help traders identify and confirm the direction of market trends. Here are two popular trend indicators:

Average Directional Index (ADX): The Average Directional Index is a widely used trend indicator that measures the strength of a trend rather than its direction. It consists of three lines: the ADX line, the Positive Directional Indicator (+DI), and the Negative Directional Indicator (-DI). The ADX line indicates the strength of the trend, while the +DI and -DI lines indicate the direction of the trend. A high ADX reading suggests a strong trend, while a low ADX reading indicates a weak or ranging market.

Traders can use the ADX to determine whether a trend is worth trading and to filter out trades during choppy or sideways markets. A rising ADX indicates an increasing trend strength, while a falling ADX suggests a weakening trend. Traders may consider entering trades when the ADX is rising and the +DI line is above the -DI line for an uptrend, or when the ADX is rising and the -DI line is above the +DI line for a downtrend.

Parabolic SAR: The Parabolic SAR (Stop and Reverse) is a trend-following indicator that helps identify potential entry and exit points. It appears as dots above or below price on the chart. When the dots are below price, it suggests an uptrend, and when the dots are above price, it suggests a downtrend.

Traders can use the Parabolic SAR to enter trades in the direction of the trend. For example, they may consider entering a long trade when the dots flip from above to below price, indicating a potential trend reversal from downtrend to uptrend. Conversely, they may consider entering a short trade when the dots flip from below to above price, indicating a potential trend reversal from uptrend to downtrend.

When incorporating trend indicators into your trading strategy, it's important to use them in conjunction with other technical analysis tools and indicators for confirmation. For example, you can combine the ADX with moving averages or chart patterns to confirm the presence of a trend and identify potential entry points. Similarly, you can use the Parabolic SAR alongside other indicators, such as oscillators or volume analysis, to validate trend signals.

Keep in mind that no single indicator is foolproof, and false signals can occur. Therefore, it's recommended to use multiple indicators and analyze the overall market context before making trading decisions. Experiment with different combinations of indicators and find the ones that work best for your trading style and preferences.

10.7 Breakout Trading in Trending Markets:

Breakout trading is a popular strategy used to capitalize on strong price movements when a security breaks out of a well-defined price range or chart pattern. Here are some steps for identifying and trading breakouts in trending markets:

Identify the trend: Before looking for breakouts, it's important to determine the direction of the trend. You can use trend indicators, moving averages, or visual analysis of price action to identify whether the market is in an uptrend or downtrend.

Identify potential breakout levels: Look for areas of consolidation or chart patterns that suggest a potential breakout. These can include horizontal support or resistance levels, trendlines, channels, triangles, or rectangles. These patterns indicate that the market is building up energy and may break out in the direction of the prevailing trend.

Confirm the breakout: Wait for the price to convincingly break above resistance or below support, confirming the breakout. Ideally, there should be a strong increase in volume accompanying the breakout, indicating increased market participation and conviction.

Entry strategies: There are several entry strategies you can use for breakout trades:

Breakout on close: Enter the trade at the close of the candle/bar that confirms the breakout. This approach helps filter out false breakouts that may occur intra-candle.

Breakout on a retest: Wait for the price to retest the breakout level after the initial breakout. Enter the trade when the price holds above the breakout level on the retest. This approach provides an additional confirmation of the breakout.

Breakout on a pullback: If the price retraces back to the breakout level, enter the trade when the price starts to move in the direction of the breakout again. This approach allows you to enter at a potentially better price after a pullback.

Setting stop loss levels: Place a stop loss order below the breakout level in an uptrend or above the breakout level in a downtrend. This helps protect your capital if the breakout fails and the price reverses. The placement of the stop loss will depend on your risk tolerance and the specific characteristics of the market and the breakout.

Setting profit targets: There are a few ways to set profit targets for breakout trades:

Measured move: Measure the height of the pattern or the distance from the breakout level to the previous swing high or low. Project this distance from the breakout level in the direction of the breakout to estimate a potential target.

Fibonacci extensions: Use Fibonacci extension levels to identify potential targets beyond the initial measured move. These levels are derived from Fibonacci ratios and can act as areas of interest where the price may encounter resistance or support.

Trailing stop: As the price continues to trend in your favor, you can use a trailing stop loss order to lock in profits and let the trade run until the trend loses momentum or reverses.

Remember, breakouts can sometimes fail or result in false signals, so it's crucial to manage risk by using proper position sizing, setting stop loss levels, and adhering to your trading plan. Continuously monitor the trade's progress and make adjustments as needed based on market conditions and price action.

10.8 Trend Reversals and Trend Continuation:

Recognizing potential trend reversals is an essential skill in technical analysis, as it allows traders to capture the early stages of a new trend and avoid holding positions in the wrong direction. Here are some strategies for entering trades during trend reversals:

Reversal patterns: Look for specific chart patterns that indicate a potential trend reversal. These patterns include:

Double top and double bottom: These patterns occur when the price reaches a resistance level twice (double top) or a support level twice (double bottom), indicating a potential reversal.

Head and shoulders: This pattern consists of a higher high (head) surrounded by two lower highs (shoulders). It signals a potential trend reversal from bullish to bearish.

Inverse head and shoulders: The inverse of the head and shoulders pattern, this indicates a potential trend reversal from bearish to bullish.

Triple top and triple bottom: Similar to double tops and bottoms, but with three highs or lows. They suggest a stronger reversal signal.

Rounding bottom or top: These patterns show a gradual shift in the price from a downtrend to an uptrend (rounding bottom) or from an uptrend to a downtrend (rounding top).

Divergence: Use technical indicators, such as the Relative Strength Index (RSI) or Moving Average Convergence Divergence (MACD), to identify divergences. Divergence occurs when the price forms a higher high or lower low while the indicator forms a lower high or higher low. This can signal a potential trend reversal.

Trendline breaks: Draw trendlines to connect swing highs or swing lows. When the price breaks the trendline, it may indicate a reversal in the trend. This is particularly effective when combined with other reversal patterns or indicators.

Moving average crossovers: Pay attention to moving average crossovers, such as when a shorter-term moving average crosses above or below a longer-term moving average. These crossovers can indicate a change in trend direction.

When it comes to identifying trend continuation patterns and trading opportunities, some common patterns to watch for include:

Flags and pennants: These are short-term consolidation patterns that occur within an existing trend. They can provide an opportunity to enter trades in the direction of the prevailing trend.

Triangles (ascending, descending, and symmetrical): Triangles represent periods of consolidation before the trend continues. Traders can look for breakouts from these patterns to enter trades in the direction of the trend.

Rectangles: Similar to triangles, rectangles are consolidation patterns that indicate a temporary pause in the trend. Traders can look for breakouts from the upper or lower boundaries of the rectangle to enter trades.

Continuation candlestick patterns: Certain candlestick patterns, such as bullish/bearish engulfing patterns or harami patterns, can indicate a continuation of the prevailing trend.

Remember, it's important to confirm these patterns and signals with other technical analysis tools and indicators and to manage risk by using appropriate position sizing, stop loss orders, and profit targets. Continuously monitor the trade and adjust your strategy as the market conditions evolve.

10.9 Volatility and Trend Trading:

The relationship between volatility and trend trading is important to understand as it can impact the effectiveness of trading strategies and risk management. Here are some key points regarding volatility and trend trading:

Volatility and trend strength: Higher volatility often accompanies strong trends, as it reflects the magnitude and speed of price movements. In such conditions, trend trading strategies can be more effective, as trends are more likely to continue in the same direction.

Adjusting strategies for volatility: Different volatility environments may require adjustments to trading strategies. In high volatility markets, wider stop loss levels may be necessary to accommodate larger price swings. Conversely, in low volatility markets, tighter stops or shorter-term strategies may be more appropriate.

Using volatility indicators: Volatility indicators, such as Average True Range (ATR) or Bollinger Bands, can provide insights into market volatility levels. These indicators can be used to confirm trends, set appropriate stop loss levels, or adjust position sizing based on the current volatility conditions.

Volatility-based trade filters: Traders may choose to implement volatility-based filters to enter or exit trades. For example, they may require a certain level of volatility or a specific volatility breakout before entering a trade. This helps ensure that trends are strong enough to warrant trading.

Managing risk in volatile markets: Volatile markets can pose increased risks, as price movements can be more erratic. Proper risk management is crucial, including setting appropriate stop loss levels, using trailing stops to protect profits, and adjusting position sizes based on the volatility of the market.

It's important to note that each trader may have their own approach to incorporating volatility into their trend trading strategies. Some traders thrive in high volatility environments, while others may prefer lower volatility conditions. Understanding and adapting to market volatility can enhance the effectiveness of trend trading strategies and improve overall trade management.

10.10 Risk Management in Trend Trading:

Position sizing techniques, stop loss levels, risk-reward ratios, and ongoing risk management are crucial components of trend trading. Here's a breakdown of these elements:

Position sizing techniques: Position sizing refers to determining the appropriate amount of capital to allocate to each trade based on your risk tolerance and account size. Several position sizing techniques are commonly used in trend trading, such as fixed fractional position sizing, where a fixed percentage of your trading capital is allocated to each trade. Another approach is the volatility-based position sizing, which adjusts the position size based on the volatility of the market or specific instrument being traded. The goal is to manage risk by limiting the amount of capital at stake in each trade.

Setting stop loss levels: Stop loss levels are predetermined price levels at which you will exit a trade to limit potential losses. In trend trading, stop loss levels are typically set below support levels or key technical levels to protect against adverse price movements. Volatility-based stop loss levels can also be employed, where the distance of the stop loss is determined by the volatility of the market or instrument. By setting appropriate stop loss levels, you limit your risk exposure in case the trend reverses or temporarily retraces.

Managing risk-reward ratios: Risk-reward ratios determine the potential profit compared to the potential loss on a trade. For trend trading, it's important to aim for favorable risk-reward ratios to ensure that the potential reward justifies the risk taken. A commonly used rule is to target a risk-reward ratio of at least 1:2 or higher, meaning that the potential profit target is at least twice the size of the potential loss. This helps to ensure that winning trades can outweigh losing trades over the long run.

Monitoring and adjusting risk management parameters: As trends evolve, it's important to continually monitor and adjust your risk management parameters. This includes periodically reviewing and adjusting stop loss levels based on market volatility and changes in the trend structure. Additionally, monitoring the risk-reward ratios of your trades and overall portfolio can help you make necessary adjustments to maintain a balanced risk profile.

By effectively implementing position sizing techniques, setting appropriate stop loss levels, managing risk-reward ratios, and regularly monitoring and adjusting risk management parameters, you can enhance your risk management practices in trend trading. These practices help to protect your capital and ensure that your trading approach is aligned with your risk tolerance and trading objectives.

Chapter 11: Contrarian Trading Strategies: Profiting from Market Reversals

Introduction: In Chapter 11, we will explore contrarian trading strategies, which involve taking positions opposite to prevailing market sentiment. Contrarian traders aim to identify market reversals and capitalize on them for potential profits. By going against the crowd, contrarian trading can offer unique opportunities and high-reward potential. This chapter will introduce you to various contrarian trading strategies and techniques to help you effectively identify and trade market reversals.

11.1 Understanding Contrarian Trading:

Contrarian trading is an approach to trading and investing that involves taking positions contrary to the prevailing market sentiment. The underlying principle of contrarian trading is that markets often exhibit herd behavior, causing prices to become overbought or oversold based on the emotions and actions of the majority of market participants. Contrarian traders believe that these extreme market sentiments create opportunities for profitable trades by taking positions opposite to the prevailing sentiment.

Contrarian trading differs from trend following, which involves identifying and trading in the direction of prevailing market trends. Contrarian traders, on the other hand, aim to identify turning points or reversals in market sentiment and take positions that go against the prevailing trend. They believe that market sentiment tends to reach extreme levels before a reversal occurs, and by identifying these extremes, they can profit from the subsequent price movement as sentiment shifts.

There are several potential benefits and challenges of contrarian trading:

Benefits of contrarian trading:

Profit from market reversals: Contrarian traders aim to enter trades at turning points, which can lead to significant price movements if the reversal occurs. By correctly identifying these turning points, contrarian traders can capture profits as the sentiment shifts.

Lower entry points and higher potential rewards: Contrarian trading allows traders to enter positions at lower prices or better value levels compared to trend followers who enter positions during established trends. If the contrarian position is successful, the potential rewards can be higher.

Challenges of contrarian trading:

Timing and accuracy: Contrarian trading requires accurate timing to identify when market sentiment is reaching extreme levels and to enter positions before a reversal occurs. It can be challenging to time market sentiment accurately, and mistimed trades can lead to losses.

Market noise and false signals: Market sentiment can be influenced by various factors, including news events, rumors, and psychological biases. This can lead to market noise and false signals, making it challenging to differentiate between genuine turning points and temporary price fluctuations.

Psychological challenges: Contrarian trading can go against the prevailing market consensus, which can create psychological challenges. It requires discipline, conviction, and the ability to withstand criticism and doubt during periods when the prevailing sentiment goes against the contrarian position.

Contrarian trading is not suitable for all traders and requires a deep understanding of market dynamics, sentiment analysis, and risk management. It is often used as a complement to other trading strategies and can be effective when combined with proper analysis and risk management techniques.

11.2 Market Sentiment and Indicators:

Market sentiment refers to the overall psychological attitude or sentiment of market participants towards a particular asset, sector, or the overall market. It reflects the collective emotions, beliefs, and expectations of traders and investors, and it can significantly impact price movements.

Market sentiment can be driven by various factors, including economic data, geopolitical events, news releases, investor sentiment surveys, and technical analysis patterns. It can range from extreme optimism (bullish sentiment) to extreme pessimism (bearish sentiment), or it can be neutral when there is no clear bias.

There are several popular sentiment indicators that traders and investors use to gauge market sentiment:

Put-Call Ratio: The put-call ratio is a sentiment indicator derived from the volume of put options relative to call options traded in the options market. A high put-call ratio suggests bearish sentiment, as more traders are buying put options to hedge or speculate on market declines. A low put-call ratio indicates bullish sentiment, as more traders are buying call options to bet on market gains.

Volatility Index (VIX): The VIX, also known as the "fear gauge," measures market expectations of future volatility based on options prices. When the VIX is high, it suggests increased fear and uncertainty in the market, indicating bearish sentiment. Conversely, a low VIX indicates complacency and bullish sentiment.

Sentiment Surveys: Various surveys and sentiment indicators are conducted to measure the sentiment of traders and investors. These surveys ask participants about their opinions, expectations, and positioning in the market. Examples include the American Association of Individual Investors (AAII) sentiment survey and the Investor's Intelligence sentiment survey.

Commitment of Traders (COT) Report: The COT report provides insights into the positions taken by different types of traders, including commercial hedgers, large speculators, and small speculators. It can help identify extreme positioning and sentiment in the futures markets.

When incorporating sentiment indicators into trading analysis, traders often use them as contrarian indicators. For example, if sentiment indicators show extreme bullishness, it may signal a potential market top, suggesting a contrarian bearish trading opportunity. Conversely, extreme bearish sentiment may indicate a potential market bottom and a contrarian bullish trading opportunity.

However, it's important to note that sentiment indicators should not be used in isolation. They should be used in conjunction with other technical and fundamental analysis tools to confirm or validate trading decisions. It's also important to consider the context, market conditions, and the overall trend when interpreting sentiment indicators.

Traders can monitor sentiment indicators on a regular basis and incorporate them into their overall trading analysis to gain additional insights into market sentiment and potential trading opportunities.

11.3 Identifying Overbought and Oversold Conditions:

Recognizing overbought and oversold conditions is an important aspect of technical analysis. It helps traders identify potential points of reversal or correction in price trends. Oscillators are commonly used technical indicators to identify overbought and oversold conditions. Two popular oscillators used for this purpose are the Relative Strength Index (RSI) and the Stochastic Oscillator.

Relative Strength Index (RSI): The RSI is a momentum oscillator that measures the speed and change of price movements. It oscillates between 0 and 100. A reading above 70 is typically considered overbought, indicating that the price may have risen too quickly and is due for a correction. Conversely, a reading below 30 is generally considered oversold, suggesting that the price may have declined too rapidly and could potentially rebound.

Stochastic Oscillator: The Stochastic Oscillator compares the current price to its price range over a specific period of time. It also oscillates between 0 and 100. Similar to the RSI, a reading above 80 is typically considered overbought, while a reading below 20 is considered oversold. Traders often look for potential reversals when the Stochastic Oscillator crosses above or below these levels.

In addition to oscillators, traders can also look for specific price and volume patterns that signal potential reversals. Here are a few examples:

Divergence: Divergence occurs when the price of an asset moves in the opposite direction of the oscillator. Bullish divergence happens when the price makes a lower low, but the oscillator makes a higher low, indicating a potential bullish reversal. Bearish divergence occurs when the price makes a higher high, but the oscillator makes a lower high, suggesting a potential bearish reversal.

Reversal candlestick patterns: Certain candlestick patterns, such as doji, hammer, and shooting star, can indicate potential reversals. For example, a hammer pattern appearing after a downtrend may suggest a bullish reversal, while a shooting star pattern after an uptrend may signal a bearish reversal.

Volume analysis: Unusually high or low trading volume during a price move can provide insights into potential reversals. High volume during a price decline or low volume during a price rally may indicate a reversal in sentiment.

It's important to note that no single indicator or pattern is foolproof, and false signals can occur. Therefore, it's recommended to use a combination of indicators, patterns, and other technical analysis tools to confirm potential reversals and make informed trading decisions. Traders should also consider the broader market context, fundamental factors, and risk management principles when interpreting these signals.

11.4 Reversal Patterns:

Reversal chart patterns are price patterns that suggest a potential reversal in the prevailing trend. Traders use these patterns to identify potential turning points in the market and take advantage of the anticipated reversal. Here are a few common reversal chart patterns:

Double Top/Bottom: The double top pattern occurs when the price forms two peaks at approximately the same level, separated by a trough in between. The double bottom pattern is the opposite, with two troughs separated by a peak in between. These patterns indicate a potential reversal of an uptrend (double top) or a downtrend (double bottom).

Head and Shoulders: The head and shoulders pattern is characterized by three peaks or troughs, with the central peak or trough (the head) being higher or lower than the other two (the shoulders). The pattern resembles a head between two shoulders. A head and shoulders pattern can signal a reversal from an uptrend to a downtrend (bearish head and shoulders) or from a downtrend to an uptrend (bullish head and shoulders).

To identify and trade these reversal patterns, traders typically look for the following characteristics:

Clear and well-defined pattern: The pattern should have distinct peaks and troughs, forming a recognizable shape.

Neckline: The neckline is a line drawn connecting the lows of a double top pattern or the highs of a double bottom pattern. In a head and shoulders pattern, the neckline connects the lows of the two shoulders.

Break of neckline: A valid reversal signal occurs when the price breaks below the neckline in a double top pattern or above the neckline in a double bottom or head and shoulders pattern.

Volume confirmation: Higher trading volume during the pattern formation and when the neckline is broken can provide confirmation of the reversal.

To validate reversal patterns, traders often use volume and confirmation indicators, such as:

Volume: An increase in trading volume during the pattern formation and when the neckline is broken can add strength to the reversal signal. Higher volume suggests increased market participation and potential confirmation of the pattern.

Oscillators: Oscillators like the Relative Strength Index (RSI) or the Stochastic Oscillator can help identify overbought or oversold conditions, confirming the potential reversal indicated by the pattern.

Moving averages: Moving averages can be used to assess the overall trend and confirm the reversal signaled by the pattern. For example, a downward-sloping 200-day moving average in a bearish reversal pattern may provide additional confirmation.

It's important to note that reversal patterns are not always 100% accurate, and false signals can occur. Traders should consider other factors such as market conditions, overall trend, and fundamental analysis before making trading decisions. Risk management techniques, including setting appropriate stop-loss levels and position sizing, are crucial when trading reversal patterns to manage potential risks.

11.5 Divergence Trading:

Divergence is a popular contrarian trading signal that occurs when there is a discrepancy between the price action and the indicator readings, particularly oscillators. It suggests a potential reversal or change in the prevailing trend. There are two types of divergence: bullish divergence and bearish divergence.

Bullish Divergence: Bullish divergence occurs when the price forms lower lows while the oscillator (such as the RSI or Stochastic) forms higher lows. This suggests that the momentum of the downtrend is weakening, and a potential bullish reversal may be imminent. It indicates that despite the lower price lows, the underlying buying pressure is increasing.

To trade bullish divergence, traders often look for the following steps:

Identify a downtrend: Ensure that there is a clear and established downtrend in place.

Look for lower lows on the price chart: Identify consecutive lower lows forming a downward trendline.

Observe the oscillator: Check if the oscillator is forming higher lows during the same period, indicating a bullish divergence.

Confirmation: Look for additional confirmation signals, such as a bullish candlestick pattern or a breakout above a resistance level, to validate the potential reversal.

Entry: Enter a long trade (buy) when the price breaks above the trendline or a significant resistance level.

Bearish Divergence: Bearish divergence occurs when the price forms higher highs while the oscillator forms lower highs. This suggests that the momentum of the uptrend is weakening, and a potential bearish reversal may be on the horizon. It indicates that despite the higher price highs, the underlying selling pressure is increasing.

To trade bearish divergence, traders often follow these steps:

Identify an uptrend: Confirm the presence of a clear and established uptrend.

Look for higher highs on the price chart: Identify consecutive higher highs forming an upward trendline.

Observe the oscillator: Check if the oscillator is forming lower highs during the same period, indicating a bearish divergence.

Confirmation: Look for additional confirmation signals, such as a bearish candlestick pattern or a breakdown below a support level, to validate the potential reversal.

Entry: Enter a short trade (sell) when the price breaks below the trendline or a significant support level.

It's important to note that divergence signals should not be considered in isolation and should be used in conjunction with other technical analysis tools and confirmation indicators. Traders should also be aware that divergence signals are not infallible and can sometimes result in false signals. Risk management techniques, such as setting stop-loss orders and position sizing, should be employed to manage potential risks.

11.6 Support and Resistance Trading:

Support and resistance levels are important areas on a price chart where the price tends to find buying (support) or selling (resistance) pressure. These levels can be used in contrarian trading to identify potential trade opportunities. Here are some strategies for trading bounces and breakouts at key support and resistance levels:

Bounce Trading: When the price approaches a support or resistance level, traders look for signs of a potential bounce and reversal in the opposite direction. The idea is to enter trades in the direction opposite to the prevailing trend.

Identify a strong support or resistance level: Look for levels where the price has previously reversed or stalled.

Wait for a bounce signal: Observe price action, candlestick patterns, or indicators that indicate a potential reversal, such as bullish/bearish engulfing patterns, hammer/shooting star patterns, or bullish/bearish divergence.

Entry: Enter a trade in the opposite direction of the prevailing trend once the bounce signal is confirmed.

Stop loss: Place a stop loss below the support or resistance level to protect against a potential breakdown.

Take profit: Set a profit target based on nearby support or resistance levels or other technical analysis methods.

Breakout Trading: Breakouts occur when the price breaks above resistance or below support, signaling a potential continuation of the prevailing trend. Contrarian traders can look for breakouts that go against the prevailing trend and enter trades accordingly.

Identify a strong support or resistance level: Look for levels where the price has previously struggled to break through.

Wait for a breakout signal: Monitor price action for a decisive breakout above resistance or below support, accompanied by an increase in volume and momentum.

Entry: Enter a trade in the direction of the breakout, going against the prevailing trend.

Stop loss: Place a stop loss above the breakout level (for a bearish breakout) or below the breakout level (for a bullish breakout).

Take profit: Set a profit target based on the projected price movement or the distance between the breakout level and the next significant support or resistance level.

When trading bounces and breakouts at support and resistance levels, it's important to adjust risk management parameters to account for potential price reversals or false breakouts. Consider factors such as the strength of the support or resistance level, the volatility of the market, and your risk tolerance. Use appropriate position sizing, set stop loss levels, and adhere to your risk-reward ratio to manage risk effectively.

It's also crucial to validate support and resistance levels using multiple indicators or chart patterns to increase the probability of successful trades. Additionally, regular monitoring of trade progress and adjustments to stop loss levels or profit targets as the price develops can help optimize risk management for support and resistance trades.

11.7 News and Event Trading:

Taking advantage of market reactions to news and events requires a contrarian approach, where you trade against the initial market sentiment driven by news releases. Here are strategies for entering trades based on news-driven market reversals:

Wait for the initial reaction: When significant news or events are released, there is often an immediate market reaction. This reaction can be driven by knee-jerk emotions and overreactions. Wait for this initial reaction to subside and for the market to stabilize.

Assess the news and its impact: Analyze the news release and its potential implications for the market. Consider factors such as the relevance of the news to the overall market sentiment, the quality of the news source, and the magnitude of the news impact.

Monitor price action and volume: Observe the price action and volume patterns following the initial reaction. Look for signs of exhaustion or a reversal in the market sentiment. This could include reversal candlestick patterns, divergence in oscillators, or a decrease in volume.

Identify key support or resistance levels: Determine significant support or resistance levels that may come into play following the news release. These levels can act as potential turning points for the market sentiment.

Wait for confirmation: Wait for confirmation signals that the market sentiment is reversing. This could include a break of a key support or resistance level, a reversal candlestick pattern, or a shift in volume and momentum.

Enter the trade: Once you have identified the reversal signal and have confirmation, enter the trade in the opposite direction of the initial market sentiment. Place your stop loss to manage risk and set profit targets based on nearby support or resistance levels or other technical analysis methods.

It's important to note that trading against the initial market sentiment driven by news carries inherent risks. Market reactions to news can be unpredictable, and there is a possibility of extended moves against your trade. Therefore, it's crucial to apply proper risk management techniques, including setting appropriate stop loss levels, considering position sizing, and being prepared to exit the trade if the market sentiment continues to move against your position.

Additionally, staying informed about upcoming news releases and events and having a solid understanding of the market dynamics and the specific instrument you are trading can help you make more informed decisions when trading news-driven reversals.

11.8 Timing and Confirmation:

Determining optimal entry and exit timing for contrarian trades involves waiting for confirmation signals before entering trades and utilizing multiple time frames for trade confirmation and analysis. Here's how you can approach these aspects:

Waiting for confirmation signals: Instead of trying to catch the exact bottom or top of a market reversal, it is prudent to wait for confirmation signals before entering a contrarian trade. Confirmation signals help validate that the market sentiment is indeed shifting in the anticipated direction. These signals can include:

Reversal candlestick patterns: Look for patterns such as bullish or bearish engulfing patterns, hammer or shooting star patterns, or doji patterns indicating potential reversals.

Divergence: Observe divergences between price and oscillators, such as the RSI or Stochastic, where the price is making lower lows or higher highs while the oscillator is showing higher lows or lower highs, indicating a potential shift in momentum.

Break of key levels: Wait for a break of significant support or resistance levels, trendlines, or moving averages to confirm a potential reversal.

Volume confirmation: Monitor volume patterns to see if there is an increase or decrease in volume during the potential reversal, providing further confirmation of the changing market sentiment.

Utilizing multiple time frames: Analyzing multiple time frames can provide additional confirmation and context for contrarian trades. Consider using a higher time frame to identify the overall trend and a lower time frame for more precise entry points. For example:

Higher time frame analysis: Use a higher time frame (e.g., daily or weekly) to determine the overall trend and market context. This helps to ensure that your contrarian trade aligns with the broader market direction.

Lower time frame analysis: Use a lower time frame (e.g., hourly or 15-minute) to fine-tune your entry and exit timing. Look for confirmation signals and patterns on this time frame that align with the anticipated reversal on the higher time frame.

By incorporating multiple time frames into your analysis, you can increase the probability of entering trades when the market sentiment is indeed shifting in your favor. This approach also helps you avoid trading against a strong and persistent trend.

Remember to implement proper risk management techniques, including setting stop loss levels based on market structure or volatility, and adjusting your profit targets based on the time frame and the potential magnitude of the reversal.

Regularly reviewing and adjusting your trading plan and strategies based on the feedback from your trades and market observations can help you refine your entry and exit timing over time.

11.9 Risk Management in Contrarian Trading:

Position sizing techniques, setting appropriate stop loss levels, managing risk-reward ratios, and monitoring risk management parameters are all crucial aspects of trading contrarian trades. Here's how you can approach each of these elements:

Position sizing techniques: Determining the appropriate position size for contrarian trades involves considering your risk tolerance, account size, and the potential risk of the trade. Some common position sizing techniques include:

Fixed dollar amount: Allocate a fixed dollar amount or percentage of your trading capital to each trade. This approach ensures consistency in position sizing and allows you to adjust the position size based on the risk of the trade.

Percentage of account: Determine a percentage of your trading account that you are willing to risk on each trade. This approach allows for flexibility in position sizing based on the size of your account and the risk of the trade.

Volatility-based position sizing: Consider the volatility of the market and the specific stock or asset you're trading. Adjust your position size based on the anticipated volatility to ensure you're not taking on excessive risk.

Setting appropriate stop loss levels: Stop loss levels are crucial for managing risk in contrarian trades. The stop loss level should be determined based on the volatility of the market and the specific stock or asset being traded. Consider the following factors when setting stop loss levels:

Market structure: Identify key support or resistance levels that, if breached, would invalidate the contrarian trade. Set your stop loss just below support for long trades and above resistance for short trades.

Volatility: Take into account the average true range (ATR) or other measures of volatility to set your stop loss at a reasonable distance from the entry point. A more volatile market may require a wider stop loss to avoid premature exits.

Risk tolerance: Set your stop loss level at a point where you are comfortable with the potential loss if the trade does not work out. Ensure that the stop loss level aligns with your risk management parameters and the risk-reward ratio of the trade.

Managing risk-reward ratios: Assessing the risk-reward ratio is essential for evaluating the potential profitability of a contrarian trade. Consider the potential reward relative to the potential risk before entering a trade. Aim for trades with a favorable risk-reward ratio, where the potential reward outweighs the potential risk. Ideally, you should target trades with a risk-reward ratio of at least 1:2 or higher, meaning that the potential reward is at least twice the potential risk.

Monitoring and adjusting risk management parameters: As market reversals develop, it is important to monitor and adjust your risk management parameters accordingly. This includes regularly reviewing your stop loss levels, profit targets, and position sizes to ensure they are aligned with current market conditions and the evolving trend. Adjusting your risk management parameters allows you to protect profits, cut losses, and manage overall risk exposure.

It's crucial to consistently monitor and reassess your risk management strategy and parameters as the market conditions change. This ensures that your risk remains in check and your trades are aligned with your risk tolerance and trading plan. Regularly review and refine your risk management approach based on your trading performance and the feedback from your trades.

11.10 Psychological Challenges and Discipline:

Contrarian trading can present unique psychological challenges due to its nature of going against the prevailing market sentiment. Here are some strategies to help you manage emotions and maintain discipline in contrarian trades:

Develop a trading plan: Having a well-defined trading plan is essential for contrarian trading. Your plan should outline your entry and exit criteria, risk management guidelines, and strategies for managing contrarian trades. By following a plan, you can reduce impulsive decisions driven by emotions and stick to a structured approach.

Predefine your risk parameters: Determine your risk tolerance and establish specific risk parameters for each trade. This includes setting stop loss levels, profit targets, and maximum risk exposure. Adhering to predetermined risk levels helps you avoid emotional decision-making and maintain discipline in your trading.

Practice patience and wait for confirmation: Contrarian trading often requires patience and the ability to wait for confirmation signals. Avoid jumping into trades prematurely based on initial market reactions. Wait for confirmation from technical indicators, price patterns, or other signals that support your contrarian thesis.

Manage your expectations: Understand that not every contrarian trade will be successful. Accept that losses are a part of trading and focus on the long-term profitability of your strategy. Avoid letting short-term losses or setbacks impact your overall mindset and decision-making.

Use positive self-talk and visualization: Cultivate a positive mindset by using affirmations and visualization techniques. Remind yourself of your trading plan, past successes, and your ability to execute your strategy effectively. Visualize yourself making disciplined and profitable decisions in contrarian trades.

Take breaks and practice self-care: Trading can be mentally and emotionally demanding. Take regular breaks from the market to recharge and maintain clarity of mind. Engage in activities outside of trading that promote relaxation and self-care, such as exercise, meditation, or hobbies.

Keep a trading journal: Maintain a trading journal to track your emotions, thoughts, and decision-making process during contrarian trades. Reviewing your journal can provide insights into your emotional patterns and help you identify areas for improvement. It also serves as a reminder of your progress and achievements.

Seek support and accountability: Surround yourself with a supportive network of fellow traders or join trading communities where you can share experiences, seek advice, and hold yourself accountable. Engaging with like-minded individuals can help you gain perspective and stay motivated.

Remember, managing emotions and maintaining discipline in contrarian trading is an ongoing process. It takes time, practice, and self-awareness. By incorporating these strategies into your trading routine, you can improve your ability to make objective decisions and navigate the psychological challenges of contrarian trading.

Chapter 12: Options Trading: Strategies and Considerations

Introduction: In Chapter 12, we will delve into options trading—a versatile financial instrument that offers unique opportunities for traders. Options provide the right, but not the obligation, to buy or sell an underlying asset at a predetermined price within a specified timeframe. This chapter will introduce you to options trading strategies and considerations, helping you understand how to effectively utilize options in your trading.

12.1 Understanding Options:

Options contracts are financial instruments that give the holder the right, but not the obligation, to buy or sell an underlying asset at a predetermined price (strike price) within a specified period (expiration date). Options provide traders with flexibility and the opportunity to profit from price movements in the underlying asset without owning the asset itself.

Here are the key components of an options contract:

Underlying Asset: The options contract is based on an underlying asset, which can be a stock, index, commodity, or currency.

Call Option: A call option gives the holder the right to buy the underlying asset at the strike price before or on the expiration date. Call options are typically used when the trader expects the price of the underlying asset to rise.

Put Option: A put option gives the holder the right to sell the underlying asset at the strike price before or on the expiration date. Put options are generally used when the trader expects the price of the underlying asset to fall.

Strike Price: The strike price is the predetermined price at which the underlying asset can be bought or sold if the option is exercised.

Expiration Date: The expiration date is the date on which the options contract expires and becomes invalid. After the expiration date, the options contract loses its value.

Premium: The premium is the price that the buyer pays to the seller for the options contract. It represents the cost of acquiring the rights associated with the options contract.

Benefits of Options Trading:

Leverage: Options allow traders to control a larger position in the underlying asset with a smaller investment, offering potential for amplified returns.

Flexibility: Options provide various strategies to profit from different market conditions, including bullish, bearish, and neutral market scenarios.

Risk Management: Options can be used to hedge against potential losses in the underlying asset or existing positions, providing a level of risk mitigation.

Risks of Options Trading:

Limited Time: Options have expiration dates, which means traders must be accurate in predicting both the direction and timing of price movements.

Volatility: Options can be affected by changes in market volatility, which may increase the premium and make trading more challenging.

Complex Strategies: Options trading involves various strategies and combinations that can be complex and require a good understanding of their mechanics.

It's important for options traders to have a solid understanding of options concepts, strategies, and risks before engaging in options trading. Seeking education, conducting thorough analysis, and practicing with simulated trading platforms can help traders gain experience and confidence in trading options effectively.

12.2 Options Trading Strategies:

Here are explanations of some commonly used options trading strategies:

Long Position: Buying options with the expectation that the price of the underlying asset will move in a favorable direction. Long call options are used when anticipating a rise in the underlying asset's price, while long put options are used when expecting a decline.

Short Position: Selling options with the obligation to fulfill the terms of the contract if exercised by the buyer. Short call options are used when expecting the underlying asset's price to stay below the strike price, while short put options are used when expecting the price to stay above the strike price.

Covered Calls: Selling call options against existing stock positions to generate income. This strategy involves owning the underlying stock and selling call options against it, allowing you to collect premiums if the options expire worthless or are not exercised.

Protective Puts: Purchasing put options to hedge against potential downside risk in an existing stock position. This strategy involves buying put options to provide insurance against potential losses if the stock price declines.

Spreads: Options spreads involve combining multiple options positions to manage risk and potentially increase profit potential. Examples include:

Bull Call Spread: Buying a lower strike call option and simultaneously selling a higher strike call option with the same expiration. This strategy profits from a moderate rise in the underlying asset's price.

Bear Put Spread: Buying a higher strike put option and simultaneously selling a lower strike put option with the same expiration. This strategy profits from a moderate decline in the underlying asset's price.

Straddles and Strangles: These strategies are used to profit from significant price volatility in the underlying asset.

Straddle: Simultaneously buying a call option and a put option with the same strike price and expiration. This strategy benefits from large price movements in either direction.

Strangle: Similar to a straddle, but with different strike prices for the call and put options. This strategy allows for a wider range of price movements to profit from.

Butterfly and Condor Spreads: These strategies involve combining multiple options positions with different strike prices to achieve limited-risk and limited-reward scenarios.

Butterfly Spread: Combining a bull spread and a bear spread by buying a call/put option at the middle strike price and selling two call/put options with different strike prices. This strategy profits from a narrow range of price movement.

Condor Spread: Similar to a butterfly spread, but with four different strike prices. It involves buying and selling call/put options to profit from a range-bound market.

These strategies provide a glimpse into the variety of options trading approaches available. Each strategy has its own risk and reward profile, and it's important to thoroughly understand the mechanics and potential outcomes before implementing them in your trading activities.

12.3 OPTIONS PRICING and Greeks:

Options pricing models, such as the Black-Scholes model and the binomial model, are mathematical formulas used to estimate the fair value of options. These models take into account various factors, including the current price of the underlying asset, the strike price, the time to expiration, the risk-free interest rate, and the volatility of the underlying asset.

The Black-Scholes model is a widely used options pricing model based on continuous time and assumes that the market follows certain assumptions, including constant volatility. It calculates the theoretical price of European-style options (options that can only be exercised at expiration) and considers factors such as the stock price, strike price, time to expiration, risk-free interest rate, and volatility.

The binomial model, on the other hand, is a discrete-time model that allows for more flexibility in modeling the price movement of the underlying asset. It works by constructing a binomial tree of possible future prices and calculating the option value at each node of the tree. The model takes into account factors such as the stock price, strike price, time to expiration, risk-free interest rate, and volatility.

Implied volatility is a crucial component of options pricing. It represents the market's expectation of future volatility of the underlying asset. When options are priced using an options pricing model like Black-Scholes, implied volatility is the value that, when input into the model, matches the observed market price of the option. High implied volatility suggests that the market anticipates larger price swings in the underlying asset, leading to higher option prices, while low implied volatility indicates expectations of smaller price movements and lower option prices.

Options Greeks are measures that indicate the sensitivity of option prices to changes in various factors. They help traders assess the risks and potential rewards associated with options positions. Here are the key Greeks and their impact on option value:

Delta: Measures the sensitivity of the option price to changes in the price of the underlying asset. It ranges from -1 to 1 for put options and 0 to 1 for call options. Delta of 0.5 means the option price will move roughly half as much as the underlying asset price.

Gamma: Represents the rate of change of the delta with respect to changes in the underlying asset price. Gamma is highest for at-the-money options and decreases as the option moves further into the money or out of the money.

Theta: Measures the rate of time decay in the option price. It indicates how much the option value will decrease with the passage of time. Theta is typically negative, reflecting the diminishing time value of options as they approach expiration.

Vega: Indicates the sensitivity of the option price to changes in implied volatility. Higher Vega values imply greater price sensitivity to changes in volatility.

Rho: Measures the sensitivity of the option price to changes in the risk-free interest rate. Rho is more relevant for longer-term options, as changes in interest rates have a greater impact over extended periods.

Understanding options pricing models, implied volatility, and the Greeks can help traders assess the potential risks and rewards of options positions and make more informed trading decisions. It is important to note that these models and metrics provide estimates and should be used as tools for analysis rather than as definitive predictors of option prices.

12.4 Options Strategies for Different Market Conditions:

Let's briefly discuss each of these options strategies:

Bullish Options Strategies:

Call Options: Buying call options allows you to profit from a rise in the price of the underlying asset. You have the right to buy the asset at a specified strike price before the expiration date.

Bull Call Spreads: This strategy involves buying a call option with a lower strike price and simultaneously selling a call option with a higher strike price. The goal is to benefit from a moderate upward move in the underlying asset while limiting the upfront cost.

Bearish Options Strategies:

Put Options: Purchasing put options enables you to profit from a decline in the price of the underlying asset. You have the right to sell the asset at a predetermined strike price before the expiration date.

Bear Put Spreads: This strategy involves buying a put option with a higher strike price and simultaneously selling a put option with a lower strike price. It allows you to profit from a moderate downward move in the underlying asset while reducing the upfront cost.

Neutral Options Strategies:

Iron Condors: This strategy involves combining a bear call spread and a bull put spread. It is used when you expect the price of the underlying asset to stay within a certain range.

Calendar Spreads: Also known as horizontal spreads, calendar spreads involve buying and selling options with the same strike price but different expiration dates. It aims to profit from time decay while maintaining a neutral stance on the underlying asset's price.

Volatility-Based Options Strategies:

Straddles: A straddle involves buying a call option and a put option with the same strike price and expiration date. It is used when you anticipate a significant price move in either direction, regardless of the underlying asset's direction.

Strangles: Similar to straddles, strangles involve buying out-of-the-money call and put options. The strike price of the options is typically set above and below the current market price. This strategy profits from a substantial price move but allows for a wider range of movement compared to straddles.

It's important to note that each options strategy has its own risk profile, potential rewards, and considerations. Traders should carefully analyze the market conditions, their expectations, and the specific characteristics of each strategy before implementing them in their trading.

12.5 Options Analysis and Risk Management:

Assessing risk-reward ratios, determining breakeven points, and managing risk are crucial aspects of options trading. Here's how you can approach these considerations:

Assessing Risk-Reward Ratios:

Calculate the potential profit and loss for the options trade. Consider the premium paid or received, transaction costs, and potential profit at expiration.

Compare the potential profit to the maximum risk. This ratio helps you evaluate whether the potential reward justifies the risk taken.

A higher risk-reward ratio indicates a potentially more favorable trade. However, it's essential to consider the probability of the trade being successful as well.

Determining Breakeven Points and Profit Potential:

For options strategies, the breakeven point is the underlying asset price at which the trade neither makes a profit nor incurs a loss.

Calculate the breakeven point(s) by considering the strike price, premium paid or received, and transaction costs associated with the options trade.

Understanding the profit potential involves considering the maximum profit achievable in the trade and the underlying asset's price movement required to reach that level.

Managing Risk:

Proper position sizing is essential in options trading. Determine the appropriate number of contracts based on your risk tolerance, account size, and the potential loss if the trade goes against you.

Implementing stop loss levels can help limit potential losses. Set predefined exit points or trailing stops based on your risk tolerance and the price level at which you're no longer comfortable holding the position.

Using Options as a Hedging Tool:

Options can be used to hedge against potential losses in an existing portfolio. For example, buying put options can help protect against a decline in the value of stocks you hold.

Consider the cost of the options and the effectiveness of the hedge when using options for portfolio protection. Ensure the hedge aligns with your portfolio's risk profile and objectives.

It's important to note that options trading involves complex strategies and may not be suitable for all traders. It's crucial to have a solid understanding of options, their characteristics, and associated risks before engaging in options trading.

12.6 Options Expiration and Exercise:

Options expiration refers to the date when options contracts cease to be valid. It is an important aspect of options trading and has implications for managing options positions. Here are some key points to consider:

Options Expiration:

Options have a predetermined expiration date, typically occurring on the third Friday of the expiration month.

Different options have different expiration cycles: monthly, weekly, or quarterly. This affects the available expiration dates for trading options.

Once options expire, they no longer have any value and are removed from the investor's account.

Managing Options Positions Near Expiration:

As options approach expiration, their time value decreases, which can impact their marketability and liquidity.

Close monitoring of options positions is essential as expiration approaches. Consider the remaining time until expiration, the underlying asset's price, and any potential events that may affect the options' value.

Evaluate the performance of the options position and reassess whether it aligns with your original trading thesis or strategy.

Options Exercise or Sell Decision:

When holding in-the-money options contracts at expiration, you have the choice to exercise them and take delivery of the underlying asset or sell the contracts in the market.

Assess the profitability and potential risks associated with exercising the options versus selling them. Consider transaction costs, taxes, and any associated fees when making this decision.

Not all options need to be exercised. Selling options contracts prior to expiration can often be more efficient and convenient.

It's important to remember that options trading involves complex strategies and risks, and decisions regarding expiration and managing positions should be made based on a comprehensive understanding of options and individual circumstances. Consulting with a financial advisor or experienced options trader can provide valuable guidance in managing options positions near expiration.

12.7 Options Trading Platforms and Tools:

Options trading platforms provide the necessary tools and features to execute options trades and implement trading strategies effectively. Here are some common features and considerations when exploring options trading platforms:

Trading Interface:

Look for a user-friendly and intuitive interface that allows you to easily navigate and execute options trades.

Ensure that the platform provides access to a wide range of options contracts, including different expiration dates, strike prices, and underlying assets.

Options Analysis Tools:

Effective options trading platforms offer various analysis tools to assist in evaluating options strategies. These tools may include options chains, volatility charts, risk/reward calculators, and probability analysis.

Look for platforms that provide real-time data, market news, and options-specific indicators to enhance your analysis.

Options Screeners:

Options screeners help you filter and identify potential trading opportunities based on specific criteria, such as options volume, implied volatility, price changes, and more.

A robust options screener can save you time and provide valuable insights into potential options trades.

Strategy Builders:

Some platforms offer strategy builders that allow you to construct multi-leg options strategies, such as spreads, straddles, and condors, by selecting individual options contracts and specifying trade parameters.

Strategy builders help visualize the risk/reward profile of complex options positions and streamline the process of implementing multi-leg strategies.

Order Types and Trade Execution:

Ensure that the platform supports various order types, including market orders, limit orders, stop orders, and contingent orders.

Look for platforms that provide fast and reliable trade execution, as delays in options trading can significantly impact trade outcomes.

Education and Support:

Consider platforms that offer educational resources, tutorials, webinars, or access to options trading courses to enhance your understanding of options trading strategies.

Reliable customer support is also essential to address any platform-related issues or questions you may have.

It's important to thoroughly research and compare different options trading platforms to find one that aligns with your trading style, needs, and preferences. Demo accounts or free trial periods can be beneficial for testing out platform functionalities before committing real funds.

12.8 Options Trading Considerations:

Liquidity and bid-ask spreads in options markets:

Liquidity refers to the ease with which options can be bought or sold without significantly impacting the price. It is important to trade options with sufficient liquidity to ensure efficient execution and minimize slippage.

Bid-ask spreads represent the difference between the highest price a buyer is willing to pay (bid) and the lowest price a seller is willing to accept (ask). Wider spreads can lead to higher trading costs. It's generally beneficial to trade options with narrower bid-ask spreads to reduce transaction costs.

Time decay (theta) and its impact on options positions:

Time decay refers to the reduction in the value of options as time passes, especially as options approach their expiration dates. This decay occurs because options have a limited lifespan.

Theta measures the rate at which an option's value erodes with the passage of time. Options that are closer to expiration will experience faster time decay.

Traders who sell options (short positions) can benefit from time decay as the options they sell lose value over time. However, buyers of options (long positions) need to be mindful of time decay and manage their trades accordingly.

Implied volatility and its effect on options pricing:

Implied volatility represents the market's expectation of future price fluctuations in the underlying asset. It is a critical component in determining options prices.

Higher implied volatility generally leads to higher options prices, as there is a greater likelihood of larger price swings in the underlying asset.

Traders may consider buying options when implied volatility is low and expected to rise, as it can increase the potential for larger price movements and higher option values.

Tax considerations and implications for options trading:

Options trading can have tax implications that vary by country and individual circumstances. It's essential to consult with a tax professional or accountant to understand the specific tax rules and obligations related to options trading in your jurisdiction.

Tax considerations may include reporting requirements, tax rates for capital gains, treatment of option premiums, and potential deductions for losses.

Traders should maintain accurate records of their options trades, including trade dates, prices, and associated costs, for tax reporting purposes.

It is crucial to consult with financial professionals or tax advisors who specialize in options trading and taxation to ensure compliance with applicable laws and to understand the specific implications based on your individual situation.

12.9 Developing an Options Trading Plan:

Setting goals and objectives for options trading:

Start by defining your financial goals and what you aim to achieve through options trading. This could include generating income, hedging existing positions, or speculating on price movements.

Set specific, measurable, achievable, realistic, and time-bound (SMART) goals that align with your overall investment objectives.

Consider your risk tolerance, available capital, and time commitment when setting goals. Different goals may require different strategies and approaches.

Choosing suitable options strategies based on market conditions and risk tolerance:

Assess the current market conditions and determine whether they are conducive to bullish, bearish, or neutral strategies.

Consider your risk tolerance and understanding of options before selecting specific strategies. Some strategies may involve more complexity or higher risk than others.

Evaluate the potential reward and risk of each strategy, including the probability of success and potential losses. Ensure the strategy aligns with your risk tolerance and investment objectives.

Incorporating risk management techniques into your options trading plan:

Determine your risk tolerance and establish risk management guidelines for options trading. This may include setting maximum risk per trade or per position.

Utilize stop loss orders to limit potential losses if the options trade goes against you. Set the stop loss level based on your risk tolerance and the price movement of the underlying asset.

Consider position sizing techniques to ensure that you allocate an appropriate amount of capital to each options trade based on its risk-reward profile.

Regularly review and evaluate your options trades, monitor their performance, and make adjustments as needed. This includes reevaluating risk management parameters and adjusting stop loss levels if market conditions change.

Remember that options trading involves risks, and it's important to thoroughly understand the strategies and associated risks before engaging in options trading. Consider consulting with a financial advisor or options trading specialist to tailor strategies to your individual circumstances and risk tolerance.

12.10 Advanced Options Trading Techniques:

Advanced options strategies provide additional flexibility and potential profit opportunities. Here are some examples:

Ratio spreads: Ratio spreads involve an unequal number of long and short options contracts. For example, a ratio call spread might involve buying two call options and selling one call option with a higher strike price. This strategy allows for potential profit in multiple scenarios, such as when the underlying asset remains within a specific price range or experiences a significant move in one direction.

Diagonal spreads: Diagonal spreads combine options with different expiration dates and strike prices. For example, a diagonal call spread might involve buying a longer-term call option with a lower strike price and simultaneously selling a shorter-term call option with a higher strike price. This strategy offers potential profit from both time decay and price movement.

Synthetic positions: Synthetic positions replicate the risk and reward characteristics of an underlying asset using a combination of options and/or the underlying asset itself. For example, a synthetic long stock position can be created by buying a call option and selling a put option with the same strike price and expiration date. This strategy allows traders to gain exposure to an asset's price movement without directly owning it.

Options adjustments and roll-up/roll-down strategies involve making changes to existing options positions to manage risk or take advantage of market movements. Traders may adjust their positions by rolling up (moving to a higher strike price) or rolling down (moving to a lower strike price) to adapt to changing market conditions.

Options can also be used in combination with other trading instruments, such as stocks or futures, to create more complex trading strategies. For instance, traders may use options to hedge a stock position or to enhance the returns of a futures trade.

It's important to thoroughly understand the mechanics and potential risks of advanced options strategies before implementing them. Consider conducting thorough research, seeking professional advice, and practicing with virtual or paper trading accounts to gain experience and confidence in using these strategies effectively.

Chapter 13: Futures Trading: Understanding Contract Specifications and Trading Strategies

Introduction: In Chapter 13, we will explore futures trading—an essential part of the financial markets that involves the buying and selling of standardized contracts for the future delivery of assets. Futures contracts provide traders with opportunities to speculate on price movements and manage risks. This chapter will introduce you to futures trading, including contract specifications, trading strategies, and considerations for successful futures trading.

13.1 Introduction to Futures Trading:

Futures contracts are standardized agreements to buy or sell a specified asset, such as commodities, currencies, stock indexes, or interest rates, at a predetermined price and date in the future. They are traded on futures exchanges, and the contracts are legally binding.

Here are some key points about futures contracts:

Standardization: Futures contracts have standardized terms, including the quantity of the underlying asset, the quality or specifications of the asset, the delivery date, and the settlement method. This standardization allows for easy trading and liquidity.

Obligation to buy or sell: When entering into a futures contract, both the buyer (long position) and the seller (short position) are obligated to fulfill the terms of the contract at the specified future date, regardless of the market price of the underlying asset at that time.

Price discovery: Futures markets play a crucial role in price discovery, as they provide a platform for participants to buy and sell contracts based on their expectations of future asset prices. The continuous trading of futures contracts reflects market sentiment and helps establish fair market prices.

Risk management: Futures contracts are widely used for risk management purposes. They allow businesses and individuals to hedge against price fluctuations in the underlying assets. For example, commodity producers may use futures contracts to lock in prices and protect against adverse price movements.

Leverage: Futures contracts typically require a fraction of the total contract value as margin, allowing traders to control a larger position with a smaller amount of capital. This leverage amplifies both potential gains and losses, making futures trading a high-risk endeavor.

Differences between futures and other financial instruments:

Stocks: Futures contracts represent an agreement to buy or sell an asset in the future, while stocks represent ownership in a company. Futures are derivative contracts, whereas stocks are the underlying assets themselves.

Options: Options provide the right, but not the obligation, to buy or sell an asset at a specific price on or before a certain date. In contrast, futures contracts have an obligation to buy or sell the asset.

Futures contracts serve various purposes for different participants, including speculators seeking profit from price movements, hedgers managing price risks, and arbitrageurs exploiting price discrepancies between markets. It's important to understand the unique characteristics and risks of futures trading before engaging in it.

13.2 Futures Contract Specifications:

Key components of futures contracts include:

Underlying asset: Futures contracts are based on various underlying assets, such as commodities (e.g., crude oil, gold, wheat), financial instruments (e.g., stock indices, interest rates), currencies, and more. The underlying asset determines the nature and characteristics of the futures contract.

Contract size: Each futures contract has a specified quantity or size of the underlying asset that is traded. For example, a crude oil futures contract may represent 1,000 barrels of oil, while a stock index futures contract may represent a specific dollar value of the index.

Delivery months: Futures contracts have specific delivery months or expiration dates. Contracts can have monthly expirations, with designated months for trading and settlement. For example, a contract may expire in March, June, September, or December.

Tick size: The tick size refers to the minimum price increment or movement of the futures contract. It represents the smallest unit by which the contract price can change. The tick size varies depending on the underlying asset and the exchange on which the contract is traded.

Expiration and rollover: Futures contracts have expiration dates, which are the last trading days for the contracts. Prior to expiration, traders may choose to roll over their positions by closing out the expiring contract and opening a new contract with a later expiration date. Rollover allows traders to maintain their exposure to the underlying asset without taking physical delivery.

Different types of futures contracts include:

Commodity futures: These contracts involve the buying or selling of physical commodities, such as crude oil, natural gas, gold, silver, agricultural products, and more. Commodity futures allow participants to manage price risks associated with these commodities.

Stock index futures: These contracts are based on the performance of a specific stock index, such as the S&P 500 or the Dow Jones Industrial Average. Traders can speculate on the direction of the overall market or hedge their equity portfolio using stock index futures.

Currency futures: Currency futures contracts represent an agreement to buy or sell a specified amount of a currency at a predetermined exchange rate. They allow participants to speculate on or hedge against currency exchange rate fluctuations.

Interest rate futures: These contracts are based on underlying interest rates, such as Treasury bonds or Eurodollar deposits. Interest rate futures help manage interest rate risks, and their prices are influenced by changes in interest rates.

Contract expiration and rollover processes vary depending on the futures exchange and the specific contract. Typically, as the expiration date approaches, traders have the option to close their positions or roll them over to a subsequent contract with a later expiration date. Rollover involves liquidating the expiring contract and simultaneously opening a new contract. It's important to understand the rules and procedures of the specific futures exchange and contract when managing expiration and rollover.

13.3 Margin and Leverage in Futures Trading:

When trading futures, margin refers to the amount of money or collateral that traders are required to deposit with their brokers to initiate and maintain positions. There are three key terms related to margin in futures trading: initial margin, maintenance margin, and margin calls.

Initial margin: Initial margin is the amount of money or collateral required by the broker to open a futures position. It acts as a security deposit and is a percentage of the total value of the futures contract. The purpose of initial margin is to cover potential losses in case the position moves against the trader.

Maintenance margin: Maintenance margin is the minimum amount of margin that must be maintained in the trading account to keep the position open. It is typically lower than the initial margin requirement. If the account falls below the maintenance margin level, a margin call is triggered.

Margin call: A margin call occurs when the account balance falls below the maintenance margin level. When this happens, the broker will require the trader to deposit additional funds into the account to bring it back above the maintenance margin level. Failure to meet a margin call can result in the broker liquidating the position to cover the losses.

Leverage is a key feature of futures trading. It allows traders to control a larger position with a smaller amount of capital. Leverage amplifies both profits and losses. By using leverage, traders can potentially generate higher returns, but it also increases the risk. It's important to carefully manage leverage and consider the potential downside risks.

Managing margin requirements and leveraging strategies involves several considerations:

Understanding risk tolerance: Traders need to assess their risk tolerance and determine an appropriate level of leverage that aligns with their risk appetite. Higher leverage can lead to higher returns, but it also increases the potential for larger losses.

Monitoring margin levels: Traders should regularly monitor their account's margin levels and ensure they have enough funds to meet margin requirements. Keeping a buffer above the maintenance margin level can help avoid margin calls.

Implementing risk management techniques: Using stop-loss orders and other risk management tools can help limit losses and protect against excessive margin utilization.

Educating oneself: Traders should have a solid understanding of the futures market, leverage, and margin requirements before engaging in futures trading. Continuous learning and staying updated on market conditions are essential.

Seeking professional advice: If unsure about margin requirements or leveraging strategies, it's advisable to consult with a financial advisor or professional with expertise in futures trading.

Ultimately, managing margin requirements and leverage involves balancing risk and potential reward, ensuring adequate capitalization, and adhering to risk management principles to protect against adverse market moves.

13.4 Popular Futures Trading Strategies:

Trend following strategies in futures trading involve identifying and capitalizing on established market trends. Traders who employ trend following strategies aim to take advantage of upward or downward price movements in the futures market. Here are some common trend following strategies in futures trading:

Moving Average Crossover: This strategy involves using two or more moving averages of different lengths (e.g., 50-day and 200-day) to identify trend reversals. A bullish signal is generated when the shorter-term moving average crosses above the longer-term moving average, indicating a potential uptrend. Conversely, a bearish signal occurs when the shorter-term moving average crosses below the longer-term moving average, suggesting a potential downtrend.

Breakout Trading: Breakout trading involves entering positions when the price breaks above a resistance level in an uptrend or below a support level in a downtrend. Traders look for strong price moves accompanied by increased volume to confirm the breakout and capture the continuation of the trend.

Trendline Trading: Trendlines are drawn on price charts to connect higher lows in an uptrend or lower highs in a downtrend. Traders enter long positions when the price bounces off an upward trendline in an uptrend and short positions when the price breaks below a downward trendline in a downtrend.

Spread trading in futures involves taking positions in two or more related futures contracts simultaneously. Here are a few common spread trading strategies:

Calendar Spreads: Calendar spreads, also known as time spreads, involve taking opposite positions in futures contracts with different expiration dates but the same underlying asset. Traders profit from price differences between the near-month and far-month contracts, taking advantage of changes in time value and market expectations.

Intermarket Spreads: Intermarket spreads involve taking positions in related futures contracts traded on different exchanges or markets. For example, traders may simultaneously buy and sell futures contracts on related commodities or indices to capitalize on price differentials or relative value opportunities.

Intracommodity Spreads: Intracommodity spreads involve taking positions in different delivery months of the same futures contract. Traders profit from price differences between different delivery months, taking advantage of seasonal patterns, supply-demand dynamics, or storage costs.

Arbitrage opportunities in futures markets arise when there are price discrepancies between related futures contracts or underlying assets. Traders aim to take advantage of these price differences by simultaneously buying and selling contracts or assets to lock in a risk-free profit. Arbitrage strategies require sophisticated technology and quick execution to exploit fleeting price discrepancies.

Scalping and day trading techniques in futures involve taking advantage of small price movements within a single trading session. Traders employing these strategies aim to profit from short-term market fluctuations. Scalpers typically enter and exit positions quickly, capitalizing on small price differentials, while day traders may hold positions for a longer duration within a single trading day.

It's important to note that implementing these strategies requires a deep understanding of market dynamics, technical analysis, risk management, and access to real-time market data. Traders should thoroughly test and refine their strategies before applying them in live trading environments.

13.5 Technical Analysis in Futures Trading:

Utilizing chart patterns, trendlines, and support/resistance levels in futures analysis can provide valuable insights into market trends and potential trading opportunities. Here's how you can use these tools in your futures trading:

Chart Patterns: Chart patterns, such as double tops/bottoms, head and shoulders, triangles, and rectangles, can indicate potential trend reversals or continuations. By identifying these patterns on price charts, traders can anticipate future price movements and make informed trading decisions.

Trendlines: Trendlines are drawn on price charts to connect successive highs or lows. In an uptrend, an upward trendline is drawn below the price, while in a downtrend, a downward trendline is drawn above the price. Trendlines help traders identify the direction and strength of the trend, as well as potential areas of support or resistance.

Support and Resistance Levels: Support levels are price levels where buying pressure is expected to outweigh selling pressure, causing the price to bounce back up. Resistance levels, on the other hand, are price levels where selling pressure is expected to outweigh buying pressure, causing the price to reverse or stall. By identifying key support and resistance levels, traders can make trading decisions based on potential price reactions at these levels.

Incorporating technical indicators can enhance your futures trading analysis and provide additional trading signals. Here are some commonly used technical indicators in futures trading:

Moving Averages: Moving averages help identify trends, support/resistance levels, and potential entry/exit points. Traders often use popular moving averages like the 50-day and 200-day moving averages to identify long-term trends and gauge price momentum.

Oscillators: Oscillators, such as the Relative Strength Index (RSI) and Stochastic Oscillator, indicate overbought and oversold conditions in the market. These indicators can help identify potential trend reversals and generate trading signals.

Volume and Open Interest Analysis: Volume reflects the number of contracts traded in a specific time period, while open interest represents the total number of outstanding contracts. Analyzing volume and open interest can provide insights into market participation, liquidity, and potential price movements. Increasing volume or open interest can validate the strength of a trend or signal a potential trend reversal.

When incorporating volume and open interest analysis, it's important to consider them in conjunction with price action and other technical indicators to confirm trading signals.

Remember, technical analysis tools and indicators are not foolproof and should be used in conjunction with other forms of analysis and risk management techniques. It's crucial to understand their limitations and use them as part of a comprehensive trading strategy.

13.6 Fundamental Analysis in Futures Trading:

Evaluating supply and demand factors in futures markets is essential for understanding price movements and making informed trading decisions. Here are some key considerations:

Supply Factors: Supply factors in futures markets refer to the availability and production of the underlying asset. Factors such as weather conditions, production levels, inventory levels, and geopolitical events can influence the supply of commodities or goods. Traders need to monitor these factors to assess potential changes in supply and their impact on futures prices.

Demand Factors: Demand factors relate to the consumption or demand for the underlying asset. Economic growth, consumer behavior, industry trends, government policies, and global events can affect demand for commodities or goods. Traders should stay informed about these factors to anticipate changes in demand and their impact on futures prices.

Economic Data and Geopolitical Events: Economic data, such as GDP reports, employment data, inflation rates, and central bank announcements, can significantly impact futures prices. Positive economic data can fuel demand and drive prices higher, while negative data can lead to price declines. Additionally, geopolitical events, such as political instability, trade disputes, or natural disasters, can create volatility and affect supply and demand dynamics in futures markets.

Seasonal Patterns: Many commodities and agricultural products exhibit seasonal patterns due to factors like weather, planting cycles, harvest seasons, and consumer demand patterns. Analyzing historical seasonal patterns can provide insights into potential price movements during specific times of the year. Traders can use this information to identify seasonal trading opportunities and adjust their strategies accordingly.

Analyzing these factors requires staying up to date with relevant news, economic reports, and market research. It's important to consider both fundamental analysis (evaluating supply and demand factors) and technical analysis (using charts and indicators) to develop a comprehensive understanding of futures markets and make well-informed trading decisions.

13.7 Risk Management in Futures Trading:

Implementing effective position sizing techniques is crucial for managing risk in futures trading. Here are some approaches to consider:

Fixed Dollar Amount: With this approach, you determine the maximum amount you're willing to risk on each futures trade. The position size is calculated based on the difference between your entry price and the stop loss level, adjusted to fit within the predetermined risk amount.

Percentage of Account: This method involves allocating a certain percentage of your trading account to each futures trade. For example, you might decide to risk 2% of your account on any given trade. The position size is calculated based on the risk amount and the distance between the entry price and stop loss level.

Volatility-Based Position Sizing: Volatility-based position sizing adjusts the position size based on the volatility of the underlying futures contract. Higher volatility may require a smaller position size to accommodate larger potential price swings. You can use indicators like Average True Range (ATR) to measure volatility and determine the appropriate position size.

Setting appropriate stop loss levels and profit targets is essential for managing risk and protecting capital. Stop loss levels are predetermined prices at which you exit a trade to limit potential losses. Profit targets, on the other hand, are predefined levels at which you aim to take profits. These levels can be based on technical analysis, such as support and resistance levels, or other factors like reward-to-risk ratios.

Risk management through diversification and portfolio allocation is important in futures trading. Diversifying your trading portfolio involves spreading your investments across different futures contracts, sectors, or asset classes. This helps mitigate the impact of adverse price movements in any single position. Additionally, allocating a portion of your overall portfolio to futures trading can help manage risk and balance your exposure across different asset classes.

Hedging strategies using futures contracts involve taking offsetting positions in related assets to reduce or manage risk. For example, if you hold a long position in a particular commodity, you can hedge against potential price declines by taking a short position in a futures contract for that same commodity. Hedging strategies can help protect against adverse price movements and minimize potential losses.

It's important to remember that position sizing, stop loss levels, and hedging strategies should be tailored to your risk tolerance, trading goals, and overall trading plan. Regularly monitoring and adjusting these parameters based on market conditions and trade performance is essential for effective risk management in futures trading.

13.8 Trading Platforms and Tools for Futures Trading:

Futures trading platforms provide traders with the necessary tools and functionalities to execute trades in the futures markets. Here are some common features and tools found in futures trading platforms:

Order Types: Futures trading platforms offer various order types to enter and exit trades. Some common order types include market orders, limit orders, stop orders, and stop-limit orders. These order types allow you to specify the desired entry or exit price for your futures trades.

Charting and Technical Analysis Tools: Futures trading platforms typically include advanced charting features. They offer a wide range of technical analysis tools, such as trendlines, support and resistance levels, moving averages, oscillators, and other indicators. These tools help you analyze price patterns, identify trends, and make informed trading decisions.

Market Depth and Level 2 Quotes: Futures trading platforms often provide access to market depth and Level 2 quotes. These features show the current bid and ask prices, as well as the order book, allowing you to assess market liquidity and the depth of the market. Level 2 quotes provide more detailed information about the supply and demand dynamics in the futures market.

Real-time Data and News: Access to real-time market data and news is essential for staying informed about market developments and making timely trading decisions. Futures trading platforms offer real-time price quotes, news feeds, economic calendars, and other relevant information to keep you up to date with market events.

Customizable Dashboards and Layouts: Many futures trading platforms allow you to customize your trading workspace, including the arrangement of charts, order entry panels, watchlists, and other tools. This allows you to personalize your trading platform to suit your preferences and trading style.

Backtesting and Simulation: Some futures trading platforms offer backtesting and simulation capabilities. These features allow you to test your trading strategies using historical data and assess their performance before risking real capital. Backtesting and simulation tools can help you refine your trading strategies and gain confidence in their effectiveness.

When selecting a futures trading platform, consider factors such as reliability, speed of execution, user interface, available markets and products, and the level of customer support provided. It's important to choose a platform that meets your specific trading needs and provides the tools and features that align with your trading strategy and analysis preferences.

13.9 Futures Trading Considerations:

Liquidity in futures markets refers to the ease with which traders can buy or sell futures contracts without significantly impacting the market price. Higher liquidity is generally desirable as it allows for faster execution and tighter bid-ask spreads, reducing transaction costs.

The liquidity of a futures market can vary depending on factors such as the trading volume, the number of market participants, and the depth of the order book. Some futures markets, such as those for popular commodities or stock indices, tend to have higher liquidity compared to markets for less widely traded contracts.

Futures markets have specific trading hours during which trading activity occurs. These trading hours are determined by the exchange on which the futures contracts are listed. Most futures exchanges operate during regular trading hours, which typically coincide with the business hours of the country where the exchange is located. However, some futures markets also have extended or overnight trading sessions.

It's important to be aware of the trading hours of the futures market you are interested in trading to ensure you can actively participate and manage your positions accordingly. Additionally, understanding the trading hours is crucial for reacting to market-moving events and news releases that may occur outside regular trading hours.

Price limits and circuit breakers are mechanisms put in place by futures exchanges to prevent excessive price volatility and provide stability to the market. These mechanisms impose temporary trading halts or restrictions when price movements exceed certain predetermined limits.

Price limits can be set as daily limits or intraday limits, depending on the exchange and the specific futures contract. Daily limits typically define the maximum price range within which a futures contract can trade in a single trading session. Intraday limits, on the other hand, restrict price movements within a shorter time frame, such as a few minutes or hours.

When a futures contract reaches its price limit, trading may be temporarily halted or allowed only within a narrower price range. The purpose of these limits is to prevent extreme price fluctuations and give market participants time to assess new information or adjust their positions.

Exchange rules and regulations govern futures trading and are established by the futures exchanges where the contracts are listed. These rules define various aspects of trading, including contract specifications, trading hours, margin requirements, position limits, order types, and other operational guidelines.

Traders engaging in futures trading must comply with the rules and regulations of the respective exchanges. It's important to familiarize yourself with the specific rules of the futures exchange you intend to trade on to ensure you understand the requirements, restrictions, and obligations associated with trading futures contracts.

13.10 Developing a Futures Trading Plan:

Setting clear goals and objectives is an important step in developing a futures trading plan. Here are some considerations for setting goals and objectives in futures trading:

Profit Targets: Determine the desired profit targets for your futures trading. Consider your financial goals, risk tolerance, and trading style when setting profit targets. These targets can be specific monetary amounts or percentage returns.

Risk Tolerance: Assess your risk tolerance and establish risk management guidelines for your futures trades. Consider factors such as the maximum acceptable loss per trade, maximum drawdown, and overall risk exposure. This helps you manage risk and protect your capital.

Timeframe: Determine the timeframe for your futures trades. Are you looking to trade on a short-term basis, such as day trading or swing trading, or do you prefer longer-term positions? Define the holding periods that align with your trading goals and strategy.

Market Analysis: Develop a systematic approach to analyzing futures markets. Identify the key factors and indicators you will consider in your analysis, such as technical analysis, fundamental analysis, or a combination of both. This will help you make informed trading decisions based on market conditions.

Position Sizing: Determine how much capital you are willing to allocate to each futures trade. Position sizing refers to the number of contracts or the dollar value of each trade relative to your account size. It helps you manage risk and allocate your capital effectively.

Risk Management: Incorporate risk management techniques into your trading plan. Define your stop loss levels based on technical or fundamental factors, and establish rules for adjusting stop loss levels as trades move in your favor. Consider using trailing stops to protect profits and manage risk.

Review and Evaluation: Regularly review and evaluate your trading performance against your goals and objectives. Identify areas for improvement and make necessary adjustments to your trading plan. This ongoing process allows you to adapt to changing market conditions and refine your approach.

Remember, setting realistic and achievable goals is crucial in futures trading. It's also important to remain disciplined and stick to your trading plan, even during periods of market volatility.

Chapter 14: Introduction to Cryptocurrencies and Blockchain Technology

Introduction: In Chapter 14, we will explore the fascinating world of cryptocurrencies and blockchain technology. Cryptocurrencies have gained significant attention in recent years, offering digital alternatives to traditional currencies and revolutionizing various industries. This chapter will provide you with a comprehensive introduction to cryptocurrencies, their underlying technology, and the key concepts associated with them.

14.1 What are Cryptocurrencies?

Cryptocurrencies are digital or virtual currencies that use cryptography for security and operate on decentralized networks, typically based on blockchain technology. Here are some key characteristics of cryptocurrencies:

Decentralization: Cryptocurrencies are decentralized, meaning they are not controlled or regulated by any central authority, such as a government or central bank. Instead, they rely on a network of computers and consensus algorithms to validate transactions and maintain the integrity of the system.

Blockchain Technology: Cryptocurrencies are typically built on blockchain technology, which is a distributed ledger that records all transactions across a network of computers. This technology ensures transparency, immutability, and security of transactions.

Security: Cryptocurrencies use cryptographic techniques to secure transactions and control the creation of new units. Public-key cryptography is commonly used to verify transactions and protect user identities.

Digital and Programmable: Cryptocurrencies exist only in a digital form and can be transferred electronically. They can also be programmable, allowing for the creation of smart contracts and decentralized applications (DApps) on blockchain platforms.

Limited Supply: Many cryptocurrencies have a limited supply, meaning there is a cap on the maximum number of units that can ever be created. This scarcity can contribute to their value and potential as an investment.

Pseudonymity: Transactions in cryptocurrencies are often pseudonymous, meaning that while transaction details are recorded on the blockchain, the identities of the participants may be obscured. However, it is important to note that some cryptocurrencies offer more privacy features than others.

Global Accessibility: Cryptocurrencies can be accessed and used by anyone with an internet connection, regardless of geographical location. This has the potential to provide financial services to unbanked populations and facilitate cross-border transactions.

Cryptocurrencies differ from fiat currencies (traditional government-issued currencies) in several ways. Fiat currencies are centralized and regulated by central banks, whereas cryptocurrencies are decentralized and operate independently of any central authority. Additionally, fiat currencies are typically physical notes and coins, while cryptocurrencies exist only in digital form. The value of fiat currencies is generally stable and backed by the government, while cryptocurrencies can be subject to higher price volatility due to factors such as market speculation and adoption rates.

It's important to note that the cryptocurrency space is diverse, with thousands of different cryptocurrencies available, each with its own unique features and purposes.

14.2 Blockchain Technology:

Blockchain technology is the underlying technology behind cryptocurrencies and has broader applications beyond digital currencies. It is a decentralized and distributed ledger that records and verifies transactions across multiple computers or nodes in a network. Here are the key fundamentals of blockchain technology:

Decentralized Ledger: A blockchain is a decentralized ledger, meaning it is not controlled by any central authority. Instead, it is maintained and updated by a network of computers or nodes that participate in the network. This decentralization ensures transparency, security, and resilience.

Immutable and Transparent: Once a transaction is recorded on the blockchain, it is difficult to alter or tamper with. Each transaction is linked to the previous one, forming a chain of blocks, and any changes to a block would require the consensus of the network participants. This immutability provides a high level of security and trust in the system. Additionally, the transparent nature of the blockchain allows anyone to view the transaction history, promoting transparency and accountability.

Consensus Mechanisms: Consensus mechanisms are protocols used in blockchain networks to agree on the state of the ledger and validate transactions. They ensure that all participants in the network reach a consensus or agreement on the validity of transactions and the order in which they are recorded. Common consensus mechanisms include Proof of Work (PoW), Proof of Stake (PoS), and Delegated Proof of Stake (DPoS). These mechanisms vary in their approach to achieving consensus, such as through computational power, ownership of cryptocurrency, or voting power.

Security and Cryptography: Blockchain networks use cryptographic techniques to secure transactions and ensure the integrity of the data stored on the blockchain. Public-key cryptography is commonly employed to verify the identity of participants and to create digital signatures that provide authenticity and non-repudiation. Encryption techniques protect the privacy of transactions and data stored on the blockchain.

Smart Contracts: Smart contracts are self-executing contracts with the terms of the agreement directly written into lines of code on the blockchain. They automatically enforce the terms and conditions of the contract without the need for intermediaries. Smart contracts enable the execution of various decentralized applications (DApps) and programmable transactions, expanding the use cases of blockchain technology beyond simple transactions.

Blockchain technology has the potential to revolutionize various industries by providing transparent, secure, and efficient systems for recording and verifying transactions. It can be used in areas such as supply chain management, healthcare, finance, voting systems, and more.

14.3 Bitcoin: The First Cryptocurrency:

Bitcoin is the first and most well-known cryptocurrency, introduced by an anonymous person or group of people using the pseudonym Satoshi Nakamoto in 2008. Here's an introduction to Bitcoin and its key features:

Digital Currency: Bitcoin is a digital currency that exists solely in electronic form. It is not issued or controlled by any central authority, such as a government or financial institution. Instead, it operates on a decentralized peer-to-peer network called the Bitcoin network.

Blockchain Technology: Bitcoin utilizes blockchain technology to record and verify transactions. The Bitcoin blockchain is a public ledger that contains a chronological record of all Bitcoin transactions. It ensures transparency, security, and immutability of transactions.

Mining: Bitcoin mining is the process by which new Bitcoins are created and transactions are verified on the blockchain. Miners use specialized hardware to solve complex mathematical problems, and when they successfully find a solution, they add a new block of transactions to the blockchain and are rewarded with newly minted Bitcoins. Mining also helps maintain the security and integrity of the Bitcoin network.

Transactions: Bitcoin transactions involve the transfer of Bitcoin value from one address to another. Each transaction is verified by network nodes through cryptography and recorded on the blockchain. Transactions are generally pseudonymous, as they are associated with Bitcoin addresses rather than personal information.

Limited Supply: Bitcoin has a limited supply cap of 21 million coins. This scarcity is built into the Bitcoin protocol and is enforced by the halving mechanism. Every four years, the reward for mining new Bitcoins is halved, reducing the rate at which new coins are created. This scarcity contributes to Bitcoin's perceived value.

Decentralization and Security: Bitcoin's decentralized nature means that no single entity controls the network or can manipulate transactions. The security of the Bitcoin blockchain is maintained through the consensus mechanism known as Proof of Work (PoW) and the computational power contributed by miners.

Store of Value and Digital Gold: Bitcoin is often referred to as "digital gold" due to its potential as a store of value. Supporters argue that its limited supply and decentralized nature make it an attractive alternative to traditional forms of currency and a potential hedge against inflation.

The significance of the Bitcoin blockchain lies in its ability to provide a transparent, secure, and decentralized system for peer-to-peer transactions. It has demonstrated the potential for cryptocurrencies and blockchain technology to disrupt traditional financial systems and open up new possibilities for digital transactions and decentralized applications. Bitcoin has also paved the way for the development of numerous other cryptocurrencies and blockchain projects.

14.4 Altcoins and Tokenization:

Altcoins, or alternative cryptocurrencies, refer to any digital currencies other than Bitcoin. While Bitcoin was the first and most well-known cryptocurrency, altcoins have emerged to offer various features, functionalities, and use cases. Here's an overview of altcoins and their purposes:

Diversification: Altcoins provide diversification in the cryptocurrency market, offering investors and users options beyond Bitcoin. They present alternative investment opportunities and can cater to specific needs or preferences.

Improved Functionality: Altcoins often aim to improve upon certain aspects of Bitcoin, such as transaction speed, scalability, privacy, or governance. They may introduce new consensus mechanisms, encryption algorithms, or protocols to enhance the efficiency and functionality of their networks.

Specific Use Cases: Some altcoins are designed with specific use cases in mind. For example, there are altcoins focused on providing decentralized computing power (e.g., Golem), facilitating smart contracts and decentralized applications (e.g., Ethereum), or enabling secure and private transactions (e.g., Monero).

Tokenization: Altcoins can also represent digital assets or commodities through a process called tokenization. This involves converting real-world assets, such as real estate, art, or securities, into digital tokens that can be traded or stored on a blockchain. Tokenization enables fractional ownership, enhances liquidity, and facilitates more efficient transfer and management of assets.

Types of Tokens:

Utility Tokens: These tokens are designed to provide access to a particular product, service, or platform. They are used within a specific ecosystem and often grant holders certain privileges or discounts. Examples include Binance Coin (BNB) and Ethereum's native token, Ether (ETH).

Security Tokens: Security tokens represent ownership in an underlying asset, such as shares of a company or ownership in a real estate project. They are subject to regulatory requirements and can offer potential dividends or profit-sharing rights.

Stablecoins: Stablecoins are cryptocurrencies that are pegged to a stable asset, such as fiat currency (e.g., US Dollar) or commodities. Their value is designed to remain relatively stable, offering a more predictable store of value and facilitating transactions within the cryptocurrency ecosystem.

Governance Tokens: Governance tokens give holders the ability to participate in decision-making processes within a blockchain network. They may have voting rights to determine protocol upgrades, funding allocation, or network governance.

Tokenization: Tokenization is the process of representing real-world assets or commodities as digital tokens on a blockchain. It involves creating a digital representation of the asset and issuing tokens that represent ownership or rights to that asset. Tokenization provides benefits such as increased liquidity, fractional ownership, transparency, and efficiency in the transfer and management of assets. It has applications in areas such as real estate, art, financial securities, supply chain management, and more.

It's important to note that the altcoin market is highly diverse and constantly evolving, with new projects and tokens being launched regularly. Investors and users should conduct thorough research and due diligence before engaging with altcoins, considering factors such as project team, technology, adoption, market dynamics, and regulatory considerations.

14.5 Cryptocurrency Exchanges:

Cryptocurrency exchanges play a vital role in the buying, selling, and trading of cryptocurrencies. They provide a platform for users to exchange their fiat currencies (such as USD or EUR) for cryptocurrencies or trade one cryptocurrency for another. Here's an overview of cryptocurrency exchanges and their types:

Centralized Exchanges: Centralized exchanges are the most common type of cryptocurrency exchanges. They are operated by a central authority or company that facilitates the exchange of cryptocurrencies. These exchanges act as intermediaries, matching buy and sell orders and executing trades on behalf of users. Centralized exchanges typically require users to create accounts, complete identity verification procedures (KYC), and deposit funds into their exchange wallets. Examples of centralized exchanges include Coinbase, Binance, and Kraken.

Decentralized Exchanges (DEX): Decentralized exchanges operate on blockchain networks and do not rely on a central authority. They allow users to trade cryptocurrencies directly with one another using smart contracts. DEXs facilitate peer-to-peer transactions, eliminating the need for intermediaries and providing users with more control over their funds. Users retain ownership of their private keys and have the freedom to trade without KYC procedures in some cases. Examples of decentralized exchanges include Uniswap, SushiSwap, and PancakeSwap.

The process of buying, selling, and trading cryptocurrencies on an exchange generally involves the following steps:

Account Creation: Users need to create an account on the exchange by providing their personal information and completing any required verification processes.

Depositing Funds: Users deposit funds into their exchange wallets. This typically involves transferring fiat currency from a bank account or depositing other cryptocurrencies into the exchange wallet.

Placing Orders: Users can place different types of orders, such as market orders (buying or selling at the current market price) or limit orders (setting a specific price at which they want to buy or sell). They specify the amount and price of the cryptocurrency they wish to buy or sell.

Order Matching: On centralized exchanges, the exchange matches buy and sell orders from different users. Once a matching buy and sell order are found, a trade is executed.

Trade Execution: The exchange executes the trade, and the corresponding cryptocurrencies are transferred between the buyer and seller. The exchange deducts fees for facilitating the transaction.

Withdrawal: After the trade is completed, users can withdraw their purchased cryptocurrencies to their personal wallets for storage or transfer them to another exchange for trading.

It's important to note that each exchange may have its own specific features, trading pairs, fees, and user interfaces. Users should carefully review and understand the terms and conditions, security measures, and fees associated with each exchange before using it for buying, selling, or trading cryptocurrencies.

14.6 Wallets and Security:

Cryptocurrency wallets are digital tools that allow users to securely store, manage, and interact with their cryptocurrencies. They are essential for holding and accessing cryptocurrencies as they store the private keys required to sign transactions on the blockchain. Here's an overview of different types of cryptocurrency wallets:

Software Wallets: Software wallets are applications or programs installed on computers, smartphones, or tablets. They can be further categorized into:

Desktop Wallets: Installed on a desktop or laptop computer, these wallets offer control and security by storing private keys locally. Examples include Electrum, Exodus, and Atomic Wallet.

Mobile Wallets: Designed for mobile devices, these wallets provide convenience and portability. Private keys are stored locally on the device. Examples include Trust Wallet, Mycelium, and Jaxx Liberty.

Web Wallets: Web wallets run on web browsers and are accessible from any device with an internet connection. They store private keys on a remote server, which introduces some security risks. Examples include MetaMask, MyEtherWallet (MEW), and Coinbase Wallet.

Hardware Wallets: Hardware wallets are physical devices specifically designed to store cryptocurrency private keys securely. They offer an offline storage solution and are considered one of the most secure options. Transactions are signed on the device itself, and private keys never leave the device. Popular hardware wallet brands include Ledger, Trezor, and KeepKey.

Paper Wallets: Paper wallets involve printing out the private and public keys on a physical piece of paper. They are offline storage options that provide a high level of security if generated and stored correctly. However, they require caution as they can be vulnerable to physical damage or loss.

When it comes to securing cryptocurrencies, here are some best practices:

Backup Your Wallet: Always create backups of your wallet's private keys or recovery seed. Store them securely in multiple locations, preferably offline or in hardware form.

Enable Two-Factor Authentication (2FA): Add an extra layer of security to your software wallets by enabling two-factor authentication. It typically involves using a separate device or app to provide an additional verification step when accessing the wallet.

Keep Software Updated: Keep your wallet software and any associated devices updated with the latest security patches and firmware upgrades to protect against known vulnerabilities.

Be Cautious of Phishing and Malware: Beware of phishing attempts and malicious software that can compromise your wallet's security. Be vigilant when clicking on links or downloading files related to your wallet.

Use Strong Passwords: Create strong, unique passwords for your wallets and avoid using the same password across multiple platforms.

Verify Wallet Sources: Only download wallets and related software from trusted sources to avoid fake or malicious applications.

Consider Cold Storage: For long-term storage or significant amounts of cryptocurrencies, consider using hardware wallets or offline storage methods like paper wallets.

Remember, the security of your cryptocurrencies is ultimately your responsibility. It's crucial to educate yourself about wallet security, stay informed about the latest threats, and adopt best practices to protect your funds.

14.7 Cryptocurrency Investment and Trading:

Cryptocurrency investment strategies can vary depending on individual goals, risk tolerance, and time horizons. Here are a few common approaches:

Buy and Hold (Long-Term Investment): This strategy involves purchasing cryptocurrencies with a long-term perspective, aiming to benefit from potential future price appreciation. It requires conducting fundamental analysis to evaluate the project's technology, team, adoption, and potential for growth. Investors using this strategy often believe in the long-term value and adoption of cryptocurrencies.

Dollar-Cost Averaging: With this strategy, investors regularly purchase a fixed amount of cryptocurrencies regardless of the price. By spreading out the investment over time, the goal is to mitigate the impact of short-term price fluctuations and potentially benefit from buying at different price levels. This strategy is suitable for those who prefer a disciplined approach and are focused on long-term growth.

Swing Trading: Swing trading involves taking advantage of short-term price swings within an overall trend. Traders using this strategy aim to identify and capitalize on price movements over a few days to weeks. Technical analysis tools such as chart patterns, indicators (e.g., moving averages, RSI), and volume analysis are commonly used to identify potential entry and exit points.

Day Trading: Day trading involves executing multiple trades within a single day, aiming to profit from intraday price movements. Day traders closely monitor charts, use technical indicators, and analyze short-term trends to make quick trading decisions. This strategy requires active participation and monitoring of the market throughout the day.

Arbitrage: Arbitrage involves taking advantage of price discrepancies between different cryptocurrency exchanges or markets. Traders can buy an asset at a lower price on one exchange and sell it at a higher price on another exchange, profiting from the price difference. This strategy requires quick execution and often relies on automated trading bots or algorithms.

When it comes to conducting fundamental analysis of cryptocurrencies, here are some key factors to consider:

Project Team and Partnerships: Evaluate the team's expertise and track record, as well as the project's partnerships with established companies or organizations.

Technology and Innovation: Assess the underlying technology of the cryptocurrency project, such as its scalability, security, and potential for real-world applications. Consider the project's unique selling proposition and competitive advantage.

Adoption and Use Cases: Examine the level of adoption and usage of the cryptocurrency. Look for real-world use cases, partnerships with businesses or industries, and community engagement.

Market and Competition: Analyze the market demand for the cryptocurrency, competition from other projects, and potential regulatory or legal challenges.

Tokenomics and Supply: Understand the token economics, including token supply, distribution, inflation, and any mechanisms that drive the token's value or utility.

Technical analysis tools and indicators commonly used in cryptocurrency trading include:

Candlestick Patterns: Candlestick charts provide visual patterns that indicate potential trend reversals, such as doji, hammer, and engulfing patterns.

Moving Averages: Moving averages help identify the overall trend and potential support or resistance levels. Commonly used moving averages include the 50-day and 200-day moving averages.

Relative Strength Index (RSI): RSI measures the momentum and overbought or oversold conditions of a cryptocurrency. It helps identify potential trend reversals and divergence between price and momentum.

Bollinger Bands: Bollinger Bands show the volatility of a cryptocurrency's price. When the price approaches the upper band, it may indicate overbought conditions, while the lower band may suggest oversold conditions.

Volume Analysis: Analyzing trading volume can provide insights into the strength of a price move. High volume during price increases or decreases can confirm the validity of a trend.

Fibonacci Retracement: Fibonacci retracement levels are used to identify potential support and resistance levels based on the Fibonacci sequence. Traders use these levels to determine potential entry or exit points.

It's important to note that no strategy or analysis method guarantees success in cryptocurrency trading. It's advisable to combine multiple approaches, stay informed about market news, and continually adapt your strategy based on market conditions and risk tolerance.

14.8 Initial Coin Offerings (ICOs) and Token Sales:

Initial Coin Offerings (ICOs) are fundraising events in the cryptocurrency industry where new projects sell their underlying digital tokens to investors. These tokens often represent a form of utility within the project's ecosystem or have potential investment value if the project succeeds.

Here is an overview of the process and considerations for participating in ICOs:

Research and Due Diligence: Before participating in an ICO, it's crucial to thoroughly research the project, team, technology, and whitepaper. Evaluate the project's goals, use cases, market demand, and potential risks. Consider the project's roadmap, partnerships, and community engagement.

Token Economics: Understand the tokenomics of the project, including token supply, distribution, and any mechanisms that may affect the token's value. Consider how the tokens will be used within the project's ecosystem and the potential for token appreciation.

Whitelisting and KYC/AML: Some ICOs require participants to complete a Know Your Customer (KYC) and Anti-Money Laundering (AML) process. This process may involve providing identification documents and other personal information to comply with legal requirements.

Contribution Process: ICOs usually specify a contribution process for interested participants. This typically involves sending the designated cryptocurrency (such as Bitcoin or Ethereum) to a specified wallet address. Follow the instructions provided by the project to ensure your contribution is properly processed.

Wallet Considerations: Ensure you have a compatible wallet to receive the tokens if your contribution is successful. Some ICOs require specific wallet types, so check the project's guidelines. It's important to secure your wallet and keep your private keys safe.

Now, let's address the risks and regulatory considerations associated with ICOs:

Regulatory Uncertainty: ICOs operate in a regulatory gray area in many jurisdictions. Regulatory bodies are still developing guidelines and regulations to address the evolving nature of ICOs. The lack of regulatory oversight can expose investors to potential risks.

Fraud and Scams: The ICO space has seen instances of fraudulent projects and scams. Some projects may make false claims or exaggerate their potential to attract investments. It's important to conduct thorough due diligence and be cautious of projects with unrealistic promises or insufficient information.

Market Volatility: The cryptocurrency market is highly volatile, and the value of tokens obtained through ICOs can fluctuate significantly. It's important to understand and be prepared for the potential risks associated with market volatility.

Lack of Liquidity: Tokens obtained through ICOs may not be immediately tradable on established exchanges, which can limit liquidity. It's essential to consider the availability and liquidity of tokens post-ICO.

Project Failure: Investing in ICOs comes with the risk of the project not reaching its goals or failing to deliver on promises. Projects may face technical, regulatory, or market challenges that hinder their progress or sustainability.

Legal and Compliance Considerations: Different jurisdictions have varying regulations concerning ICOs, and participating in ICOs may have legal implications. It's important to consult legal and financial professionals to understand the regulatory environment and compliance requirements in your jurisdiction.

Before participating in an ICO, it's advisable to seek professional advice, perform thorough research, and carefully assess the potential risks and rewards involved.

14.9 Decentralized Finance (DeFi):

Decentralized Finance (DeFi) refers to a category of financial applications built on blockchain networks that aim to recreate traditional financial systems and services in a decentralized and open manner. It leverages smart contracts and blockchain technology to enable peer-to-peer transactions without the need for intermediaries like banks or other centralized financial institutions. DeFi provides individuals with greater control over their financial assets, increased transparency, and the potential for higher yields.

Here are a few key aspects of DeFi:

Decentralized Lending and Borrowing: DeFi protocols allow individuals to lend their digital assets and earn interest or borrow assets by collateralizing their existing holdings. Smart contracts automate the lending and borrowing process, eliminating the need for intermediaries. Interest rates are determined by supply and demand dynamics within the protocol.

Yield Farming: Yield farming, also known as liquidity mining, involves providing liquidity to DeFi protocols and earning rewards in the form of additional tokens. Users contribute their digital assets to liquidity pools, which are used to facilitate trades on decentralized exchanges or as collateral for lending. In return, they receive tokens that represent their share of the pool's earnings.

Decentralized Exchanges (DEXs): DEXs are platforms that enable users to trade cryptocurrencies directly with each other without relying on a centralized intermediary. These exchanges utilize smart contracts to facilitate peer-to-peer trading and provide greater security, transparency, and control over funds compared to traditional centralized exchanges.

Liquidity Pools: Liquidity pools are pools of digital assets locked within a smart contract on a decentralized exchange or lending platform. Users contribute their assets to the pool and receive liquidity pool tokens in return. These tokens can be traded or used to earn additional rewards through yield farming.

The impact of DeFi on the financial industry is significant and disruptive. It introduces new possibilities for financial services and removes barriers to entry, allowing anyone with an internet connection to access a wide range of financial products and services. Some potential impacts include:

Financial Inclusion: DeFi opens up financial services to the unbanked and underbanked population who may not have access to traditional banking services. It allows individuals to participate in lending, borrowing, and investing without the need for a bank account or credit history.

Transparency and Security: DeFi protocols are built on public blockchains, which provide transparency and immutability of transactions. Smart contracts automate processes, reducing the risk of fraud or manipulation. However, it's important to note that the security of the underlying smart contracts and the associated risks of vulnerabilities should be carefully evaluated.

Disintermediation: By removing intermediaries, DeFi reduces the reliance on centralized financial institutions, such as banks and brokerage firms. This disintermediation can lead to lower costs, faster transactions, and more control over financial assets.

Programmable Money: DeFi protocols allow for the creation of programmable money through the use of smart contracts. This enables the automation of complex financial transactions, such as conditional payments, escrow services, and decentralized derivatives.

Despite its potential, DeFi also presents risks and challenges. Smart contract vulnerabilities, market volatility, and regulatory uncertainties are some of the factors that individuals need to consider when participating in DeFi. It's important to conduct thorough research, understand the risks involved, and exercise caution when engaging with DeFi protocols and platforms.

14.10 Future Trends and Considerations:

Emerging trends and developments in the cryptocurrency space:

Increased Institutional Adoption: Over the past few years, there has been a notable increase in institutional adoption of cryptocurrencies. Major financial institutions, hedge funds, and corporations have started to embrace cryptocurrencies as an asset class, investing in Bitcoin and other digital assets. This institutional involvement brings more liquidity and legitimacy to the market.

Decentralized Finance (DeFi) Expansion: DeFi has experienced significant growth, with new protocols and applications being developed regularly. This trend has seen an increase in decentralized lending and borrowing platforms, decentralized exchanges (DEXs), yield farming, and other innovative DeFi solutions. The expansion of DeFi offers alternative financial services and investment opportunities.

Non-Fungible Tokens (NFTs): NFTs have gained significant attention in recent years. NFTs are unique digital assets that can represent ownership or proof of authenticity for digital or physical items. They have found applications in digital art, collectibles, gaming, and more. The NFT market has seen substantial growth, with high-profile sales and increased interest from artists, creators, and collectors.

Central Bank Digital Currencies (CBDCs): Several central banks worldwide are exploring the concept of Central Bank Digital Currencies. CBDCs are digital forms of fiat currencies issued and regulated by central banks. These digital currencies aim to provide the benefits of cryptocurrencies while maintaining the control and stability associated with traditional fiat currencies.

Regulatory considerations and challenges for cryptocurrencies:

Regulatory Frameworks: Governments and regulatory bodies around the world are still grappling with creating comprehensive regulatory frameworks for cryptocurrencies. There are varying approaches and regulations, ranging from outright bans to supportive measures aimed at fostering innovation while ensuring consumer protection and mitigating risks such as money laundering and fraud.

Investor Protection: Due to the decentralized and pseudonymous nature of cryptocurrencies, investor protection can be a challenge. There have been cases of scams, fraud, and hacking incidents in the cryptocurrency space. Regulators are working to establish guidelines to protect investors and create a safer environment for cryptocurrency activities.

AML/KYC Compliance: Cryptocurrencies face scrutiny regarding anti-money laundering (AML) and know-your-customer (KYC) regulations. Governments and regulatory bodies are increasingly focusing on implementing AML and KYC measures for cryptocurrency exchanges and service providers to prevent illicit activities.

International Cooperation: Cryptocurrencies operate globally, and their regulatory landscape requires international cooperation and coordination. Collaboration among countries and regulatory bodies is necessary to address cross-border challenges such as money laundering, tax evasion, and the global nature of cryptocurrency exchanges.

Potential impact of cryptocurrencies on traditional financial systems:

Disintermediation: Cryptocurrencies have the potential to disrupt traditional financial systems by reducing reliance on intermediaries like banks, payment processors, and clearinghouses. Peer-to-peer transactions facilitated by cryptocurrencies can lower costs and increase efficiency.

Financial Inclusion: Cryptocurrencies can provide financial services to the unbanked and underbanked populations who have limited access to traditional banking services. Cryptocurrencies allow individuals to have control over their finances, access global markets, and engage in cross-border transactions without relying on traditional banking systems.

Remittances and Cross-Border Transactions: Cryptocurrencies enable faster and cheaper cross-border transactions compared to traditional remittance methods. They have the potential to simplify and streamline global payments, making them more accessible and affordable.

Monetary Policy and Currency Stability: The emergence of cryptocurrencies challenges traditional monetary policy and the control exercised by central banks. The potential widespread adoption of cryptocurrencies could impact the stability of fiat currencies and influence the dynamics of monetary systems.

It's important to note that the cryptocurrency landscape is continuously evolving, and its impact on traditional financial systems and regulatory environments is still unfolding. It's crucial for individuals, businesses, and regulators to stay informed, adapt to changes, and evaluate the risks and opportunities associated with cryptocurrencies.

Chapter 15: Trading Cryptocurrencies: Opportunities and Risks

Introduction: In Chapter 15, we will dive into the world of trading cryptocurrencies. Cryptocurrencies have gained popularity as tradable assets, offering unique opportunities for investors and traders. However, it's important to understand the opportunities and risks associated with cryptocurrency trading. This chapter will provide you with insights into trading cryptocurrencies, including strategies, risk management techniques, and considerations for successful trading.

15.1 Cryptocurrency Market Overview:

Understanding the dynamics of the cryptocurrency market:

Market Size and Growth: The cryptocurrency market has experienced significant growth since the inception of Bitcoin in 2009. It has evolved into a global market with a diverse range of cryptocurrencies and a large number of participants, including individual investors, institutional investors, traders, and developers.

Market Sentiment and Speculation: The cryptocurrency market is highly influenced by market sentiment and speculation. News, events, regulatory developments, and investor sentiment can have a significant impact on cryptocurrency prices. Positive news and investor optimism can drive prices up, while negative news and fear can lead to price declines.

Volatility: Cryptocurrencies are known for their high volatility. Price fluctuations can be substantial within short periods of time. While volatility presents opportunities for profit, it also increases the risk associated with trading and investing in cryptocurrencies.

Market Cycles: The cryptocurrency market has shown a cyclical pattern characterized by periods of rapid growth (bull markets) followed by significant corrections (bear markets). These cycles are influenced by various factors, including market sentiment, technological advancements, regulatory developments, and macroeconomic conditions.

Differentiating between major cryptocurrencies and altcoins:

Major Cryptocurrencies: Major cryptocurrencies refer to the most widely recognized and established cryptocurrencies. Bitcoin (BTC) is considered the first and most dominant cryptocurrency. Other major cryptocurrencies include Ethereum (ETH), Ripple (XRP), Litecoin (LTC), and Bitcoin Cash (BCH). These cryptocurrencies often have the largest market capitalizations and the highest trading volumes.

Altcoins: Altcoins, short for alternative coins, refer to any cryptocurrency other than Bitcoin. Altcoins can serve various purposes, such as providing alternative functionalities, addressing specific use cases, or experimenting with new technologies. Examples of altcoins include Ethereum-based tokens, privacy-focused cryptocurrencies like Monero (XMR), and utility tokens for specific platforms or services.

Exploring market liquidity and volatility in cryptocurrency trading:

Market Liquidity: Liquidity refers to the ease with which an asset can be bought or sold without significantly impacting its price. In cryptocurrency trading, liquidity is essential for executing trades efficiently and with minimal slippage. High liquidity markets have a large number of buyers and sellers, tight bid-ask spreads, and sufficient trading volume.

Volatility: Volatility is a measure of the price fluctuations of an asset over a specific period. Cryptocurrencies are known for their high volatility, which can present both opportunities and risks for traders and investors. Volatility can be attributed to factors such as market sentiment, news events, regulatory developments, and overall market conditions. Traders often seek volatile markets to capitalize on price movements.

It's important to note that market dynamics, liquidity, and volatility can vary across different cryptocurrencies and time periods. Traders and investors should consider these factors when formulating their trading strategies and risk management approaches. Additionally, it's recommended to thoroughly research and understand the characteristics and dynamics of individual cryptocurrencies before engaging in trading or investing activities.

15.2 Technical Analysis for Cryptocurrency Trading:

Technical analysis is a popular approach used by traders to analyze price patterns and make trading decisions. It involves studying historical price data, chart patterns, and various indicators to identify trends and potential trading opportunities. Here are some key technical analysis tools and indicators commonly used in cryptocurrency trading:

Candlestick Charts: Candlestick charts display price movements over a given period. Each candlestick represents a specific time interval and provides information on the opening, closing, high, and low prices. Traders analyze candlestick patterns, such as doji, hammer, and engulfing patterns, to identify potential reversals or continuation of trends.

Trend Lines: Trend lines are drawn on a price chart to identify the direction of the trend. An upward sloping trend line connects higher swing lows, indicating an uptrend, while a downward sloping trend line connects lower swing highs, indicating a downtrend. Traders use trend lines to determine potential entry and exit points based on trend reversals or breakouts.

Moving Averages: Moving averages (MAs) smooth out price data by calculating the average price over a specified period. They help identify trends and provide support and resistance levels. The two commonly used types of moving averages are the simple moving average (SMA) and the exponential moving average (EMA). Traders look for crossovers between different moving averages or the price to gauge potential trend changes.

Relative Strength Index (RSI): The RSI is a momentum oscillator that measures the speed and change of price movements. It oscillates between 0 and 100 and indicates overbought and oversold conditions. Traders use the RSI to identify potential trend reversals or to confirm existing trends.

Support and Resistance Levels: Support levels are price levels where buying pressure is expected to outweigh selling pressure, causing prices to bounce back up. Resistance levels are price levels where selling pressure is expected to outweigh buying pressure, causing prices to reverse or stall. Traders use support and resistance levels to identify potential entry and exit points and to set stop-loss and take-profit levels.

Volume Analysis: Volume is the number of shares or contracts traded during a given period. It provides insights into the strength of price movements and can help confirm or invalidate trends. Traders analyze volume patterns to assess market participation and the likelihood of trend continuation or reversal.

It's important to note that no single tool or indicator can guarantee accurate predictions in cryptocurrency trading. Traders often use a combination of these tools, along with their own analysis and risk management strategies, to make informed trading decisions. Additionally, it's recommended to practice and test strategies using historical data or on a demo trading platform before applying them in real-market conditions.

15.3 Fundamental Analysis for Cryptocurrency Trading:

When evaluating the fundamental factors influencing cryptocurrency prices, there are several key aspects to consider:

Whitepapers and Project Fundamentals: Whitepapers are documents that outline the concept, technology, and goals of a cryptocurrency project. By thoroughly analyzing the whitepaper, you can gain insights into the project's purpose, use case, technical specifications, and potential for adoption. Assessing the viability of the project, the team's expertise, and the underlying technology is crucial for understanding its long-term potential.

Team Credibility and Development Activity: The team behind a cryptocurrency project plays a significant role in its success. Research the team members' backgrounds, experience, and track record in the industry. Evaluate their ability to deliver on their promises and drive the project forward. Additionally, monitoring the project's development activity, including updates, partnerships, and milestones achieved, can provide insights into its progress and potential impact on the price.

Market News and Sentiment: Staying updated with the latest news and developments in the cryptocurrency market is essential for understanding market sentiment and its potential impact on prices. News related to regulatory decisions, partnerships, technological advancements, adoption by mainstream companies, or market trends can significantly influence cryptocurrency prices. Monitor reputable news sources, social media discussions, and industry forums to stay informed.

Regulatory Developments: The regulatory environment surrounding cryptocurrencies can have a significant impact on their prices. Keep track of regulatory announcements and developments from governments and regulatory bodies worldwide. Changes in regulations related to cryptocurrency trading, taxation, or ICOs can affect market sentiment and investor confidence, leading to price fluctuations.

Market Adoption and Real-World Use Cases: The adoption of cryptocurrencies in real-world applications and industries can drive their prices. Evaluate the level of adoption and use cases for the cryptocurrency you are interested in. Look for partnerships with established companies, integration into existing platforms, or innovative applications that demonstrate the cryptocurrency's utility and potential for growth.

It's important to conduct thorough research and due diligence when assessing the fundamental factors influencing cryptocurrency prices. Combining fundamental analysis with technical analysis can provide a more comprehensive understanding of market dynamics and help you make informed investment decisions.

15.4 Trading Strategies for Cryptocurrencies:

Day Trading Strategies for capturing short-term price movements in cryptocurrencies:

Scalping: This strategy involves making quick trades to profit from small price movements within a short period. Traders often look for highly liquid cryptocurrencies with volatility and use technical analysis tools like charts, indicators, and order flow data to identify short-term price patterns and execute trades.

Breakout Trading: Traders using this strategy look for cryptocurrency prices that break out of established support or resistance levels with high volume. The idea is to capture the momentum and ride the price movement as it accelerates in the breakout direction. Traders can use technical indicators like moving averages, Bollinger Bands, or chart patterns to identify potential breakouts.

Swing Trading Strategies for taking advantage of medium-term trends in cryptocurrencies:

Trend Following: Swing traders using this strategy aim to identify and ride medium-term price trends in cryptocurrencies. They analyze price charts, moving averages, trendlines, and other technical indicators to identify the direction of the trend. They enter trades when the price pulls back or retraces within the trend and exit when the trend shows signs of reversal.

Fibonacci Retracement Trading: This strategy involves using Fibonacci retracement levels to identify potential support or resistance levels within a trend. Swing traders look for price retracements to these levels and enter trades in the direction of the prevailing trend. They often use additional technical indicators or candlestick patterns for confirmation.

Long-term Investment Strategies for holding cryptocurrencies:

Buy and Hold: This strategy involves buying cryptocurrencies with a long-term investment horizon. Investors focus on the fundamental aspects of cryptocurrencies, such as their technology, use cases, adoption potential, and market position. They aim to hold the cryptocurrencies over an extended period, often months or years, expecting their value to increase over time.

Dollar-Cost Averaging (DCA): DCA is a strategy where investors regularly allocate a fixed amount of funds to buy cryptocurrencies at regular intervals, regardless of the price. This approach helps smooth out the impact of short-term price fluctuations and allows investors to accumulate cryptocurrencies over time, taking advantage of potential market dips.

It's important to note that these strategies come with their own risks and require careful analysis, risk management, and adherence to a trading plan. Each strategy should be tailored to individual risk tolerance, investment goals, and time commitment. Additionally, staying updated with market news, regulatory developments, and continuously monitoring the performance of selected cryptocurrencies is crucial for successful implementation of any trading or investment strategy.

15.5 Risk Management in Cryptocurrency Trading:

Position Sizing Techniques for Managing Risk in Cryptocurrency Trades:

Fixed Percentage Risk: With this technique, you determine a fixed percentage of your total trading capital that you are willing to risk on each cryptocurrency trade. For example, if you decide to risk 2% of your capital on each trade, you will adjust your position size accordingly. This approach helps you maintain consistent risk across different trades and protects your capital from substantial losses.

Volatility-Based Position Sizing: This technique takes into account the volatility of the cryptocurrency you are trading. More volatile cryptocurrencies may require smaller position sizes to manage risk effectively, while less volatile ones may allow for larger positions. You can use indicators such as Average True Range (ATR) or historical price volatility to gauge the volatility of a cryptocurrency and adjust your position size accordingly.

Setting Stop Loss Orders and Profit Targets:

Stop Loss Orders: A stop loss order is an order placed with your exchange or broker to automatically sell a cryptocurrency position if it reaches a specified price level. It helps limit potential losses by exiting the trade if the price moves against your expectations. When setting a stop loss, consider the volatility of the cryptocurrency and the level at which your trading thesis would be invalidated. Adjust the stop loss accordingly to give the trade enough room to fluctuate while still protecting you from significant losses.

Profit Targets: A profit target is the price level at which you plan to exit a profitable trade and take your profits. It's important to have a predefined profit target to prevent greed from clouding your judgment. Consider factors such as historical price levels, key support or resistance zones, or technical indicators that suggest potential resistance ahead. You can also use trailing stop orders to capture additional profits as the price continues to move in your favor.

Diversification and Portfolio Allocation Strategies:

Spread Across Cryptocurrencies: Diversifying your cryptocurrency portfolio helps spread the risk across different assets. Allocate your capital among a variety of cryptocurrencies with different use cases, market capitalizations, and risk profiles. This reduces the impact of a single cryptocurrency's poor performance on your overall portfolio.

Asset Allocation: Determine the percentage of your total investment portfolio allocated to cryptocurrencies. Consider your risk tolerance, investment goals, and the overall volatility of the cryptocurrency market. It's generally recommended to allocate only a portion of your investment portfolio to cryptocurrencies due to their high volatility and inherent risks. A diversified portfolio should include other asset classes like stocks, bonds, or real estate.

Rebalance Periodically: Regularly review and rebalance your cryptocurrency portfolio based on market conditions and changes in your investment goals. If certain cryptocurrencies have gained significant value, they may become a larger portion of your portfolio, increasing risk. Rebalancing ensures that your portfolio remains aligned with your desired risk exposure.

Remember, risk management is a crucial aspect of successful trading and investing. Implementing these techniques helps protect your capital, manage risk, and maintain a disciplined approach in the volatile cryptocurrency market.

15.6 Market Psychology and Sentiment Analysis:

Market psychology plays a significant role in cryptocurrency trading as it can drive market sentiment and influence price movements. Understanding market psychology can help you make informed trading decisions and identify potential contrarian trading opportunities. Here are some key points to consider:

Emotions and Crowd Behavior: Emotions such as fear and greed often drive market participants' actions, leading to price fluctuations. When the market is driven by fear, prices may decline as investors rush to sell. Conversely, during periods of greed, prices may rise as investors FOMO (fear of missing out) and enter the market. It's important to be aware of these emotions and avoid making impulsive trading decisions based on them.

Sentiment Indicators: Sentiment indicators provide insights into the overall market sentiment and can help gauge the bullish or bearish sentiment of traders. These indicators can include surveys, sentiment indexes, or sentiment analysis of social media platforms. High bullish sentiment may indicate an overbought market, while high bearish sentiment may suggest an oversold market. By monitoring sentiment indicators, you can identify potential turning points in the market.

Social Media Trends: Social media platforms play a significant role in shaping market sentiment. Monitoring discussions, opinions, and trends on platforms like Twitter, Reddit, and Telegram can provide valuable insights into the sentiment of the cryptocurrency community. However, it's important to exercise caution and critically analyze information as social media can be influenced by biased or misleading content.

Contrarian Trading: Contrarian trading involves taking positions that go against the prevailing market sentiment. When the market sentiment is excessively bullish or bearish, contrarian traders look for opportunities to enter trades in the opposite direction. This strategy assumes that the market sentiment may be overextended and that a reversal or correction is likely to occur. Contrarian trading requires careful analysis of market sentiment indicators, technical analysis, and risk management.

Analyzing Market Sentiment and Price Action: Analyzing market sentiment alongside price action can provide additional confirmation for contrarian trading strategies. For example, if the market sentiment is extremely bearish, but price action indicates potential bullish reversal patterns, it may signal an opportunity for contrarian traders. Combining sentiment analysis with technical analysis can help identify favorable entry and exit points.

It's important to note that market sentiment is just one factor to consider in your trading decisions. It should be used in conjunction with other analysis techniques such as technical analysis, fundamental analysis, and risk management strategies. Being aware of market psychology and sentiment can provide valuable insights, but it's essential to maintain a disciplined approach and not solely rely on sentiment indicators for trading decisions.

15.7 Risk Factors and Considerations:

Security risks and protecting cryptocurrency assets:

Secure Wallets: Use reputable and secure cryptocurrency wallets, such as hardware wallets or software wallets with strong security features. Keep your private keys and recovery phrases offline and in a safe place.

Two-Factor Authentication (2FA): Enable 2FA for your cryptocurrency exchange accounts and wallets to add an extra layer of security. This typically involves using a mobile app or receiving SMS codes to verify your identity during login.

Phishing Attacks: Be cautious of phishing attempts where malicious actors impersonate legitimate websites or services to steal your login credentials. Double-check URLs, use bookmarks, and avoid clicking on suspicious links in emails or messages.

Updates and Patches: Keep your wallets, devices, and software up to date with the latest security patches and updates. Regularly review and update your passwords.

Cold Storage: Consider storing a significant portion of your cryptocurrency assets in cold storage, which involves keeping them offline in hardware wallets or paper wallets. This protects them from online attacks.

Regulatory and legal considerations in cryptocurrency trading:

Research Regulations: Familiarize yourself with the regulatory environment and legal requirements for cryptocurrency trading in your jurisdiction. Different countries have different regulations, and staying compliant is crucial.

Know Your Customer (KYC) and Anti-Money Laundering (AML): Understand the KYC and AML procedures enforced by cryptocurrency exchanges and comply with their verification processes. This helps prevent fraudulent activities and ensures the legitimacy of the platform.

Tax Obligations: Understand and fulfill your tax obligations related to cryptocurrency trading. Consult with a tax professional or seek guidance from relevant tax authorities to ensure compliance.

Market manipulation and scams to be aware of:

Pump and Dump Schemes: Be cautious of schemes where individuals or groups artificially inflate the price of a cryptocurrency through false or misleading information, then sell their holdings once the price has risen significantly, causing others to suffer losses.

Ponzi Schemes: Beware of investment schemes that promise high returns but rely on the recruitment of new participants to pay existing participants. These schemes are unsustainable and often result in significant losses for those involved.

Phony Exchanges and ICOs: Exercise caution when dealing with new or lesser-known exchanges and initial coin offerings (ICOs). Do thorough research, verify the credibility of the project, and check for red flags such as lack of transparency or unrealistic promises.

Social Engineering Attacks: Be vigilant against social engineering attacks where scammers attempt to deceive you into revealing sensitive information or transferring your funds. Always verify the legitimacy of requests and avoid sharing personal or financial details online.

Staying informed, conducting due diligence, and using reputable platforms and services are crucial to mitigating risks and protecting your cryptocurrency assets. Additionally, following best practices for online security and maintaining a skeptical mindset can help you avoid falling victim to scams or market manipulations.

15.8 Cryptocurrency Exchanges and Trading Platforms:

When evaluating cryptocurrency exchanges, consider the following factors:

Security: Look for exchanges that prioritize robust security measures, such as two-factor authentication (2FA), cold storage for funds, and encryption protocols. Check if the exchange has a strong track record in security and if they have experienced any security breaches in the past.

Reputation and Reliability: Research the reputation of the exchange in the cryptocurrency community. Read user reviews and feedback to gauge their reliability and customer satisfaction. Consider the exchange's trading volume and liquidity, as higher liquidity generally allows for smoother trading.

Supported Cryptocurrencies: Ensure that the exchange supports the cryptocurrencies you are interested in trading. Some exchanges offer a wide range of cryptocurrencies, while others may have a more limited selection.

User Interface and Experience: Evaluate the exchange's user interface and trading platform. It should be intuitive, easy to navigate, and provide the necessary trading tools and charting features. A user-friendly interface can enhance your trading experience and efficiency.

Fees and Trading Costs: Review the fee structure of the exchange, including trading fees, deposit and withdrawal fees, and any other applicable charges. Compare the fees with other exchanges to find the most cost-effective option.

Liquidity: Consider the liquidity of the exchange, as higher liquidity provides better opportunities for executing trades at desired prices without significant slippage.

Regulatory Compliance: Check if the exchange operates within regulatory frameworks and complies with Know Your Customer (KYC) and Anti-Money Laundering (AML) regulations. Compliance with regulations adds an extra layer of trust and security.

Customer Support: Evaluate the level of customer support provided by the exchange. Look for exchanges that offer responsive customer support channels, such as live chat, email, or phone support, to address any concerns or issues that may arise.

When it comes to order types and trading functionalities, here are some common features to consider:

Market Orders: These orders are executed at the current market price. They provide immediate execution but do not guarantee a specific price.

Limit Orders: With limit orders, you specify the price at which you are willing to buy or sell a cryptocurrency. The order will be executed only when the market reaches your specified price.

Stop Orders: Stop orders are used to trigger a market order once the price reaches a specific level. A stop-loss order, for example, is designed to limit potential losses by automatically selling a cryptocurrency if its price drops to a predetermined level.

Margin Trading: Some exchanges offer margin trading, which allows you to trade with borrowed funds, magnifying potential profits but also increasing the risk. Margin trading is suitable for experienced traders who understand the risks involved.

Advanced Charting and Analysis Tools: Look for exchanges that provide advanced charting features, technical analysis indicators, and tools to help you make informed trading decisions.

Mobile Applications: If you prefer trading on the go, consider exchanges that offer mobile applications compatible with your device's operating system.

Ultimately, the right trading platform for you depends on your specific trading needs, preferences, and level of experience. Take the time to research and compare different exchanges to find the one that aligns with your requirements.

15.9 Algorithmic Trading and Trading Bots:

Algorithmic trading, also known as automated trading or algo trading, refers to the use of computer programs or trading bots to execute trading strategies automatically in the cryptocurrency market. These programs are designed to analyze market data, identify trading opportunities, and execute trades based on predefined rules and algorithms.

Trading bots can be programmed to perform various functions, such as market making, arbitrage, trend following, and mean reversion strategies. They can execute trades at high speed and with precision, eliminating the need for manual intervention and emotions.

Here are some key components and considerations of algorithmic trading in the cryptocurrency market:

Strategy Development: Algorithmic trading requires the development of a trading strategy that defines the rules and conditions for entering and exiting trades. The strategy can be based on technical indicators, statistical models, or a combination of factors. Backtesting the strategy using historical data is important to evaluate its performance and refine the rules.

Data Analysis and Decision Making: Algorithmic trading relies on real-time market data to analyze price movements, order book depth, and other relevant information. Trading bots can be programmed to make trading decisions based on specific conditions or patterns in the data.

Risk Management: Implementing risk management measures is crucial in algorithmic trading. This includes setting stop loss levels, defining position sizes, and monitoring market conditions to avoid excessive risk exposure. Proper risk management is essential to protect capital and minimize potential losses.

Execution Speed and Latency: Algorithmic trading often requires fast execution speeds to take advantage of short-lived opportunities in the market. The speed of trade execution can be influenced by factors such as internet connectivity, exchange infrastructure, and the proximity of the trading server to the exchange's matching engine. Minimizing latency is important to ensure timely trade execution.

Market Liquidity and Impact: Algorithmic trading strategies need to consider market liquidity, particularly in the cryptocurrency market where liquidity can vary significantly between different coins and exchanges. Large orders can impact the market and result in slippage, where the executed price deviates from the intended price. Proper order placement and execution algorithms can help mitigate such risks.

Monitoring and Maintenance: Algorithmic trading requires ongoing monitoring and maintenance. Strategies should be regularly reviewed and adjusted as market conditions change. Monitoring performance metrics and analyzing trade data can help identify areas for improvement and optimize trading strategies.

While algorithmic trading offers potential benefits such as speed, efficiency, and reduced emotional bias, it also comes with risks and considerations:

Technical Risks: Algorithmic trading relies on technology, and technical failures or glitches can result in unexpected behavior or errors. It is important to have robust testing procedures and safeguards in place to minimize such risks.

Market Risks: The cryptocurrency market is highly volatile and can experience rapid price movements. Algorithmic trading strategies need to account for market risks and adapt to changing market conditions.

Regulatory and Compliance Risks: Algorithmic trading may be subject to regulatory requirements and compliance obligations. It is important to ensure that the trading activities comply with relevant laws and regulations.

Over-Optimization and Data Bias: There is a risk of over-optimizing trading strategies based on historical data, which may not perform as expected in real-time market conditions. Additionally, biases in the historical data can impact strategy performance.

Lack of Human Judgment: Algorithmic trading removes human judgment from the decision-making process, which can be both an advantage and a limitation. There may be situations where human intervention or discretion is necessary to adapt to unforeseen events or market dynamics.

It is essential to thoroughly understand the technical and operational aspects of algorithmic trading and carefully consider the associated risks before engaging in automated trading in the cryptocurrency market. Seeking professional advice and conducting comprehensive testing and risk assessments are recommended to mitigate potential risks.

15.10 Tax Considerations for Cryptocurrency Trading:

Tax regulations for cryptocurrency trading vary depending on the jurisdiction. It is important to understand and comply with the tax obligations specific to your country or region. Here are some general considerations regarding tax regulations for cryptocurrency trading:

Classification of Cryptocurrency: Determine how cryptocurrencies are classified for tax purposes in your jurisdiction. Some countries treat cryptocurrencies as assets, while others consider them as currencies or commodities.

Capital Gains Tax: In many jurisdictions, profits from cryptocurrency trading are subject to capital gains tax. Capital gains tax is usually applied when you sell or dispose of a cryptocurrency for a profit. The tax rate may vary based on the holding period of the cryptocurrency and your income tax bracket.

Reporting Requirements: Understand the reporting requirements for cryptocurrency transactions. This typically includes reporting the gains or losses from cryptocurrency trading on your annual tax return. Keep track of your transactions, including the purchase and sale prices, dates, and any associated fees.

Cost Basis Calculation: Calculate the cost basis of your cryptocurrency holdings. The cost basis represents the original purchase price of the cryptocurrency and is used to determine the capital gains or losses when you sell or dispose of it. Different methods for calculating the cost basis may be allowed, such as First-In-First-Out (FIFO), Last-In-First-Out (LIFO), or specific identification.

Holding Period: The holding period refers to the length of time you hold a cryptocurrency before selling or disposing of it. In some jurisdictions, the tax rate may vary based on whether the holding period is considered short-term (held for less than a year) or long-term (held for more than a year). Long-term capital gains may receive preferential tax treatment.

Tax Losses: Losses incurred from cryptocurrency trading may be used to offset capital gains and reduce your tax liability. Keep records of any losses to potentially offset gains in future years.

Seek Professional Advice: Due to the complexity and evolving nature of cryptocurrency tax regulations, it is advisable to seek professional advice from a tax accountant or tax advisor with experience in cryptocurrencies. They can provide guidance specific to your situation and help ensure compliance with tax laws.

It is important to note that tax regulations can change, and the information provided here is a general overview. Consult with a tax professional who is knowledgeable about the tax laws in your jurisdiction to get accurate and up-to-date advice regarding your specific tax obligations related to cryptocurrency trading.

Chapter 16: Creating a Diversified Stock Portfolio

Introduction: In Chapter 16, we will explore the importance of creating a diversified stock portfolio. A diversified portfolio allows investors to spread their investments across different stocks and sectors, reducing the impact of individual stock volatility and potentially increasing overall returns. This chapter will guide you through the process of building a diversified stock portfolio, including asset allocation, stock selection strategies, and portfolio management techniques.

16.1 Understanding Diversification:

Diversification is an investment strategy that involves spreading investments across different assets or asset classes to reduce risk and increase portfolio stability. It is based on the principle that not all investments will perform the same way under different market conditions.

The main benefits of diversification are:

Risk Reduction: By investing in a variety of assets, you can reduce the impact of any single investment's poor performance on your overall portfolio. Different assets have different risk profiles, and when you diversify, you can mitigate the risk associated with any one asset.

Smoother Returns: Diversification can help smooth out the returns of your portfolio. When some investments are performing poorly, others may be performing well, which can help offset losses and provide a more stable return profile over time.

Potential for Higher Returns: Diversification allows you to access a broader range of investment opportunities. By including assets with different return characteristics, you increase the potential for higher overall returns. While some investments may underperform, others may deliver strong gains.

The impact of correlation and asset allocation on portfolio diversification:

Correlation: Correlation measures the relationship between the returns of different assets. If assets have a high positive correlation, they tend to move in the same direction. If assets have a high negative correlation, they tend to move in opposite directions. By including assets with low or negative correlation in a portfolio, you can further enhance diversification benefits. When one asset is experiencing a downturn, the other may provide a counterbalancing effect.

Asset Allocation: Asset allocation refers to the process of dividing your portfolio across different asset classes, such as stocks, bonds, commodities, and real estate. Each asset class has its own risk and return characteristics. By allocating your investments across different asset classes based on your risk tolerance, investment goals, and time horizon, you can achieve a balanced portfolio that is better positioned to weather market fluctuations.

To effectively diversify your portfolio, it is important to consider not only the type of assets but also their correlation with one another. A well-diversified portfolio includes assets that have low or negative correlations, as this helps reduce the overall risk. Regular monitoring and rebalancing of the portfolio are also necessary to maintain the desired diversification levels as market conditions and correlations may change over time.

Diversification does not guarantee profits or protect against losses, but it is a risk management strategy that aims to reduce the impact of individual investment risks on the overall portfolio.

16.2 Defining Investment Objectives and Risk Tolerance:

Determining your investment objectives, assessing your risk tolerance, and aligning your portfolio strategy with your goals are essential steps in creating an investment plan that suits your individual needs. Here's an overview of each aspect:

Investment Objectives: Investment objectives refer to the financial goals you want to achieve through your investments. These goals can vary depending on your personal circumstances, such as capital appreciation (aiming for growth and increasing the value of your investments), income generation (seeking regular income from dividends or interest payments), capital preservation (protecting your wealth and minimizing losses), or a combination of these objectives. Clearly defining your investment objectives helps guide your decision-making process and determine the appropriate investment strategies and asset classes to pursue.

Risk Tolerance: Risk tolerance is your willingness and ability to bear the potential risks associated with investments. It depends on various factors, including your financial situation, investment knowledge, investment experience, time horizon, and emotional capacity to handle market fluctuations. Assessing your risk tolerance helps you determine the level of risk you are comfortable with and select investments that align with your risk profile. Generally, risk and potential returns are positively correlated, meaning higher-risk investments have the potential for higher returns, but also higher volatility and potential losses.

Time Horizon: Your investment time horizon is the length of time you plan to hold your investments before needing the funds for a specific financial goal. It can range from short-term (less than one year) to medium-term (one to five years) or long-term (five years or more). Longer time horizons generally allow for a more aggressive investment approach, as there is more time to recover from short-term market fluctuations. Shorter time horizons may require a more conservative approach to help protect capital and ensure liquidity for upcoming financial needs.

Portfolio Strategy: Once you have determined your investment objectives, risk tolerance, and time horizon, you can align your portfolio strategy accordingly. This involves selecting asset classes, diversifying across different investments within those asset classes, and allocating your investments based on their risk-return characteristics and your goals. For example, if you have a long-term investment horizon and a higher risk tolerance, you may choose to allocate a larger portion of your portfolio to growth-oriented assets such as stocks. On the other hand, if you have a shorter time horizon and a lower risk tolerance, you may opt for a more conservative portfolio with a larger allocation to fixed-income assets.

Regularly reviewing and reassessing your investment objectives, risk tolerance, and time horizon is important as your circumstances may change over time. It's also recommended to seek professional advice from a financial advisor or investment professional to help you determine the most suitable portfolio strategy based on your individual goals and circumstances.

16.3 Asset Allocation Strategies:

Diversification involves spreading your investments across different asset classes to reduce risk and optimize returns. Here are some key asset classes to consider when building a diversified portfolio:

Stocks: Stocks represent ownership shares in publicly traded companies. They offer the potential for long-term capital appreciation and dividend income. Stocks are typically more volatile than other asset classes but have historically provided higher returns over the long term.

Bonds: Bonds are debt securities issued by governments, municipalities, and corporations. They provide fixed interest payments (coupon) and return the principal amount at maturity. Bonds are generally considered lower risk than stocks and provide income and stability to a portfolio.

Commodities: Commodities include physical goods such as precious metals (gold, silver), energy (oil, natural gas), agricultural products (corn, wheat), and industrial metals (copper, aluminum). Commodities can provide diversification benefits and act as a hedge against inflation.

Real Estate: Real estate investments can involve direct ownership of properties, real estate investment trusts (REITs), or real estate funds. Real estate offers potential income from rental payments and the potential for long-term appreciation.

Cash and Cash Equivalents: Cash and cash equivalents, such as money market funds and short-term Treasury bills, provide liquidity and stability to a portfolio. They can be used as a source of funds for short-term expenses and as a safe haven during market downturns.

Alternative Investments: Alternative investments, such as hedge funds, private equity, venture capital, and commodities trading strategies, offer diversification benefits and unique risk-return profiles. They are typically less correlated with traditional asset classes and can provide additional sources of return.

When allocating assets, it's important to consider your risk and return expectations, investment goals, and time horizon. A common approach is to create a diversified portfolio with a mix of different asset classes based on your risk tolerance. Generally, higher-risk assets such as stocks and commodities may have a higher allocation for investors seeking higher returns, while lower-risk assets like bonds and cash may have a larger allocation for investors focused on capital preservation.

The specific allocation will depend on your individual circumstances and investment preferences. Regular portfolio rebalancing is important to maintain the desired asset allocation and adapt to changes in market conditions and your investment objectives.

It's important to note that asset allocation and diversification do not guarantee profits or protect against losses. It's always advisable to consult with a financial advisor or investment professional to develop a suitable asset allocation strategy based on your unique financial situation and goals.

16.4 Stock Selection Strategies:

You've covered some key approaches to analyzing and selecting stocks. Let's dive into each one in more detail:

Fundamental Analysis: This approach involves analyzing a company's financial statements, earnings reports, and other fundamental factors to assess its intrinsic value. Fundamental analysts examine metrics such as revenue growth, profitability, cash flow, and balance sheet strength. They also consider qualitative factors like management quality, competitive advantage, industry trends, and macroeconomic conditions. The goal is to determine whether a stock is undervalued or overvalued and make investment decisions based on the company's underlying fundamentals.

Technical Analysis: This approach focuses on studying historical price and volume data to identify patterns, trends, and market sentiment. Technical analysts use various chart patterns, indicators, and oscillators to predict future price movements. They believe that historical price and volume patterns repeat themselves and can be used to forecast market behavior. Technical analysis helps traders make short-term trading decisions based on the assumption that past price movements can indicate future price movements.

Quantitative Analysis: Quantitative analysis involves using mathematical and statistical models to analyze large datasets and identify investment opportunities. Quantitative analysts, often referred to as quants, use computer algorithms and data-driven approaches to screen stocks based on predetermined criteria. This approach relies heavily on quantitative factors such as earnings growth, valuation ratios, volatility, and other quantitative metrics. Quants aim to exploit patterns and anomalies in the market to generate consistent returns.

Factor-based Investing: Factor-based investing focuses on selecting stocks based on specific factors or characteristics that have historically been associated with outperformance. Common factors include value, growth, quality, momentum, and low volatility. Investors using this approach construct portfolios that tilt towards stocks exhibiting desired factor characteristics. Factor-based investing combines elements of both fundamental and quantitative analysis, as it involves selecting stocks based on specific factors but also considers company fundamentals.

It's worth noting that these approaches are not mutually exclusive, and investors often use a combination of methods to make investment decisions. The choice of approach depends on individual preferences, investment goals, and time horizon. Some investors may lean more towards fundamental analysis for long-term investments, while others may use technical analysis for shorter-term trading strategies.

It's important to conduct thorough research, consider multiple perspectives, and understand the limitations and risks associated with each approach. Additionally, it can be beneficial to diversify your investment strategies and combine different analysis methods to gain a comprehensive understanding of potential investments.

16.5 Sector and Industry Analysis:

To identify and analyze sectors and industries with growth potential, you can follow these steps:

Market Research: Conduct thorough market research to identify sectors and industries that are expected to experience growth in the coming years. Look for sectors with favorable macroeconomic trends, technological advancements, or changing consumer preferences. Consider factors such as population growth, GDP growth, and emerging market trends.

Industry Analysis: Analyze the specific industry dynamics, competitive landscape, and regulatory factors. Assess the growth drivers, barriers to entry, market size, and competitive advantages of the companies operating in the industry. Consider factors such as market share, revenue growth, profitability, and innovation.

Fundamental Analysis: Evaluate the financial health and growth prospects of the companies within the sector or industry. Analyze key financial metrics such as revenue growth, earnings growth, profit margins, and return on investment. Consider factors such as company management, product pipeline, and strategic partnerships.

Technical Analysis: Utilize technical analysis tools and indicators to assess the price trends and momentum of the sector or industry. Look for patterns, support and resistance levels, and trend lines to gauge the market sentiment and potential entry or exit points.

Regulatory Factors: Consider the regulatory environment and any potential changes or developments that may impact the sector or industry. Stay informed about government policies, legislation, and regulatory risks that can affect the growth prospects or profitability of companies operating in the sector.

Based on your analysis, you can decide whether to overweight or underweight certain sectors in your investment strategy. Overweighting a sector means allocating a larger portion of your portfolio to that sector compared to its weight in the broader market index. Underweighting means allocating a smaller portion than the market weight. This decision depends on your risk appetite, investment objectives, and market conditions. If you believe a particular sector or industry has strong growth potential, you may choose to overweight it in your portfolio. Conversely, if you have concerns about a sector's outlook, you may decide to underweight it or avoid it altogether.

It's important to regularly monitor and reassess your sector weightings based on changing market conditions, industry trends, and your investment strategy. Diversification across sectors and industries can also help mitigate risks and capture opportunities in different market segments.

16.6 Geographic and Market Capitalization Diversification:

Investing in stocks from different geographic regions, as well as diversifying across market capitalizations, can be an effective way to diversify your portfolio and manage risks. Here's an overview of each:

Geographic Diversification:

Domestic Stocks: Investing in stocks from your home country can provide familiarity and insights into local industries and economic conditions.

International Stocks: Investing in stocks from countries outside your home country allows you to access different markets, industries, and economic cycles.

Emerging Markets: Investing in stocks from emerging markets can offer opportunities for high growth, but also come with higher risks due to political, economic, and regulatory factors.

Benefits of Geographic Diversification:

Risk Mitigation: By investing in stocks from different geographic regions, you can reduce the impact of country-specific risks or events on your portfolio.

Exposure to Different Markets: Each country has its own unique market dynamics, growth drivers, and investment opportunities, allowing you to access a broader range of investment options.

Potential for Higher Returns: Diversifying across regions increases your chances of capturing market outperformance in specific countries or regions.

Risks of Geographic Diversification:

Currency Risk: Investing in international stocks exposes you to currency exchange rate fluctuations, which can impact the returns when converting back to your home currency.

Political and Regulatory Risks: Different countries may have varying levels of political stability, regulatory frameworks, and legal protections for investors, which can impact the performance of stocks in those regions.

Diversification Across Market Capitalizations:

Large-Cap Stocks: These are stocks of well-established, large companies with a market capitalization typically above $10 billion. They tend to offer stability and may pay dividends.

Mid-Cap Stocks: These stocks belong to companies with a market capitalization between $2 billion and $10 billion. They offer a balance between growth potential and relative stability.

Small-Cap Stocks: These stocks represent companies with a market capitalization below $2 billion. They have higher growth potential but can also be more volatile and carry higher risks.

Benefits of Market Capitalization Diversification:

Risk Distribution: By investing in stocks of companies across different market capitalizations, you spread the risk associated with each category.

Exposure to Different Growth Stages: Large-cap stocks may provide stability and consistent returns, while mid-cap and small-cap stocks can offer higher growth potential.

Risks of Market Capitalization Diversification:

Volatility and Liquidity: Small-cap stocks tend to be more volatile and may have lower trading volumes, which can result in wider bid-ask spreads and potentially reduced liquidity.

Global diversification can offer several benefits, including reducing concentration risk, accessing new growth opportunities, and potentially enhancing risk-adjusted returns. However, it's essential to consider the associated risks, such as currency fluctuations, political risks, and varying levels of market efficiency in different regions. It's prudent to conduct thorough research, monitor global market trends, and consider the help of a financial advisor when making decisions related to global diversification.

16.7 Risk Management and Portfolio Rebalancing:

Implementing risk management techniques is crucial to effectively manage your investment portfolio. Here are some key risk management techniques you can use:

Stop Loss Orders: A stop loss order is an order placed with your broker to sell a security if it reaches a specified price level. It helps limit potential losses by automatically triggering a sell order when the price falls below your predetermined stop loss level.

Position Sizing: Position sizing refers to determining the appropriate allocation of capital to each investment position. It involves considering factors such as risk tolerance, portfolio diversification, and the potential for losses. By sizing your positions appropriately, you can manage risk and avoid overexposure to any single investment.

Regular Portfolio Review and Rebalancing: It's important to regularly review your portfolio to ensure it aligns with your investment goals and risk tolerance. Rebalancing involves adjusting the portfolio's asset allocation by buying or selling assets to bring it back to the desired target allocation. This helps maintain the intended risk profile and prevents overweighting or underweighting of specific asset classes.

Diversification: Diversification is a risk management technique that involves spreading investments across different asset classes, sectors, geographic regions, and investment styles. By diversifying your portfolio, you reduce the impact of any single investment on your overall portfolio performance. Diversification can help mitigate risk and potentially improve risk-adjusted returns.

Strategic Adjustments: Market conditions and investor preferences change over time. It's important to make strategic adjustments to your portfolio based on changing market trends, economic conditions, and your own investment objectives. This may involve reducing exposure to underperforming assets, increasing allocations to sectors or regions showing potential, or making tactical shifts in response to market conditions.

Remember, risk management is an ongoing process, and it requires regular monitoring and adjustments. It's crucial to set clear risk management rules, stick to your investment strategy, and avoid making emotional or impulsive decisions. Consider working with a financial advisor who can provide guidance and expertise in implementing risk management techniques that align with your investment goals and risk tolerance.

16.8 Dividend Investing:

Dividend investing is a popular strategy that offers several benefits when incorporated into a diversified portfolio:

Income Generation: Dividend-paying stocks provide a regular income stream in the form of cash dividends. This can be particularly beneficial for investors seeking current income or for those in retirement who rely on dividends as a source of income.

Stability and Defensive Characteristics: Dividend-paying stocks, especially those from established companies in defensive sectors, tend to exhibit more stability during market downturns. Dividends can provide a cushion to offset potential declines in stock prices, making them attractive for risk-averse investors.

Potential for Capital Appreciation: Dividend-paying stocks can still offer potential capital appreciation over time. Reinvesting dividends allows investors to benefit from compounding growth, where the reinvested dividends buy additional shares, potentially leading to increased dividends and capital gains over the long term.

Discipline and Focus on Quality: Companies that consistently pay dividends are often financially stable and have a track record of generating steady cash flows. Investing in dividend-paying stocks encourages a focus on quality companies with sustainable business models and disciplined management teams.

When identifying dividend-paying stocks with sustainable yields, consider the following factors:

Dividend Yield: Look for stocks with a reasonable dividend yield, which is the annual dividend payment divided by the stock price. However, a high dividend yield alone should not be the sole criteria for selection, as it could be a sign of financial distress.

Dividend History: Examine the company's track record of paying dividends consistently and increasing them over time. Consistent dividend growth is an indicator of a company's ability to generate sufficient cash flows.

Payout Ratio: Evaluate the company's payout ratio, which is the proportion of earnings paid out as dividends. A sustainable dividend yield is often supported by a reasonable payout ratio, indicating that the company retains enough earnings to reinvest in its business.

Financial Health: Assess the company's financial health, including its profitability, cash flow generation, and debt levels. A financially stable company is more likely to sustain dividend payments even during challenging economic conditions.

Reinvesting dividends can enhance long-term compounding growth. Many brokerages offer dividend reinvestment plans (DRIPs) that automatically reinvest dividends back into additional shares of the company's stock. This allows investors to benefit from compounding returns over time and potentially accumulate more shares without incurring transaction costs.

It's important to note that dividend investing, like any investment strategy, carries risks. Market volatility, changes in interest rates, and economic conditions can affect the performance of dividend-paying stocks. Conduct thorough research and consider diversifying across sectors and regions to mitigate risk. Additionally, consulting with a financial advisor can provide personalized guidance and help tailor a dividend investing strategy to your specific needs and goals.

16.9 Portfolio Performance Evaluation:

Assessing the performance of a diversified stock portfolio involves several steps, including benchmarking, measuring risk-adjusted returns, and conducting a comprehensive analysis. Here's an overview of the process:

Set Benchmarks: Select appropriate benchmarks that represent the broad market or specific segments relevant to your portfolio. Common benchmarks for stock portfolios include broad market indices like the S&P 500 or sector-specific indices. These benchmarks serve as a reference point to evaluate your portfolio's performance against the overall market or relevant market segments.

Compare Total Returns: Calculate the total return of your portfolio by considering both capital appreciation (change in stock prices) and income (dividends or distributions received). Compare the total return of your portfolio with the selected benchmarks over the same time period to assess relative performance.

Evaluate Risk-Adjusted Returns: Assessing risk-adjusted returns helps measure the efficiency of your portfolio in generating returns relative to the risk taken. Common risk-adjusted metrics include the Sharpe ratio, which measures the excess return per unit of risk (usually calculated using the portfolio's volatility or standard deviation). A higher Sharpe ratio indicates better risk-adjusted performance.

Analyze Sector/Asset Allocation: Review your portfolio's sector and asset allocation to ensure it aligns with your investment strategy and objectives. Assess whether your allocations are consistent with your risk tolerance and desired exposure to different sectors or asset classes. Adjustments may be necessary if there are significant deviations from the target allocations.

Performance Attribution: Evaluate the performance of individual holdings within your portfolio to identify contributors and detractors. Analyze the performance of specific stocks or sectors to understand their impact on the overall portfolio performance. This analysis can guide you in making adjustments to holdings that may not be meeting expectations.

Review Investment Strategy: Regularly assess whether your investment strategy and goals have changed. Consider factors such as your time horizon, risk tolerance, and market conditions. Adjustments may be necessary to align your portfolio with your evolving investment objectives.

Rebalance and Make Adjustments: Rebalance your portfolio periodically to restore the original target allocations. This involves selling over-weighted assets and buying under-weighted assets. Rebalancing helps maintain the desired risk profile and prevents concentration in specific holdings or sectors. Adjustments should be made based on a thoughtful analysis of the portfolio's performance and your investment objectives.

It's important to note that evaluating portfolio performance should be done over a meaningful time horizon. Short-term performance fluctuations can occur due to market volatility, and it's essential to focus on long-term trends and objectives.

Regular monitoring and analysis of your portfolio's performance can help you make informed decisions and make necessary adjustments to stay on track with your investment goals. If you're unsure about the process or need assistance, consider consulting with a financial advisor who can provide personalized guidance based on your specific circumstances.

16.10 Portfolio Monitoring and Review:

Establishing a robust monitoring system and staying informed about market developments are essential for effectively managing your stock portfolio. Here are some steps to help you establish a monitoring system and conduct periodic portfolio reviews:

Define Key Performance Metrics: Determine the key performance metrics you will track for individual stocks and the portfolio as a whole. Common metrics include total return, dividend yield, earnings growth, price-to-earnings ratio, and other relevant financial ratios. These metrics will help you assess the performance and health of your holdings.

Set Monitoring Frequency: Determine how frequently you will review and monitor your portfolio. This could be on a daily, weekly, monthly, or quarterly basis, depending on your preferences and the level of activity in your portfolio. Regular monitoring allows you to stay informed about market movements and identify any significant changes or developments that may impact your holdings.

Use Watchlists and Alerts: Create watchlists of stocks you are interested in or currently own. Monitor these stocks for any news, earnings reports, or other events that may impact their performance. Utilize price alerts or news alerts provided by trading platforms or financial news services to stay updated in real-time.

Stay Informed: Stay informed about market and economic developments through reliable sources such as financial news outlets, research reports, and official economic releases. Pay attention to factors that can influence stock prices, such as interest rate changes, geopolitical events, regulatory developments, and industry-specific news.

Conduct Periodic Portfolio Reviews: Conduct regular portfolio reviews to assess the performance and alignment of your holdings with your investment goals. Consider factors such as individual stock performance, sector exposure, diversification, and risk management. Identify underperforming stocks, evaluate their prospects, and make decisions on whether to hold, sell, or adjust positions.

Rebalance and Adjust: If your portfolio has deviated significantly from your target asset allocation or if certain stocks are consistently underperforming, consider rebalancing and making adjustments. Rebalancing involves selling assets that have exceeded their target allocation and buying assets that are underrepresented. Adjustments may also involve trimming or selling stocks that no longer align with your investment strategy or goals.

Document and Review Decisions: Keep a record of your decisions, including buy/sell transactions, reasons for adjustments, and the outcomes of those decisions. Review your decisions periodically to evaluate their impact on your portfolio and identify areas for improvement in your investment process.

Remember that monitoring and reviewing your portfolio are ongoing processes. Regularly reassess your investment goals, risk tolerance, and market conditions to ensure your portfolio remains aligned with your objectives. If you're unsure about the monitoring process or need assistance, consider consulting with a financial advisor who can provide guidance based on your specific circumstances.

Chapter 17: Value Investing: Identifying Undervalued Stocks for Long-Term Gains

INTRODUCTION: IN CHAPTER 17, we will delve into the concept of value investing—a popular investment strategy that aims to identify undervalued stocks for long-term gains. Value investing involves seeking out stocks that are trading below their intrinsic value, providing an opportunity to buy quality companies at discounted prices. This chapter will guide you through the principles and strategies of value investing, including fundamental analysis techniques and factors to consider when identifying undervalued stocks.

17.1 Understanding Value Investing:

Value investing is an investment philosophy that aims to identify undervalued stocks or assets in the market. It is based on the belief that the market sometimes misprices stocks, creating opportunities for investors to buy them at a discount. Value investors seek to buy stocks that are trading at prices lower than their intrinsic value, which is determined by analyzing fundamental factors such as earnings, cash flows, book value, and other relevant metrics.

The principles of value investing include:

Intrinsic Value: Value investors focus on determining the intrinsic value of a stock, which represents its true worth based on its underlying fundamentals. They believe that the market may sometimes overreact to short-term news and create mispricings, offering opportunities for long-term investors.

Margin of Safety: Value investors seek a margin of safety by buying stocks at a significant discount to their intrinsic value. This provides a cushion against potential errors in valuation and unexpected market downturns.

Long-Term Orientation: Value investing is typically a long-term approach, emphasizing the importance of patience and holding investments for an extended period. Value investors believe that over time, the market will recognize the true value of undervalued stocks, leading to potential price appreciation.

Fundamental Analysis: Value investors extensively analyze the financial statements, earnings growth, competitive position, management quality, and other fundamental aspects of companies. They aim to understand the underlying value drivers and assess the potential for future growth and profitability.

Contrarian Mindset: Value investors often take a contrarian approach, being willing to invest in stocks that are out of favor or facing temporary challenges. They believe that market sentiment and short-term fluctuations may create opportunities to buy quality stocks at attractive prices.

Value investing differs from other investment approaches such as growth investing, which focuses on companies with high growth potential even if their valuations appear high. Value investing also contrasts with momentum investing, which emphasizes investing in stocks that have shown recent price momentum.

Value investing requires discipline, patience, and a long-term perspective. It is not about trying to time the market or making quick profits but rather identifying and owning companies with strong fundamentals and a significant gap between their market price and intrinsic value. Successful value investing requires thorough research, a contrarian mindset, and the ability to remain patient during periods of market volatility.

17.2 Fundamental Analysis for Value Investing:

When evaluating a company for value investing, analyzing its financial statements and key financial ratios is an essential part of the process. Here are some key aspects to consider:

Financial Statements: Review the company's income statement, balance sheet, and cash flow statement. Look for trends, revenue growth, profitability, and cash flow generation over multiple periods. Assess the company's financial health and stability.

Earnings Quality: Evaluate the quality and sustainability of the company's earnings. Look for consistency in earnings growth, the stability of profit margins, and the presence of any one-time or non-recurring items that may distort the earnings picture. Consider factors such as revenue sources, cost structure, and the company's ability to generate cash flow.

Financial Ratios: Calculate and analyze various financial ratios to gain insights into the company's performance. Common ratios to consider include profitability ratios (e.g., gross margin, operating margin, net profit margin), liquidity ratios (e.g., current ratio, quick ratio), leverage ratios (e.g., debt-to-equity ratio, interest coverage ratio), and efficiency ratios (e.g., inventory turnover, receivables turnover).

Competitive Position: Assess the company's competitive position within its industry. Evaluate factors such as market share, customer base, brand strength, and barriers to entry. Consider the company's ability to maintain or improve its competitive advantage over time.

Industry Outlook: Analyze the industry in which the company operates. Consider industry trends, growth prospects, competition, regulatory factors, and technological advancements that may impact the company's future performance. Assess whether the industry is cyclical or undergoing structural changes.

By evaluating financial statements and ratios, assessing earnings quality and sustainability, and analyzing the company's competitive position and industry outlook, you can gain a deeper understanding of the company's financial health and its potential for long-term value creation. It is important to conduct thorough research and stay updated on the latest developments to make informed investment decisions.

17.3 Valuation Techniques for Value Investing:

Estimating intrinsic value using discounted cash flow (DCF) analysis is a commonly used valuation method in value investing. Here's an overview of the process:

Cash Flow Projections: Forecast the future cash flows of the company over a specific time period. This typically involves estimating the company's free cash flows, which represent the cash available to the company after deducting capital expenditures and working capital requirements.

Discount Rate: Determine an appropriate discount rate to account for the time value of money and the company's risk profile. The discount rate reflects the expected return investors would require for investing in the company. It is typically derived from the company's cost of capital or a suitable risk-adjusted rate.

Present Value Calculation: Discount each projected cash flow back to its present value using the chosen discount rate. The present value represents the value of each cash flow in today's dollars.

Terminal Value: Estimate the value of the company beyond the projection period. This is often done by applying a terminal value multiple to a representative cash flow (e.g., using a perpetuity or exit multiple approach).

Calculate Intrinsic Value: Sum up the present values of the projected cash flows and the terminal value to arrive at the estimated intrinsic value of the company.

Comparing a company's valuation multiples to industry peers is another approach to assess its relative valuation. The most commonly used valuation multiples include price-to-earnings (P/E) ratio and price-to-book (P/B) ratio.

P/E Ratio: It compares the price of a company's stock to its earnings per share (EPS). A higher P/E ratio suggests that investors are willing to pay a higher price for each dollar of earnings, indicating a relatively higher valuation.

P/B Ratio: It compares the price of a company's stock to its book value per share. Book value represents the net assets of the company (total assets minus total liabilities). A higher P/B ratio indicates a higher price being paid relative to the company's book value, which may suggest a higher valuation.

When comparing valuation multiples to industry peers, it is important to consider factors such as growth prospects, profitability, risk profile, and other qualitative aspects that may impact the valuation. Additionally, it is crucial to conduct a comprehensive analysis and consider multiple valuation approaches to gain a more complete understanding of a company's value.

17.4 Identifying Undervalued Stocks:

Screening for stocks with low valuation metrics is a common practice in value investing. Here are a few valuation metrics that can be used in the screening process:

Price-to-Earnings (P/E) Ratio: This ratio compares the stock price to the company's earnings per share (EPS). A lower P/E ratio may suggest that the stock is relatively undervalued compared to its earnings potential.

Price-to-Book (P/B) Ratio: This ratio compares the stock price to the company's book value per share. A lower P/B ratio indicates that the stock may be trading at a lower price compared to its underlying net assets.

Price-to-Sales (P/S) Ratio: This ratio compares the stock price to the company's revenue per share. A lower P/S ratio implies that the stock may be undervalued relative to its revenue generation.

Dividend Yield: This ratio measures the annual dividend payment as a percentage of the stock price. A higher dividend yield indicates that the stock may be providing a higher income return relative to its price.

When assessing a company's growth potential and future prospects, consider the following factors:

Revenue and Earnings Growth: Analyze the historical and projected growth rates of the company's revenue and earnings. Look for consistent or improving growth trends.

Industry and Market Position: Evaluate the company's position within its industry and its ability to capture market share. Consider the industry growth potential and the company's competitive advantages.

Product or Service Innovation: Assess the company's ability to innovate and adapt to changing market trends. Look for evidence of successful product launches, technological advancements, or unique offerings.

Management and Leadership: Evaluate the company's management team and their track record. Look for experienced leaders with a strong vision and a history of effective execution.

Identifying temporary market dislocations and misconceptions about a company requires thorough research and analysis. Some ways to uncover such opportunities include:

Contrarian Approach: Look for stocks that have fallen out of favor with the market due to temporary setbacks or negative sentiment. Assess whether the negative perception is warranted or if there are underlying strengths that the market may be overlooking.

Fundamental Analysis: Conduct a comprehensive evaluation of the company's financials, industry dynamics, competitive landscape, and growth prospects. Look for discrepancies between the company's intrinsic value and its current market price.

Event-Driven Opportunities: Keep an eye on market events, such as mergers and acquisitions, regulatory changes, or industry disruptions, which can create temporary mispricings and opportunities for investors.

Qualitative Factors: Consider qualitative aspects, such as changes in management, new product launches, strategic partnerships, or favorable regulatory developments that may positively impact the company's prospects.

It's important to note that identifying temporary market dislocations and misconceptions requires diligent research and analysis. It's advisable to combine fundamental analysis with a contrarian mindset to uncover potential opportunities in the market.

17.5 Contrarian Investing:

The contrarian approach to value investing involves taking positions that go against the prevailing market sentiment. Contrarian investors believe that markets can be inefficient and driven by emotions, leading to mispricing of stocks. They aim to identify opportunities where the market has overreacted to negative news or overlooked the true value of a stock.

Contrarian investors often seek to buy stocks during market downturns or when a particular stock or sector is out of favor. They take advantage of market pessimism and capitalize on the potential for a rebound or market correction. By purchasing stocks at lower prices when they are undervalued, contrarian investors position themselves to benefit from the market's eventual recognition of the stock's true value.

Evaluating the potential risks and rewards of contrarian investing is crucial. Here are some key considerations:

Market Timing: Contrarian investing requires accurately timing market cycles and identifying the turning points when stocks are oversold or undervalued. However, market timing is challenging, and mistiming the entry or exit points can result in losses.

Contrarian Bias: It's important to avoid falling into the trap of contrarian bias, where investments are made solely based on being contrarian without conducting thorough analysis. Contrarian investing should be grounded in fundamental analysis and a comprehensive understanding of the company's prospects.

Uncertainty and Volatility: Contrarian investments often involve companies facing challenges, which can lead to increased uncertainty and volatility. It's important to assess the company's financial strength, competitive position, and ability to navigate through difficult times.

Patience and Long-Term Perspective: Contrarian investing requires patience, as it may take time for the market to recognize the true value of a stock. Investors need a long-term perspective and the ability to withstand short-term price fluctuations.

Fundamental Analysis: Conduct thorough fundamental analysis to assess the intrinsic value of the stock. Look for companies with strong balance sheets, sustainable competitive advantages, and the potential for long-term growth.

Portfolio Diversification: As with any investment approach, it's important to maintain a diversified portfolio to spread the risk. Diversification across different sectors and asset classes can help mitigate the risks associated with individual contrarian investments.

Contrarian investing can offer the potential for significant returns, but it also carries risks. It requires careful analysis, disciplined execution, and a long-term perspective. Successful contrarian investors have a deep understanding of the market, industry dynamics, and company fundamentals to identify undervalued opportunities. It's important to assess each investment on its own merits and consider the potential risks and rewards before making any investment decisions.

17.6 Margin of Safety:

The margin of safety is a fundamental concept in value investing that aims to protect investors against downside risk. It is the difference between the intrinsic value of a stock and its market price. In value investing, investors seek to purchase stocks that are trading at a significant discount to their estimated intrinsic value, thereby providing a margin of safety.

By investing with a margin of safety, investors reduce their risk of capital loss. The margin of safety acts as a cushion, allowing for unexpected negative events or miscalculations in valuation. It provides a margin for error and protects investors from overpaying for a stock.

To apply the concept of margin of safety in value investing, investors typically follow these steps:

Estimate Intrinsic Value: Conduct thorough fundamental analysis to determine the intrinsic value of the stock. This involves analyzing financial statements, evaluating industry and company prospects, and utilizing valuation methods such as discounted cash flow (DCF) analysis or comparable company analysis.

Determine Margin of Safety: Compare the estimated intrinsic value to the current market price of the stock. The margin of safety is the difference between the intrinsic value and the market price. Investors aim to purchase stocks with a significant margin of safety, meaning the stock is priced well below its intrinsic value.

Assess Financial Health: Evaluate the company's financial health and balance sheet strength. Look for companies with low debt levels, strong cash flow generation, and solid liquidity. A financially healthy company is more likely to weather economic downturns and financial challenges, providing an additional layer of safety.

Risk Assessment: Consider the specific risks associated with the company and its industry. Assess the competitive landscape, regulatory factors, and any other risks that could impact the company's operations and future prospects. A thorough understanding of the risks allows investors to determine an appropriate margin of safety.

By investing in stocks with a significant discount to intrinsic value and considering the company's financial health, investors aim to minimize their risk and increase their potential for capital appreciation. The margin of safety provides a buffer against unexpected events or unfavorable market conditions.

It's important to note that determining the intrinsic value of a stock is not an exact science, and there is always a degree of uncertainty involved. Investors should conduct thorough research, exercise sound judgment, and maintain a long-term perspective when applying the concept of margin of safety in value investing.

17.7 Long-Term Investing and Patience:

A long-term investment horizon is a key principle in value investing. Value investors focus on the underlying intrinsic value of a company and aim to hold investments for an extended period, allowing time for the market to recognize and reflect that value. By adopting a long-term perspective, value investors aim to avoid the short-term market fluctuations, noise, and emotional reactions that can impact investment decisions.

Here are some reasons why a long-term investment horizon is important in value investing:

Time for Value to be Realized: Value investing is based on the belief that the market sometimes misprices stocks, leading to opportunities for investors to buy undervalued assets. However, market inefficiencies can take time to correct. By having a long-term horizon, investors give the market sufficient time to recognize and adjust the stock price to reflect the company's intrinsic value.

Patience and Discipline: Value investing requires patience and discipline. Stocks may experience short-term price volatility, and it's important to stay focused on the underlying value of the investment. By maintaining a long-term perspective, investors are less likely to be swayed by short-term market movements or noise, allowing them to stay committed to their investment thesis.

Capitalizing on Market Inefficiencies: Inefficient market pricing can persist for extended periods, creating opportunities for patient value investors. By holding investments for the long term, investors increase their chances of benefiting from the eventual correction of market mispricing.

Reduced Trading Costs: Frequent trading can lead to increased transaction costs, such as commissions and taxes. By adopting a long-term approach, investors can minimize these costs and potentially enhance their overall returns.

Company Performance and Value Creation: Value investing focuses on identifying companies with solid fundamentals and growth potential. It takes time for companies to execute their business strategies, generate profits, and increase their value. A long-term horizon allows investors to monitor the progress of the company, assess its performance, and participate in the value creation over time.

It's important for value investors to stick to their investment thesis and not be swayed by short-term market fluctuations or external noise. By maintaining a long-term perspective, investors can give their investments the time they need to realize their value and potentially achieve superior returns.

However, it's crucial to periodically review investments and reassess the investment thesis to ensure that the original reasons for investing still hold true. While a long-term horizon is important, it doesn't mean blindly holding onto investments that no longer align with the investment thesis or if there are material changes in the company's fundamentals. Flexibility and ongoing evaluation are also key aspects of successful value investing.

17.8 Value Investing Strategies:

Deep Value Investing: Deep value investing involves identifying distressed or undervalued companies that have the potential for a turnaround. Investors following this strategy look for stocks trading at a significant discount to their intrinsic value, often due to temporary setbacks, market misconceptions, or unfavorable market conditions. The goal is to invest in these undervalued companies and benefit from their potential recovery, which can lead to substantial returns when the market recognizes their true value.

Key aspects of deep value investing include thorough fundamental analysis, assessing the company's financial health, analyzing its competitive position, and understanding the potential catalysts that could drive a turnaround. Investors following this strategy need to be patient, as the recovery of undervalued companies may take time. It is crucial to identify companies with strong balance sheets, sustainable business models, and the ability to generate positive cash flows.

Dividend Investing: Dividend investing focuses on selecting stocks that offer attractive dividend yields and sustainable payouts. Dividends are cash distributions that companies pay to their shareholders as a portion of their profits. Dividend investors seek stocks with a history of consistent dividend payments and companies that have the potential to continue paying dividends in the future.

Dividend investing can provide investors with a steady income stream, particularly for those seeking regular cash flow from their investments. It is important to assess the company's financial stability, dividend payout ratios, and its ability to generate consistent earnings or cash flows. Dividend investors often look for companies with a track record of increasing dividend payments over time, as this indicates financial strength and management's commitment to rewarding shareholders.

GARP (Growth at a Reasonable Price): GARP investing combines elements of both value and growth investing. It focuses on identifying companies with strong growth potential but at a reasonable price relative to their growth prospects. GARP investors seek companies that demonstrate both attractive growth rates and reasonable valuations.

This approach involves assessing the company's growth prospects, such as revenue growth, earnings growth, or expanding market share, while considering the valuation metrics such as price-to-earnings (P/E) ratio, price-to-sales (P/S) ratio, or price-to-earnings growth (PEG) ratio. GARP investors aim to find companies that offer a balance between growth potential and valuation, avoiding overvalued stocks with unrealistic growth expectations and undervalued stocks with limited growth prospects.

GARP investing requires a thorough analysis of a company's fundamentals, including its competitive position, industry trends, and management's ability to execute growth strategies. It combines elements of value investing by seeking reasonable valuations and growth investing by focusing on companies with growth potential.

It's important to note that these investment approaches are not mutually exclusive, and investors may incorporate aspects of each strategy based on their individual preferences and investment goals. The key is to conduct thorough research, understand the risks involved, and align the chosen strategy with one's investment objectives and risk tolerance.

17.9 Assessing Management and Corporate Governance:

Evaluating the quality and competence of a company's management team is an essential aspect of fundamental analysis. The management team plays a crucial role in shaping the company's strategy, making operational decisions, and driving long-term growth. Here are some factors to consider when assessing management:

Track Record and Experience: Evaluate the management team's track record, including their experience in the industry and their ability to navigate challenging business environments. Look for a consistent and successful history of executing strategic initiatives and delivering on their promises.

Leadership and Vision: Assess the leadership qualities of key executives, such as the CEO and other C-suite members. Look for a clear vision, strategic thinking, and effective communication skills. Consider whether the management team has a well-defined strategy for growth and a roadmap for achieving it.

Financial Discipline and Capital Allocation: Analyze the management team's financial decision-making abilities, including their approach to capital allocation, investment decisions, and cost management. Look for evidence of prudent financial management, efficient use of resources, and a focus on creating shareholder value.

Corporate Governance Practices: Consider the company's corporate governance structure and practices. Evaluate the independence and expertise of the board of directors, the presence of committees such as an audit committee and compensation committee, and the company's adherence to regulatory requirements and best practices.

Transparency and Communication: Assess the company's transparency in financial reporting, disclosure practices, and communication with shareholders. Look for regular and clear communication through investor presentations, conference calls, and shareholder meetings. Transparency is important for maintaining trust and confidence in the management team.

Alignment of Interests: Consider whether the management team's interests are aligned with those of shareholders. Look for ownership stakes by key executives and their participation in long-term incentive programs tied to the company's performance. This alignment indicates that management has a vested interest in driving shareholder value.

It is important to gather information from various sources, including annual reports, company announcements, news articles, and industry publications, to assess the competence and integrity of the management team. Additionally, pay attention to any red flags, such as excessive compensation, ethical controversies, or a lack of transparency, which may indicate potential governance issues or management concerns.

Remember that evaluating management is subjective to some extent, and it requires a combination of qualitative and quantitative analysis. It is also helpful to consider the opinions and assessments of industry experts, analysts, and other investors when forming an overall judgment about the quality of a company's management team.

17.10 Risk Management and Portfolio Diversification:

Managing risk is a crucial aspect of any investment strategy, including value investing. Here are some strategies to manage risk in value investing:

Proper Position Sizing: Determine the appropriate allocation of capital to each investment based on your risk tolerance and portfolio objectives. Avoid allocating a significant portion of your portfolio to a single stock or a small number of stocks. By diversifying your investments, you reduce the impact of any individual stock's performance on your overall portfolio.

Portfolio Diversification: Spread your investments across different sectors, industries, and geographies. This diversification helps reduce exposure to any specific company, sector, or market. By diversifying, you can mitigate the risk associated with the underperformance of a particular industry or sector.

Risk Assessment: Conduct a thorough analysis of the potential risks associated with value investing. This includes assessing the risk of value traps, where a stock appears undervalued but continues to decline in price. Value traps may arise due to deteriorating fundamentals, poor management, or industry-specific challenges. Perform detailed fundamental analysis to identify companies with genuine value and solid prospects for recovery.

Industry-Specific Risks: Consider the risks that are inherent to specific industries. Industries can face unique challenges and risks that may affect the performance of companies within them. For example, regulatory changes, technological disruptions, or shifts in consumer preferences can impact certain sectors. Assess these risks and invest in industries that you have a good understanding of and where you can effectively evaluate the prospects for value creation.

Continuous Monitoring: Regularly monitor your value investments and stay informed about any changes in the company's fundamentals, industry dynamics, or market conditions. Be prepared to make adjustments to your portfolio if new risks emerge or if your investment thesis is no longer valid.

Patience and Long-Term Focus: Value investing requires patience and a long-term perspective. Value stocks may take time to reach their intrinsic value, and short-term price volatility should not deter you from your investment thesis. By maintaining a long-term focus, you can potentially ride out short-term fluctuations and benefit from the recovery and growth of undervalued companies.

It is important to note that even with risk management strategies in place, investing in stocks, including value stocks, carries inherent risks. No investment is entirely risk-free, and there is always the possibility of losses. Conduct thorough research, seek professional advice when needed, and carefully assess the risks and rewards before making investment decisions.

Chapter 18: Growth Investing: Spotting High-Potential Stocks for Capital Appreciation

Introduction: In Chapter 18, we will explore growth investing—an investment strategy focused on identifying high-potential stocks with the potential for significant capital appreciation. Growth investors seek out companies that demonstrate above-average growth rates in terms of revenue, earnings, or market share. This chapter will guide you through the principles and strategies of growth investing, including factors to consider when spotting high-potential growth stocks.

18.1 Understanding Growth Investing:

Growth investing is an investment approach that focuses on identifying companies with strong growth potential. The philosophy behind growth investing is to invest in companies that are expected to experience above-average revenue and earnings growth rates compared to the broader market or their industry peers. Growth investors seek out companies that have the potential for rapid expansion and increasing market share.

Here are some key principles of growth investing:

Focus on Future Potential: Growth investors concentrate on companies that have the potential for significant future growth. They are more concerned with a company's future earnings and cash flow prospects rather than its current valuation. Growth investors believe that the market will recognize and reward the company's growth potential over time.

Emphasis on Market Expansion: Growth investors seek companies operating in expanding markets or industries. They look for sectors that are experiencing strong demand, technological advancements, or changing consumer preferences. By investing in companies in these high-growth sectors, growth investors aim to benefit from the overall growth of the market.

Company Quality and Competitive Advantage: Growth investors pay attention to the quality of the companies they invest in. They seek businesses with strong competitive advantages, such as unique products or services, intellectual property, or a dominant market position. These competitive advantages help the company sustain its growth and outperform competitors.

Long-Term Investment Horizon: Growth investing typically has a longer-term investment horizon. Investors are willing to hold onto their investments for an extended period to allow the company's growth story to unfold. They understand that the growth trajectory may take time and are willing to tolerate short-term volatility in pursuit of long-term gains.

Differences between Growth Investing and Value Investing:

Growth investing and value investing are two distinct investment approaches:

Focus: Growth investing emphasizes future growth potential, while value investing focuses on finding undervalued stocks based on their intrinsic value.

Valuation: Growth investors are more willing to pay a premium for stocks with high growth potential, even if their current valuations appear high. Value investors, on the other hand, seek stocks that are trading at a discount to their intrinsic value, often based on metrics like price-to-earnings ratio or price-to-book ratio.

Investment Criteria: Growth investors prioritize factors such as revenue growth, earnings growth, and market share expansion. Value investors focus on financial metrics like book value, dividends, and low price-to-earnings ratios.

It's important to note that growth and value investing are not mutually exclusive, and some investment strategies may incorporate elements of both approaches. Investors may also choose to have a diversified portfolio that includes both growth and value stocks to balance risk and return potential.

18.2 Characteristics of Growth Stocks:

Key Characteristics of Growth Stocks:

High Earnings and Revenue Growth: Growth stocks are characterized by their ability to generate above-average earnings and revenue growth compared to the overall market or their industry peers. These companies often have innovative products or services, strong market positions, or disruptive business models that contribute to their growth potential.

Expanding Market Opportunities: Growth stocks operate in sectors or industries with significant growth prospects. These sectors may be driven by technological advancements, changing consumer behaviors, or emerging markets. Growth companies benefit from capturing market share and expanding their customer base.

Strong Competitive Advantages: Growth stocks often possess competitive advantages that allow them to sustain their growth and outperform competitors. These advantages can include brand recognition, intellectual property, network effects, or a unique business model that differentiates them from others in the industry.

Reinvestment of Profits: Growth companies typically reinvest a significant portion of their earnings back into the business to fuel further growth. They may prioritize investing in research and development, expanding operations, or acquiring complementary businesses to drive future growth.

Sectors and Industries Known for Growth Opportunities:

Technology: The technology sector has historically been a fertile ground for growth stocks. It encompasses companies involved in software development, cloud computing, artificial intelligence, e-commerce, and other innovative technologies.

Healthcare: The healthcare sector, particularly biotechnology and pharmaceutical companies, offers growth opportunities due to advancements in medical research, drug development, and the increasing demand for healthcare services.

Consumer Discretionary: This sector includes companies that provide non-essential goods and services, such as retail, leisure, travel, and entertainment. Consumer discretionary stocks can benefit from increased consumer spending as the economy expands.

Communication Services: Companies in the communication services sector, including internet and social media platforms, streaming services, and telecommunications providers, can experience growth as technology and connectivity continue to evolve.

Potential Risks Associated with Growth Investing:

Valuation Risk: Growth stocks often trade at high valuations due to high investor expectations. If the company's growth fails to meet those expectations or market sentiment shifts, the stock price may decline significantly, leading to potential losses for investors.

Market Volatility: Growth stocks are often more volatile than value stocks due to higher investor expectations and market sentiment. Market downturns or shifts in investor sentiment can lead to sharp price declines in growth stocks.

Competitive and Technological Risks: Companies operating in rapidly evolving sectors face the risk of competition from both established players and new entrants. Technological disruptions or changes in consumer preferences can quickly impact growth prospects.

Regulatory and Legislative Risks: Companies in certain sectors, such as technology or healthcare, may face regulatory challenges or changes in government policies that can affect their growth trajectory.

It's important for investors to carefully evaluate growth stocks, considering their financial health, competitive advantages, growth prospects, and valuations. Diversification and a long-term investment approach can help mitigate risks associated with growth investing.

18.3 Identifying Growth Opportunities:

Analyzing Industry Trends and Market Dynamics:

To identify potential growth opportunities, it's crucial to analyze industry trends and market dynamics. This involves assessing factors such as market size, growth rate, demand drivers, competitive landscape, and regulatory environment. Look for industries that are experiencing favorable trends, such as increasing consumer demand, technological advancements, or changing demographics. It's important to consider both the current state and the future growth potential of the industry.

Identifying Companies with Innovative Products or Services:

Companies with innovative products or services often have a competitive edge and the potential for substantial growth. Look for companies that are introducing new and disruptive technologies, addressing unmet consumer needs, or revolutionizing existing markets. Evaluate their product pipeline, research and development efforts, patents or intellectual property, and their ability to stay ahead of competitors.

Evaluating Competitive Advantage and Market Positioning:

Assessing a company's competitive advantage and market positioning is crucial in growth investing. Look for companies that have a sustainable competitive advantage, such as a strong brand, proprietary technology, unique distribution channels, or a large and loyal customer base. Evaluate their market share, pricing power, barriers to entry, and the strength of their relationships with suppliers and customers. A strong competitive advantage can help a company maintain its growth trajectory and fend off competition.

Consider other factors such as the management team's track record, financial health, and ability to execute on growth strategies. Conduct thorough research and analysis, including studying company financials, industry reports, analyst opinions, and conducting interviews or attending industry conferences to gain insights into the company's growth potential.

Remember, growth investing requires a long-term perspective and the willingness to endure volatility. Regularly monitor the company's performance, industry trends, and competitive landscape to ensure the investment thesis remains intact.

18.4 Fundamental Analysis for Growth Investing:

Assessing a Company's Revenue Growth and Earnings Growth Rates:

When evaluating growth stocks, it's important to assess a company's revenue growth and earnings growth rates. Look for companies that have consistently demonstrated strong and sustainable growth in both revenue and earnings over time. Analyze the historical growth rates and compare them to industry peers to understand the company's competitive position.

Revenue growth can be an indication of increasing market share, expanding customer base, or successful product/service offerings. Earnings growth, on the other hand, reflects the company's ability to generate profits and efficiently convert revenue into earnings. Consistent and accelerating growth rates may indicate a company's ability to sustain its growth trajectory.

Analyzing Profitability Metrics:

Profitability metrics provide insights into a company's ability to generate profits from its operations. Key metrics to evaluate include profit margins and return on equity (ROE). Profit margins, such as gross margin and net margin, measure the company's efficiency in controlling costs and pricing its products/services. A company with improving or above-average profit margins may indicate competitive advantages or effective cost management.

Return on equity (ROE) measures how effectively a company utilizes shareholder equity to generate profits. A higher ROE suggests that the company is efficient in utilizing its resources and generating returns for shareholders. Compare the company's ROE to industry benchmarks to assess its relative performance.

Evaluating the Company's Ability to Generate and Reinvest Cash Flows:

Cash flow analysis is essential to understand a company's ability to generate cash from its operations. Evaluate the company's operating cash flow, free cash flow, and cash flow growth rates. Positive and growing cash flows indicate the company's ability to fund its growth initiatives, invest in research and development, make strategic acquisitions, or return capital to shareholders through dividends or share buybacks.

Assess the company's cash flow reinvestment strategies to support future growth. Look for evidence of prudent capital allocation, such as investments in research and development, expanding production capacity, or entering new markets. Companies that generate and reinvest cash flows effectively have a higher likelihood of sustaining their growth and creating long-term shareholder value.

Remember to compare these growth and profitability metrics with industry peers and consider the company's growth prospects, competitive advantage, and industry trends. It's essential to conduct thorough research and analysis to gain a comprehensive understanding of the company's growth potential.

18.5 Evaluating Management and Leadership:

Assessing the Quality and Competence of the Company's Management Team:

The management team plays a crucial role in driving a company's growth and executing its strategies. To assess the quality and competence of the management team, consider the following factors:

Track Record and Experience: Evaluate the management team's track record of successfully executing growth strategies and achieving stated objectives. Look for experienced leaders with a proven history of delivering results and navigating challenges.

Strategic Vision and Leadership: Assess the management team's strategic vision and their ability to articulate and execute a clear growth strategy. Look for leaders who demonstrate strong leadership skills, effective decision-making, and the ability to inspire and motivate employees.

Industry Knowledge and Expertise: Evaluate whether the management team has deep knowledge and expertise in the company's industry. Industry-specific experience can help the management team identify growth opportunities, make informed decisions, and stay ahead of market trends and changes.

Communication and Transparency: Consider the management team's communication style and transparency in providing information to shareholders and stakeholders. Transparent and open communication is essential for building trust and maintaining investor confidence.

Analyzing the Company's Track Record of Executing Growth Strategies:

Examine the company's historical performance and track record of executing its growth strategies. Look for evidence of successful product launches, market expansion, revenue growth, and market share gains. Evaluate whether the company has consistently achieved its growth targets and demonstrated a track record of delivering on its promises.

Consider the company's ability to adapt to changing market conditions and navigate challenges. Assess how well the company has managed through economic downturns or industry disruptions in the past. A strong track record of executing growth strategies, even in challenging environments, can provide confidence in the company's ability to sustain its growth in the future.

Considering the Company's Vision and Ability to Adapt to Changing Market Conditions:

Evaluate the company's long-term vision and its alignment with industry trends and market dynamics. Assess whether the company has a clear understanding of emerging opportunities and challenges within its industry and whether its growth strategies are adaptable to changing market conditions.

Consider the company's agility and ability to innovate. Companies that can adapt to evolving customer preferences, technological advancements, and regulatory changes are better positioned for long-term growth. Look for evidence of a culture of innovation, investments in research and development, and the ability to capitalize on emerging trends.

In summary, assessing the quality of the management team, analyzing the company's track record of executing growth strategies, and considering its vision and adaptability are essential steps in evaluating a company's growth potential. Comprehensive research and analysis, including reviewing financial statements, listening to management presentations, and analyzing industry trends, can provide valuable insights into a company's growth prospects.

18.6 Market Share and Competitive Landscape:

Evaluating a Company's Market Share and Potential for Expansion:

Market Share: Assess the company's current market share within its industry or specific market segment. Compare its market share to competitors and analyze any trends or changes in market share over time. A growing or dominant market share can indicate the company's ability to capture a larger portion of the market.

Market Size and Growth Potential: Evaluate the size of the total addressable market (TAM) and the company's market penetration. Consider the growth potential of the market and assess the company's ability to expand its market share in a sustainable manner.

Competitive Positioning: Analyze the competitive landscape and the company's position relative to its competitors. Consider factors such as pricing power, product differentiation, customer loyalty, and distribution networks. A strong competitive position can support the company's market share growth and potential for expansion.

Assessing the Company's Competitive Advantages and Barriers to Entry:

Unique Products or Services: Evaluate whether the company offers unique or differentiated products or services that set it apart from competitors. Consider the company's intellectual property, patents, proprietary technology, or exclusive licenses that provide a competitive advantage.

Brand Strength: Assess the strength of the company's brand and its ability to command customer loyalty and premium pricing. A strong brand can act as a barrier to entry for new competitors and support the company's market position.

Cost Advantages: Evaluate whether the company has cost advantages over competitors, such as economies of scale, efficient operations, or access to key resources. Cost advantages can help the company maintain profitability and compete effectively in the market.

Monitoring Competitive Pressures and Industry Disruptors:

Competitive Analysis: Regularly monitor the competitive landscape and assess the strategies and actions of key competitors. Identify any competitive threats or changes in the competitive dynamics that could impact the company's market share and growth prospects.

Industry Disruptors: Stay informed about emerging technologies, trends, and disruptive business models that could impact the industry. Assess whether the company is positioned to adapt and capitalize on these changes or if it faces risks of being disrupted.

Customer Preferences and Changing Needs: Understand the evolving needs and preferences of customers within the industry. Monitor consumer trends and assess whether the company is meeting changing customer demands or if it needs to adapt its products, services, or business model.

Regularly reviewing and monitoring these factors will help you stay informed about the company's market share, competitive advantages, and potential risks. It will also enable you to identify opportunities for expansion and assess the company's ability to navigate competitive pressures and industry disruptors.

18.7 Technological Innovations and Disruptions:

Identifying Companies at the Forefront of Technological Advancements:

Industry Research: Conduct research and analysis of specific industries known for technological advancements, such as technology, healthcare, renewable energy, or artificial intelligence. Identify companies within these industries that are recognized as leaders or innovators.

News and Publications: Stay updated with industry news, trade publications, and technology-focused websites to identify companies that are consistently mentioned as pioneers or frontrunners in technological advancements.

Innovation Awards and Recognitions: Pay attention to industry awards and recognitions that highlight companies at the forefront of technological advancements. These awards often indicate the company's commitment to innovation and the impact of its technologies.

Assessing the Potential Impact of Disruptive Technologies on Industries:

Industry Analysis: Conduct a thorough analysis of the industry and identify the key technologies or trends that have the potential to disrupt the traditional business models or practices. This could include technologies such as blockchain, Internet of Things (IoT), cloud computing, or automation.

Market Research and Reports: Refer to market research reports and forecasts that focus on the impact of disruptive technologies on specific industries. These reports often provide insights into the potential growth and adoption of new technologies and the companies driving the change.

Expert Opinions and Thought Leaders: Follow industry experts, thought leaders, and analysts who specialize in disruptive technologies. They often provide valuable insights and predictions on how specific technologies will transform industries and which companies are leading the way.

Monitoring the Company's Research and Development Efforts:

Annual Reports and Financial Filings: Review the company's annual reports and financial filings to gain insights into its research and development (R&D) expenditures. Companies that invest significantly in R&D demonstrate their commitment to innovation and technological advancements.

Patent Filings: Monitor the company's patent filings and intellectual property portfolio. A strong patent portfolio indicates the company's investment in developing new technologies and protects its innovations from competitors.

Partnerships and Collaborations: Keep track of the company's partnerships and collaborations with research institutions, universities, or other technology-focused companies. These partnerships can provide access to cutting-edge research and development capabilities.

By identifying companies at the forefront of technological advancements, assessing the potential impact of disruptive technologies on industries, and monitoring the company's research and development efforts, you can gain insights into the company's innovation capabilities and its potential to lead in the future. It is important to conduct thorough research and analysis to make informed investment decisions.

18.8 Growth Metrics and Valuation:

Analyzing Growth Metrics:

Price-to-Earnings Growth (PEG) Ratio: The PEG ratio combines the company's price-to-earnings (P/E) ratio with its projected earnings growth rate. A PEG ratio below 1 is often considered favorable, indicating that the stock may be undervalued relative to its growth potential. However, it's important to consider other factors alongside the PEG ratio to gain a comprehensive understanding of the company's growth prospects.

Price-to-Sales (P/S) Ratio: The P/S ratio compares the company's market capitalization to its total sales or revenue. A lower P/S ratio may suggest that the stock is undervalued relative to its sales. However, it's important to consider profitability and industry-specific factors when interpreting the P/S ratio.

Comparing Valuation Multiples to Industry Peers:

Relative Valuation: Compare the company's valuation multiples (such as P/E ratio, P/S ratio, or price-to-book ratio) to those of its industry peers. If the company's valuation multiples are significantly higher or lower than its peers, it may indicate an overvalued or undervalued stock.

Growth Premium: Consider whether the company's valuation multiples are justified by its superior growth prospects compared to industry peers. If the company has a higher growth rate, it may command a higher valuation multiple.

Balancing Growth Potential with Valuation Levels:

Consider the Growth Potential: Assess the company's growth potential based on factors such as market demand, industry outlook, competitive advantage, and the company's ability to execute its growth strategies. High-growth companies may warrant a higher valuation.

Evaluate Valuation Levels: Evaluate the company's valuation multiples in relation to its historical valuation levels and industry norms. If the valuation multiples are significantly above historical averages or industry norms, it may indicate an overvalued stock.

Growth at a Reasonable Price (GARP) Approach: Consider adopting a GARP approach that combines elements of both growth and value investing. Look for companies with strong growth prospects but reasonable valuation levels, striking a balance between growth potential and valuation.

By analyzing growth metrics, comparing valuation multiples to industry peers, and balancing growth potential with reasonable valuation levels, you can make more informed investment decisions in growth stocks. However, it's important to conduct thorough research and consider other factors, such as industry trends, competitive landscape, and company-specific risks, to gain a holistic view of the investment opportunity.

18.9 Risk Management and Portfolio Diversification:

Managing Risk through Proper Position Sizing and Portfolio Diversification:

Position Sizing: Determine the appropriate allocation of capital to individual growth stocks based on your risk tolerance and portfolio objectives. Avoid overconcentration in a single stock, and consider diversifying your investments across multiple growth stocks.

Portfolio Diversification: Spread your investments across different sectors and industries to reduce the impact of any adverse events affecting a particular sector. Diversification helps to mitigate the risk of a single stock or sector negatively impacting your entire portfolio.

Assessing Potential Risks Associated with Growth Investing:

Sector-Specific Risks: Growth investing often involves investing in specific sectors or industries that are expected to experience above-average growth. Be aware of the risks associated with these sectors, such as regulatory changes, technological disruptions, or changes in consumer preferences. Conduct thorough research and stay updated on sector-specific developments.

Market Volatility: Growth stocks can be more susceptible to market volatility and price fluctuations. The rapid growth expectations may result in higher valuation levels, making the stocks more sensitive to changes in market sentiment. Be prepared for market volatility and ensure your risk management strategies, such as stop-loss orders and proper position sizing, are in place.

Company-Specific Risks: Each growth stock carries its own set of company-specific risks. Evaluate factors such as management competence, competitive pressures, financial health, and potential disruptions that may impact the company's growth trajectory. Conduct thorough fundamental analysis and monitor company-specific news and events.

Valuation Risk: Growth stocks are often priced with high expectations for future growth, which can lead to elevated valuation levels. If the company fails to meet growth expectations or faces competitive challenges, the stock's valuation may decline. Assess the company's valuation relative to its growth potential and industry peers to mitigate valuation risk.

Remember, growth investing can offer significant opportunities for capital appreciation, but it also carries inherent risks. By effectively managing risk through proper position sizing, portfolio diversification, and assessing potential risks associated with growth investing, you can enhance the risk-return profile of your investment portfolio. It is crucial to conduct thorough research, stay informed about market and industry developments, and regularly review and adjust your portfolio as needed.

18.10 Monitoring and Adjusting Growth Investments:

Staying Updated with Company News, Earnings Reports, and Industry Trends:

Company News: Stay updated with the latest news and announcements from the companies in your portfolio. This includes press releases, regulatory filings, and news articles that provide insights into the company's operations, partnerships, product launches, or any other significant developments.

Earnings Reports: Monitor the company's quarterly and annual earnings reports. These reports provide information on revenue growth, earnings growth, and other financial metrics. Pay attention to key performance indicators such as revenue, net income, gross margins, and operating margins. Compare the reported results to analysts' expectations and previous periods to assess the company's performance.

Industry Trends: Keep an eye on industry trends and dynamics that may impact the growth prospects of the company. Stay informed about emerging technologies, regulatory changes, consumer behavior shifts, and competitive landscape developments within the industry. This information can help you assess the company's competitive position and growth potential.

Monitoring Key Performance Indicators and Growth Targets:

Key Performance Indicators (KPIs): Identify the key metrics that drive the growth of the company and monitor them regularly. These may include metrics such as customer acquisition rate, revenue per user, conversion rates, or any other metrics specific to the company's business model. Tracking these KPIs will provide insights into the company's growth trajectory and help you evaluate its progress.

Growth Targets: Understand the company's stated growth targets and milestones. These targets may include revenue growth targets, market share expansion goals, or product development milestones. Regularly assess the company's progress in achieving these targets and evaluate whether it is on track to meet its growth expectations.

Making Adjustments to the Portfolio Based on Changes in the Company's Growth Trajectory:

Reassess Growth Prospects: If there are significant changes in the company's growth prospects, reevaluate your investment thesis and assess whether the company's future growth potential aligns with your investment goals. If the growth prospects have deteriorated significantly, consider reducing or exiting your position.

Portfolio Rebalancing: Regularly review your portfolio and rebalance it to maintain your desired allocation. If a company's growth prospects have improved and it becomes a larger portion of your portfolio than desired, consider trimming the position to rebalance your portfolio across different stocks or sectors.

Risk Management: Continuously assess the risks associated with individual stocks and the overall portfolio. Implement risk management techniques such as setting stop-loss orders or using trailing stop orders to protect against downside risks. Consider diversifying your portfolio across different growth stocks and sectors to mitigate concentration risk.

Remember that staying updated with company news, monitoring key performance indicators, and making adjustments to your portfolio based on changes in the company's growth trajectory require active engagement as an investor. Regularly review your investment thesis, stay informed about market and industry developments, and make informed decisions based on the available information.

Chapter 19: Trading Psychology: Mastering Emotions and Discipline

Introduction: In Chapter 19, we will delve into the critical aspect of trading psychology. Successful trading goes beyond technical analysis and strategies—it requires the ability to master emotions, maintain discipline, and make rational decisions. This chapter will explore the psychological factors that influence trading outcomes and provide techniques to enhance emotional control and discipline in your trading activities.

19.1 The Role of Psychology in Trading:

UNDERSTANDING THE IMPACT of Emotions on Trading Decisions:

Emotions play a significant role in trading decisions and can impact investment outcomes. Some common emotions experienced by traders include fear, greed, excitement, and frustration. These emotions can influence decision-making and lead to irrational behavior, such as impulsive trading or holding onto losing positions for too long.

Fear and Greed: Fear and greed are powerful emotions that can cloud judgment. Fear can lead to selling prematurely or avoiding potentially profitable trades, while greed can drive excessive risk-taking and failure to take profits at appropriate levels.

Overconfidence: Overconfidence can lead to taking on excessive risk or neglecting thorough analysis. Traders may become overconfident after a series of successful trades, leading to complacency and poor risk management.

Loss Aversion: Loss aversion refers to the tendency to strongly prefer avoiding losses over acquiring gains. Traders may hold onto losing positions in the hope of a rebound, leading to further losses instead of cutting their losses.

Confirmation Bias: Confirmation bias is the tendency to seek out information that confirms existing beliefs while disregarding contradictory information. Traders may only focus on information that supports their trading decisions, ignoring warning signs or alternative perspectives.

Recognizing Common Psychological Biases:

Anchoring Bias: Anchoring bias occurs when traders rely too heavily on one piece of information or a reference point when making decisions. They may anchor their decisions to a specific price or event, ignoring other relevant information.

Availability Bias: Availability bias is the tendency to rely on readily available information or recent experiences when making decisions. Traders may place excessive weight on recent market events without considering the broader context.

Herd Mentality: Herd mentality refers to the tendency to follow the crowd or popular opinion, even if it goes against rational analysis. Traders may feel compelled to join in on market trends or follow the actions of other traders without independent assessment.

Recognizing the Importance of Self-Awareness in Trading Psychology:

Self-awareness is crucial in trading psychology as it helps traders recognize and manage their emotions, biases, and behavior. By being self-aware, traders can:

Identify Emotional Triggers: Recognize the emotions that arise during trading and identify the triggers that lead to these emotions. This awareness allows for better self-regulation and decision-making.

Manage Impulsive Behavior: Being aware of impulsive tendencies helps traders pause and assess their decisions before acting on them. This can prevent impulsive trades driven by emotions or biased thinking.

Challenge Biases: Self-awareness allows traders to question their beliefs and challenge biases. By actively seeking alternative perspectives and being open to different viewpoints, traders can make more informed decisions.

Practice Discipline: Self-awareness helps traders establish and maintain discipline in their trading approach. It enables them to stick to their trading plan, follow risk management strategies, and avoid impulsive actions.

Developing self-awareness requires reflection, continuous learning, and keeping a trading journal to track emotions, biases, and decision-making processes. It is an ongoing process that allows traders to improve their psychological resilience and make more rational and objective trading decisions.

19.2 Emotional Intelligence in Trading:

Developing Emotional Intelligence for Effective Trading:

Self-Awareness: Emotional intelligence begins with self-awareness. Take the time to understand your emotions, how they influence your trading decisions, and the impact they have on your performance. Monitor your thoughts, feelings, and reactions during trading activities.

Identify Emotional Triggers: Recognize the specific situations, events, or market conditions that trigger certain emotions. This awareness will help you anticipate and manage those emotions more effectively. For example, if you tend to get fearful during volatile market periods, you can develop strategies to mitigate that fear.

Emotional Regulation: Once you are aware of your emotions, focus on regulating them. This involves techniques such as deep breathing exercises, meditation, or taking breaks to calm yourself during intense trading moments. Developing emotional regulation skills can help you make more rational and objective decisions.

Cognitive Restructuring: Challenge and reframe your negative or irrational thoughts that arise during trading. Replace them with more positive and realistic thoughts. For example, if you feel overwhelmed by losses, remind yourself that losses are a normal part of trading and that you can learn from them.

Practice Mindfulness: Cultivate mindfulness during trading by staying present in the moment and focusing on the current market conditions. Mindfulness can help you avoid impulsive reactions and make more deliberate decisions based on objective analysis.

Develop Patience: Patience is a crucial trait in trading. Understand that success in trading often requires waiting for the right opportunities and allowing trades to play out over time. Avoid rushing into trades based on impatience or fear of missing out (FOMO).

Build Resilience: Recognize that losses and setbacks are part of trading. Develop resilience by viewing losses as learning opportunities and maintaining a long-term perspective. Resilient traders bounce back from losses and remain focused on their overall trading strategy.

Seek Support and Feedback: Surround yourself with a supportive trading community or seek the guidance of a mentor. Engage in discussions, share experiences, and learn from others who have successfully managed their emotions in trading.

Remember, emotional intelligence is a skill that takes time and practice to develop. Be patient with yourself and continuously work on improving your emotional awareness and regulation. By cultivating emotional intelligence, you can enhance your trading performance and make more rational and disciplined decisions in the face of market fluctuations.

19.3 Overcoming Psychological Biases:

Recognizing Cognitive Biases in Trading:

Confirmation Bias: This bias occurs when traders seek out information that confirms their existing beliefs or opinions and ignore or downplay information that contradicts them. To mitigate confirmation bias, actively seek out different perspectives and challenge your own assumptions. Consider alternative scenarios and weigh evidence objectively before making trading decisions.

Herd Mentality: Herd mentality refers to the tendency to follow the crowd and make decisions based on the actions or opinions of others, rather than independent analysis. Be aware of the influence of the crowd and avoid blindly following the herd. Conduct your own research, analyze the data, and make decisions based on your own analysis and trading strategy.

Overconfidence Bias: Overconfidence bias leads traders to overestimate their abilities and underestimate risks. It can result in excessive risk-taking and poor decision-making. To mitigate overconfidence bias, maintain humility and constantly reassess your trading strategies and assumptions. Keep a trading journal to review and learn from past mistakes and successes.

Loss Aversion Bias: Loss aversion bias refers to the tendency to feel the pain of losses more intensely than the pleasure of gains. It can lead to holding on to losing trades for too long or exiting winning trades too early. Recognize the bias and set clear risk management rules, such as predetermined stop-loss levels, to limit potential losses and avoid making emotionally-driven decisions.

Anchoring Bias: Anchoring bias occurs when traders rely too heavily on a specific piece of information, such as an initial purchase price or a price target, and fail to adjust their views based on new information. Avoid anchoring bias by regularly reassessing your investment thesis and considering new market developments that may impact the value of your investments.

Applying Critical Thinking and Rational Analysis in Trading:

Objective Analysis: Base your trading decisions on objective analysis rather than emotions or biases. Use a systematic approach, such as technical analysis, fundamental analysis, or a combination of both, to evaluate investment opportunities.

Data-driven Decision Making: Rely on reliable and accurate data to inform your trading decisions. Utilize financial statements, economic indicators, market trends, and other relevant data points to gain a comprehensive understanding of the investment landscape.

Due Diligence: Conduct thorough research and due diligence on potential investments. Consider factors such as the company's financial health, competitive position, industry trends, and management team. Seek out credible sources of information and cross-validate findings to ensure accuracy.

Critical Assessment: Engage in critical thinking by questioning assumptions, evaluating risks, and considering alternative viewpoints. Challenge your own analysis and seek out potential flaws or weaknesses in your investment thesis. Actively seek feedback and diverse perspectives to refine your analysis.

Risk Management: Incorporate risk management techniques, such as setting stop-loss orders and diversifying your portfolio, to protect against potential losses. Apply rational analysis to assess the risk-reward profile of each trade and make informed decisions based on the potential outcomes.

By being aware of cognitive biases, applying critical thinking, and conducting rational analysis, you can make more informed and objective trading decisions. Regularly review and update your strategies and be open to adjusting your views based on new information. Developing a disciplined and analytical approach will help mitigate the impact of biases and enhance your trading performance.

19.4 Creating a Trading Plan and Sticking to It:

Developing a Well-Defined Trading Plan:

Clear Objectives: Define your trading objectives, whether they are focused on capital appreciation, income generation, or a combination of both. Set specific and measurable goals that align with your overall financial objectives.

Strategies and Methods: Identify the trading strategies and methods you will use to achieve your objectives. This may include technical analysis, fundamental analysis, or a combination of both. Determine the timeframes you will trade (short-term, medium-term, or long-term) and the types of assets you will focus on.

Risk Tolerance: Assess your risk tolerance and establish guidelines for managing risk. Determine the maximum amount of capital you are willing to risk on each trade and set stop-loss orders to limit potential losses. Consider your risk appetite and ability to withstand market fluctuations.

Realistic Expectations: Set realistic expectations for your trading outcomes. Understand that trading involves both profits and losses, and it is important to have a long-term perspective. Avoid setting overly ambitious or unrealistic profit targets that may lead to excessive risk-taking.

Trade Management: Define your trade management rules, including entry and exit criteria. Determine the specific conditions or indicators that will trigger a trade entry or exit. This helps maintain discipline and reduces the likelihood of impulsive actions based on emotions or short-term market fluctuations.

Consistency and Discipline: Follow your trading plan consistently and avoid deviating from it based on impulsive actions or emotional reactions. Stick to your predefined strategies, risk management rules, and trade management guidelines. Regularly review and assess your trading plan, making adjustments only after careful consideration.

Record-Keeping and Evaluation: Maintain a trading journal to track your trades, including entry and exit points, reasons for the trade, and outcomes. Evaluate the performance of your trades and review your trading plan regularly to identify strengths, weaknesses, and areas for improvement.

By developing a well-defined trading plan, setting realistic expectations, and following it consistently, you can reduce the impact of emotional biases and impulsive actions. A disciplined approach will help you make more rational decisions based on your predetermined strategies and risk tolerance. Regularly review and refine your trading plan to adapt to changing market conditions and improve your trading performance over time.

19.5 Managing Risk and Money:

Implementing Proper Risk Management Techniques in Trading:

Determine Risk Tolerance: Assess your risk tolerance by considering factors such as your financial goals, investment experience, and emotional capacity to handle losses. This will help you establish the level of risk you are comfortable with in your trading activities.

Position Sizing: Determine the appropriate position size for each trade based on your risk tolerance. This involves considering factors such as the amount of capital you are willing to risk on a single trade and the potential loss you can tolerate. A common rule of thumb is to limit your risk per trade to a certain percentage of your overall trading capital, such as 1-2%.

Stop Loss Orders: Implement stop loss orders for each trade to limit potential losses. A stop loss order is an instruction to sell a security if it reaches a specific price level, protecting you from further losses. Set your stop loss level based on technical analysis, support and resistance levels, or other relevant indicators.

Profit Targets: Set profit targets for each trade to secure your gains and exit the trade at a predetermined price. This helps you lock in profits and avoid holding onto positions for too long, potentially exposing yourself to increased risk. Determine your profit targets based on technical analysis, price patterns, or profit-taking strategies.

Trailing Stop Loss: Consider using a trailing stop loss order, which adjusts your stop loss level as the price of the security moves in your favor. This allows you to capture profits while still protecting yourself from significant reversals. Trailing stops can help you maximize gains during trending markets.

Risk-Reward Ratio: Evaluate the risk-reward ratio for each trade. Aim for trades where the potential reward is significantly greater than the potential risk. This ensures that your winning trades can offset any potential losses, providing a positive overall expectancy.

Diversification: Diversify your portfolio across different assets, sectors, or markets to spread out your risk. This reduces the impact of individual trade losses and helps protect your capital from excessive exposure to any single asset or market.

Regular Monitoring and Adjustments: Monitor your trades regularly and make adjustments as needed. If a trade is not going as expected or if market conditions change, be prepared to exit the trade early or adjust your stop loss and profit targets accordingly.

Risk Management Tools: Utilize risk management tools provided by your trading platform, such as limit orders and conditional orders, to automate your risk management process. These tools can help you execute trades according to your predetermined risk management plan.

By implementing proper risk management techniques, such as setting appropriate position sizes, using stop loss orders and profit targets, and regularly monitoring your trades, you can control your risk exposure and protect your trading capital. Remember that risk management is an essential aspect of trading and should be prioritized to ensure long-term success.

19.6 Dealing with Losses and Drawdowns:

Developing a Healthy Mindset towards Losses and Drawdowns:

Accept Losses as Part of the Game: Understand that losses are inevitable in trading and are a natural part of the process. Accepting this fact from the beginning can help you develop a healthier mindset towards losses.

Learn from Mistakes: Treat losses as learning opportunities. Analyze your losing trades to identify any mistakes or errors in your analysis or execution. Use this feedback to improve your trading strategy and decision-making process.

Maintain Discipline and Emotional Control: Emotional control is crucial when facing losses or drawdowns. Avoid making impulsive decisions driven by frustration or disappointment. Stick to your trading plan and avoid revenge trading, which involves trying to recoup losses quickly by taking high-risk trades.

Focus on Process over Outcome: Instead of focusing solely on the outcome of each individual trade, shift your focus to the process and execution of your trading strategy. Evaluate your trades based on how well you followed your plan, rather than solely on whether they were winners or losers.

Keep a Trading Journal: Maintain a trading journal to document your trades, including the reasons behind each trade and your emotions during the process. Reviewing your journal can provide valuable insights into your trading patterns, strengths, and areas for improvement.

Seek Continuous Learning: Embrace a growth mindset and prioritize continuous learning in trading. Read trading books, attend webinars or seminars, and follow reputable trading sources to expand your knowledge and improve your skills. This continuous learning mindset can help you handle losses more effectively.

Utilize Support Networks: Connect with fellow traders, join trading communities, or find a mentor who can provide guidance and support during challenging times. Sharing experiences and insights with like-minded individuals can help you navigate through losses and drawdowns.

Stick to Your Trading Plan: During challenging periods, it's important to stick to your trading plan and resist the urge to deviate from it based on short-term market fluctuations or emotions. Trust the process and the strategies you have developed, and avoid making impulsive decisions that can further exacerbate losses.

Remember that losses are a normal part of trading, and maintaining a healthy mindset towards them is crucial for long-term success. Learn from your mistakes, remain disciplined, and focus on continuous improvement to become a more resilient and successful trader.

19.7 Patience and Discipline in Trading:

Cultivating Patience and Avoiding Impulsive Trading Decisions:

Stick to Your Trading Plan: Develop a well-defined trading plan that outlines your entry and exit strategies, risk management rules, and overall trading approach. When you have a clear plan in place, it becomes easier to stay patient and avoid impulsive trading decisions.

Set Realistic Expectations: Understand that successful trading is a long-term endeavor and that consistent profits take time. Set realistic expectations for your trades and avoid chasing quick gains. Patience is crucial for allowing your trades to play out according to your plan.

Avoid Overtrading: Overtrading is a common pitfall that can lead to impulsive and emotional decision-making. Stick to your predefined trading strategy and avoid entering trades outside of your plan. Be selective and focus on high-quality setups that meet your criteria.

Manage Your Emotions: Emotions can cloud judgment and lead to impulsive decisions. Learn to recognize when emotions like fear, greed, or FOMO (Fear of Missing Out) are influencing your trading decisions. Take a step back, reassess the situation, and make rational decisions based on your trading plan.

Practice Discipline in Execution: Discipline is key in executing your trades. Follow your predefined entry and exit points, and avoid making impulsive changes to your trades based on short-term market fluctuations. Stick to your predetermined stop loss and profit targets.

Avoid FOMO (Fear of Missing Out): FOMO can lead to impulsive trading decisions driven by the fear of missing out on potential gains. Stay focused on your trading plan and avoid jumping into trades solely because you fear missing an opportunity. Remember that there will always be new opportunities in the market.

Stay Focused and Minimize Distractions: During trading hours, create an environment that allows you to stay focused on the task at hand. Minimize distractions, turn off unnecessary notifications, and allocate dedicated time and space for trading. Avoid multitasking and concentrate on analyzing the market and executing your trades.

Practice Mindfulness and Self-Awareness: Develop mindfulness and self-awareness to better understand your thoughts, emotions, and impulses while trading. Take regular breaks to clear your mind and regain focus. Being aware of your emotions and thought patterns can help you make more rational and disciplined trading decisions.

Cultivating patience and avoiding impulsive trading decisions is a skill that takes time and practice. By following your trading plan, managing your emotions, and staying focused, you can develop the discipline necessary to make informed and patient trading decisions that align with your long-term goals.

19.8 Managing Trading Stress:

RECOGNIZING AND MANAGING Stress and Anxiety Associated with Trading:

Awareness: Recognize when stress and anxiety are affecting your trading performance. Pay attention to physical and emotional signs of stress, such as increased heart rate, tension, or negative thoughts. Awareness is the first step in effectively managing stress.

Stress-Reducing Techniques: Incorporate stress-reducing techniques into your daily routine. Practices like meditation, deep breathing exercises, and mindfulness can help calm your mind, reduce anxiety, and improve focus. Regular exercise, such as yoga or aerobic activities, can also help alleviate stress and promote overall well-being.

Balance and Self-Care: Prioritize self-care and maintain a healthy work-life balance. Engage in activities that bring you joy and relaxation outside of trading, such as spending time with loved ones, pursuing hobbies, or engaging in leisure activities. Taking breaks and allowing yourself time to recharge can help reduce stress and improve mental resilience.

Set Realistic Goals: Set realistic trading goals and avoid putting excessive pressure on yourself. Focus on the process of trading rather than solely on the outcome. Celebrate small wins and recognize that losses are part of the learning process. By setting achievable goals, you can reduce the stress associated with unrealistic expectations.

Seek Support: Connect with other traders or join trading communities to share experiences and seek support. Talking to like-minded individuals who understand the challenges of trading can provide valuable insights and emotional support. Consider working with a trading coach or therapist specializing in trading psychology if needed.

Manage Risk: Implement sound risk management techniques to minimize the potential impact of trading losses on your overall well-being. Use appropriate position sizing, set stop loss orders, and maintain a diversified portfolio to mitigate risk. Knowing that you have measures in place to protect your capital can help alleviate anxiety.

Continuous Learning: Continuously educate yourself about trading strategies, market dynamics, and trading psychology. The more knowledge and skills you acquire, the more confident and less anxious you may feel when making trading decisions. Learning can also help you adapt to changing market conditions and better manage risks.

Take Breaks and Disconnect: Give yourself regular breaks from trading and disconnect from the market during non-trading hours. Engage in activities that help you relax and recharge, such as reading, listening to music, or spending time in nature. Creating boundaries between trading and personal life can help reduce stress and maintain a healthy perspective.

Remember, managing stress and anxiety is a personal journey, and different techniques work for different individuals. Experiment with various stress-reducing techniques and find what works best for you. By prioritizing self-care and maintaining a balanced lifestyle, you can better manage stress and optimize your overall well-being as a trader.

19.9 Learning from Trading Experiences:

Engaging in Regular Self-Reflection and Evaluation of Trading Performance:

Keep a Trading Journal: Maintain a trading journal where you record your trades, including entry and exit points, reasons for the trade, and emotions experienced during the trade. Regularly review your journal to identify patterns, strengths, and weaknesses in your trading decisions.

Analyze Trade Data: Use trading platforms or specialized software to track and analyze your trade data. Look for patterns in winning and losing trades, identify common mistakes or missed opportunities, and assess the overall performance of your trading strategy.

Identify Areas for Improvement: Reflect on your trading performance and identify specific areas that need improvement. This could include decision-making processes, risk management techniques, or emotional control. Be honest with yourself and focus on areas where you can make meaningful changes.

Set Goals for Improvement: Based on your self-reflection and analysis, set specific and actionable goals for improvement. These goals could be related to refining your entry and exit strategies, developing better risk management techniques, or enhancing your trading discipline.

Seek Feedback: Seek feedback from experienced traders or mentors who can provide objective insights into your trading performance. Consider joining trading communities or forums where you can share experiences and learn from others. Be open to constructive criticism and use it as an opportunity for growth.

Embrace a Growth Mindset: Adopt a growth mindset that recognizes trading as a continuous learning journey. Embrace failures and losses as learning opportunities rather than as personal setbacks. View challenges as chances to develop new skills and improve your trading approach over time.

Continuous Learning: Dedicate time to continuous learning and staying updated with market trends, trading strategies, and psychological principles. Read books, attend webinars or seminars, and follow reputable sources of information in the trading community. Expand your knowledge base and be open to exploring new ideas and approaches.

Practice Consistency: Implement what you learn through deliberate practice and consistency. Avoid constantly changing your trading strategy or approach based on short-term outcomes. Instead, focus on implementing improvements over time and building a consistent and disciplined trading routine.

Remember, improving as a trader is an ongoing process. Embrace self-reflection, continuous learning, and a growth mindset to enhance your trading skills and performance over the long term. Be patient with yourself, stay committed to your goals, and celebrate your progress along the way.

19.10 Seeking Support and Accountability:

Building a Network of Like-Minded Traders:

Join Trading Communities: Look for trading communities or online forums where traders gather to discuss strategies, share insights, and support each other. Participate actively in these communities by asking questions, sharing your experiences, and engaging in meaningful discussions.

Attend Trading Conferences and Events: Attend trading conferences, seminars, or workshops where you can meet and connect with other traders. These events often offer opportunities for networking, learning from experienced traders, and gaining new perspectives on trading.

Join Trading Groups: Consider joining trading groups or investment clubs in your local area. These groups provide a platform for traders to meet regularly, exchange ideas, and share trading strategies. It's a great way to build relationships with like-minded individuals and learn from their experiences.

Utilize Social Media: Follow and engage with traders on social media platforms like Twitter, LinkedIn, and specialized trading communities. Many traders share their insights, analyses, and experiences on these platforms, providing valuable information and potential networking opportunities.

Engaging in Trading Communities or Groups:

Participate Actively: Actively participate in trading communities or groups by sharing your knowledge, asking questions, and contributing to discussions. Be respectful and considerate in your interactions, and always strive to add value to the community.

Learn from Others: Take advantage of the collective knowledge and experiences of other traders in the community. Learn from their successes and failures, and leverage their insights to enhance your own trading approach.

Share Your Experiences: Share your own experiences and lessons learned with the community. By sharing your journey, you can help others who may be facing similar challenges or seeking guidance.

Seeking Professional Guidance or Mentorship:

Find a Trading Mentor: Look for experienced traders who are willing to mentor you and provide guidance. A trading mentor can offer personalized advice, help you navigate challenges, and provide insights based on their own experiences.

Consider Professional Coaching: If you feel the need for more structured guidance, consider working with a professional trading coach. They can provide personalized coaching, help you develop a trading plan, and offer guidance on improving your trading psychology.

Join Trading Education Programs: Explore trading education programs or courses offered by reputable institutions or professional traders. These programs often provide comprehensive training and mentorship to help you improve your trading skills.

Remember, building a network of like-minded traders, engaging in trading communities, and seeking professional guidance can offer valuable support, knowledge sharing, and accountability in your trading journey. It's important to approach these interactions with an open mind, willingness to learn, and a genuine desire to contribute to the trading community.

Chapter 20: Advanced Trading Strategies: Scalping, Arbitrage, and Algorithmic Trading

Introduction: In Chapter 20, we will delve into advanced trading strategies that cater to different trading styles and utilize sophisticated techniques. These strategies—scalping, arbitrage, and algorithmic trading—offer opportunities for traders to capitalize on short-term price movements, exploit market inefficiencies, and leverage automation for efficient trading. This chapter will explore the principles, techniques, and considerations associated with these advanced trading strategies.

20.1 Scalping Strategy:

Scalping is a trading strategy that focuses on making multiple small profits from short-term price fluctuations. Traders who employ scalping, known as scalpers, aim to capitalize on small price movements within a short time frame, often holding positions for only a few seconds to a few minutes.

Objectives of Scalping:

Quick Profits: The primary objective of scalping is to generate quick and frequent profits by capturing small price movements.

High Trading Frequency: Scalpers execute a large number of trades within a trading session, aiming to accumulate small gains that can add up over time.

Minimize Exposure: Scalpers aim to minimize their exposure to the market by keeping positions open for a very short duration. This reduces the risk of price fluctuations and potential adverse market events.

Short-Term Nature of Scalping Trades: Scalping is characterized by its short-term trading horizon. Scalpers focus on capturing small price movements that occur within minutes or even seconds. They rely on technical analysis, such as chart patterns and indicators, to identify short-term price trends and entry/exit points.

Suitable Market Conditions and Instruments for Scalping:

High Liquidity: Scalping is most effective in highly liquid markets, such as major currency pairs in the forex market or heavily traded stocks in the equities market. High liquidity ensures that there are enough buyers and sellers to execute trades quickly at desired prices.

Volatility: Scalpers thrive in markets with sufficient volatility, as it provides opportunities for price fluctuations and quick profits. However, excessive volatility can also increase the risk of sudden price reversals, so it's important to assess volatility levels and adjust trading strategies accordingly.

Tight Spreads: Scalpers aim to capture small price differentials, so trading instruments with tight bid-ask spreads are preferred. Tight spreads minimize transaction costs and allow for more efficient execution of trades.

Shorter Time Frames: Scalping is typically done on shorter time frames, such as one-minute or five-minute charts. These time frames provide the necessary granularity to identify and capitalize on short-term price movements.

It's important to note that scalping requires advanced technical analysis skills, a disciplined approach, and the ability to make quick decisions. Scalpers must also have a reliable and fast trading platform to execute trades promptly. Due to the high-frequency nature of scalping, transaction costs, including spreads and commissions, should be carefully considered to ensure they do not erode profits.

20.2 Scalping Techniques and Tools:

Analyzing Price Action and Utilizing Technical Indicators for Scalping: Scalpers heavily rely on price action analysis and technical indicators to make quick trading decisions. They analyze short-term price movements, patterns, and trends to identify potential entry and exit points. Common technical indicators used in scalping include moving averages, oscillators (such as the Relative Strength Index or RSI), and Bollinger Bands. These indicators help scalpers gauge momentum, overbought or oversold conditions, and potential price reversals.

Implementing Rapid Trade Execution and Utilizing Low-Latency Trading Platforms: Scalping requires rapid trade execution to take advantage of short-term price movements. Scalpers often use low-latency trading platforms or direct market access (DMA) platforms that offer fast order execution and minimal delays. These platforms provide real-time market data, quick order routing, and instant trade confirmation, allowing scalpers to enter and exit trades swiftly.

Managing Risk through Proper Position Sizing and Stop Loss Orders: Risk management is crucial in scalping due to the short holding period of trades. Scalpers typically use tight stop loss orders to limit potential losses if the market moves against their positions. Stop loss orders are placed at a predetermined price level and automatically trigger a trade exit when that price is reached. Additionally, proper position sizing is essential to manage risk. Scalpers typically allocate a small percentage of their trading capital to each trade, ensuring that a single trade's potential loss is limited. This helps to protect the overall trading account from significant drawdowns.

Scalping requires discipline and adherence to the trading plan. It's important to establish clear rules for entry and exit points based on technical analysis and stick to them consistently. Scalpers should also be mindful of market conditions and news events that can increase volatility and impact trading strategies. Regular monitoring of trades and adjustments to stop loss levels or profit targets may be necessary to adapt to changing market conditions.

Lastly, it's worth noting that scalping is a highly active trading strategy that requires continuous attention and monitoring of the market. Traders considering scalping should have the necessary time and focus to devote to their trading activities.

20.3 Arbitrage Trading Strategy:

Arbitrage is a trading strategy that aims to exploit price discrepancies in different markets or instruments to make a profit with minimal risk. The concept of arbitrage is based on the principle of buying an asset at a lower price in one market and simultaneously selling it at a higher price in another market, taking advantage of the price differential.

There are different types of arbitrage strategies, including:

Risk Arbitrage: This type of arbitrage involves taking advantage of price discrepancies in situations such as mergers, acquisitions, or corporate events. Risk arbitrageurs seek to profit from the price difference between the current market price and the expected future price of a company's stock involved in the event. The goal is to capture the price convergence as the event progresses.

Statistical Arbitrage: Statistical arbitrage, also known as stat arb, involves exploiting short-term price discrepancies in correlated assets based on statistical models and quantitative analysis. Traders use historical data and mathematical models to identify relationships and patterns between different securities. They take positions that profit from the expected price convergence based on the statistical relationship.

Arbitrage opportunities can be identified in various markets and instruments, including:

Geographic Arbitrage: This involves taking advantage of price differences between different geographical markets. For example, if an asset is priced differently in two different countries due to factors such as exchange rate fluctuations or regulatory disparities, traders can profit by buying in the cheaper market and selling in the more expensive market.

Futures Arbitrage: Futures contracts are often priced based on the spot price of the underlying asset, interest rates, and other factors. Traders can exploit pricing discrepancies between the futures contract and the underlying asset by simultaneously buying or selling the futures contract and the underlying asset to capture the price difference.

Cryptocurrency Arbitrage: Given the decentralized and fragmented nature of cryptocurrency markets, price disparities can occur across different exchanges. Cryptocurrency arbitrage involves buying a cryptocurrency at a lower price on one exchange and selling it at a higher price on another exchange, taking advantage of the price difference.

It's important to note that arbitrage opportunities can be short-lived, as market participants quickly exploit them, leading to price convergence. To capitalize on arbitrage opportunities, traders need to act quickly, have access to multiple markets or platforms, and employ efficient trade execution.

Arbitrage strategies require careful monitoring of market conditions, precision in trade execution, and the ability to manage risks effectively. Additionally, some forms of arbitrage may require substantial capital, advanced trading infrastructure, and specialized knowledge in specific markets or instruments.

20.4 Arbitrage Techniques and Tools:

Analyzing price discrepancies and market inefficiencies is a crucial step in identifying arbitrage opportunities. Traders can use various techniques and tools to identify these discrepancies, such as monitoring real-time market data, comparing prices across different exchanges or platforms, and conducting statistical analysis.

Algorithmic tools and automated trading systems can be particularly useful in efficiently executing arbitrage trades. These tools can quickly identify price disparities, calculate the potential profit, and automatically execute trades at the optimal moment. By utilizing algorithms, traders can take advantage of fleeting arbitrage opportunities and eliminate the need for manual monitoring and execution.

Risk management is essential in arbitrage trading, as price discrepancies can quickly disappear, resulting in potential losses. Traders should carefully assess the risks associated with each arbitrage opportunity and implement appropriate risk management strategies. This may include setting stop-loss orders to limit potential losses, using position sizing techniques to manage exposure, and diversifying arbitrage trades across different markets and instruments.

Execution challenges can arise in arbitrage trading, especially when dealing with high-frequency trading or in markets with low liquidity. It's important to consider factors such as transaction costs, slippage, and the speed of trade execution. Traders should have access to reliable and efficient trading platforms or systems that can handle the required volume and execute trades swiftly.

Moreover, regulatory considerations and legal restrictions should also be taken into account when engaging in arbitrage trading. Different jurisdictions may have specific rules and regulations related to arbitrage activities, so it's crucial to understand and comply with the relevant laws.

Lastly, monitoring and staying updated with market conditions, news, and technological advancements are essential to effectively identify and capitalize on arbitrage opportunities. By staying informed, traders can adapt their strategies to changing market dynamics and adjust their arbitrage approach accordingly.

Overall, successful arbitrage trading requires a combination of analytical skills, efficient execution tools, risk management techniques, and continuous monitoring of market conditions.

20.5 Algorithmic Trading Strategy:

Algorithmic trading, also known as automated trading or algo trading, involves using computer algorithms to execute trading strategies. It utilizes predefined rules and mathematical models to automatically generate and execute trades, eliminating the need for manual intervention. Here are some principles and advantages of algorithmic trading:

Efficiency: Algorithmic trading allows for high-speed and precise trade execution, eliminating human delays and errors. It can execute trades at a much faster pace than manual trading, taking advantage of market opportunities that may be fleeting.

Backtesting and Optimization: Algorithms can be backtested using historical data to evaluate their performance and refine their parameters. This allows traders to test different strategies, optimize their settings, and assess the potential profitability of the algorithm before deploying it in live trading.

Increased Trading Volume: Algorithmic trading can handle large trade volumes, enabling traders to execute trades across multiple markets and instruments simultaneously. This scalability is particularly beneficial for institutional traders or those dealing with high-frequency trading.

Diversification: Algorithmic trading enables diversification across multiple strategies, markets, and timeframes. Traders can deploy different algorithms to capture various market conditions and reduce reliance on a single strategy or asset class.

Removing Emotional Bias: Algorithms follow predefined rules and execute trades based on objective criteria, eliminating the impact of emotional biases that often affect human traders. This can lead to more disciplined and consistent trading decisions.

Access to Advanced Trading Strategies: Algorithmic trading allows traders to implement complex trading strategies that may be challenging to execute manually. Strategies like trend following, mean reversion, statistical arbitrage, and pattern recognition can be effectively implemented using algorithms.

The role of technology and programming languages is critical in algorithmic trading. Traders often use programming languages such as Python, Java, or C++ to develop algorithms and create automated trading systems. These programming languages provide the flexibility and computational power required to process large amounts of data, implement trading strategies, and interface with trading platforms and APIs.

Technology infrastructure, including high-speed internet connections, reliable data feeds, and low-latency execution platforms, is essential for algorithmic trading. Traders rely on advanced hardware, co-location services, and direct market access (DMA) to ensure fast and efficient execution of trades.

In summary, algorithmic trading offers numerous advantages, including efficiency, scalability, backtesting capabilities, and the removal of emotional biases. It empowers traders to implement sophisticated strategies and execute trades with precision. However, it requires expertise in programming, risk management, and continuous monitoring to ensure optimal performance.

20.6 Developing Algorithmic Trading Systems:

Designing and implementing trading algorithms:

Define the Objective: Clearly define the objective of the trading algorithm, whether it's capturing short-term price movements, exploiting market inefficiencies, or executing specific trading strategies.

Identify Trading Rules: Determine the specific rules and conditions that will trigger trade entries and exits. This may involve technical indicators, price patterns, or fundamental factors. Consider the timeframes, markets, and instruments the algorithm will focus on.

Choose Programming Language and Platform: Select a suitable programming language (e.g., Python, C++, Java) and a trading platform or framework that supports algorithmic trading. Popular platforms include MetaTrader, NinjaTrader, and Interactive Brokers' API.

Code the Algorithm: Write the code that defines the trading algorithm based on the identified rules. Ensure that the code is clear, efficient, and follows best practices for algorithmic trading.

Test the Algorithm: Use historical data to backtest the algorithm. This involves running the algorithm on past market data to assess its performance and profitability. Identify strengths, weaknesses, and areas for improvement.

Backtesting and optimizing trading strategies:

Data Collection: Gather high-quality historical market data, including price, volume, and other relevant indicators. Ensure the data is accurate and covers a sufficient period to provide meaningful insights.

Define Performance Metrics: Determine the key performance metrics to evaluate the strategy, such as return on investment (ROI), drawdown, and Sharpe ratio. These metrics will help measure the strategy's profitability, risk, and consistency.

Backtesting Process: Apply the trading algorithm to historical data to simulate trades and track performance. Compare the algorithm's trades and signals with actual market conditions to assess its effectiveness.

Performance Analysis: Analyze the backtest results to evaluate the strategy's performance. Assess metrics like profitability, risk-adjusted returns, win/loss ratio, and maximum drawdown. Identify periods of outperformance or underperformance.

Optimization: Adjust the parameters or rules of the trading algorithm to optimize its performance. Use sensitivity analysis and parameter sweeps to find the best combination of parameters that maximize profitability and minimize risk.

Considering risk management and incorporating safeguards:

Position Sizing: Determine appropriate position sizes for each trade based on risk tolerance, account size, and the algorithm's risk-reward profile. Avoid overly large positions that could result in significant losses.

Stop Loss Orders: Incorporate stop loss orders to limit potential losses on each trade. Define a predetermined level at which the algorithm will exit a losing trade to protect against adverse market moves.

Risk Controls: Implement risk controls, such as maximum drawdown limits or risk-per-trade limits, to prevent excessive losses. Regularly monitor the algorithm's risk metrics and adjust risk controls if necessary.

Market Conditions: Consider incorporating filters or rules in the algorithm to adjust trading activity during volatile or illiquid market conditions. This helps mitigate the risks associated with unstable markets.

Regular Monitoring and Review: Continuously monitor the algorithm's performance and adapt as market conditions evolve. Regularly review risk management practices and adjust them if needed to ensure ongoing protection.

By designing and implementing trading algorithms, conducting thorough backtesting and optimization, and incorporating risk management practices, traders can increase the chances of developing robust and profitable algorithmic trading strategies while managing risk effectively.

20.7 High-Frequency Trading (HFT):

Understanding the concept and characteristics of high-frequency trading (HFT):

High-frequency trading refers to a trading strategy that relies on powerful computers, advanced algorithms, and high-speed data connections to execute a large number of trades within very short timeframes, often measured in milliseconds or microseconds. HFT aims to exploit small price discrepancies and market inefficiencies, often taking advantage of fleeting opportunities in the market. Characteristics of HFT include:

Speed: HFT relies on ultra-fast computer systems and high-speed data connections to enable rapid trade execution, often leveraging co-location services that position trading servers close to exchange servers to minimize latency.

Algorithmic Trading: HFT strategies are typically implemented through complex algorithms that automatically analyze market data, identify trading opportunities, and execute trades without human intervention.

High Trade Volumes: HFT involves executing a large number of trades, often leveraging the smallest price movements to generate profits. The strategy relies on the ability to quickly enter and exit positions to capitalize on these small price differentials.

Liquidity Provision: HFT firms often act as liquidity providers in the market, offering buy and sell orders to other market participants. By providing liquidity, HFT helps improve market efficiency and narrow bid-ask spreads.

Infrastructure and technology requirements for HFT:

Low-Latency Connectivity: HFT requires direct, low-latency connections to exchanges and trading venues to ensure fast and reliable data transmission and trade execution. Co-location services, high-speed data feeds, and advanced networking infrastructure are essential.

High-Performance Hardware: HFT firms invest in powerful computer systems with high-speed processors, low-latency memory, and efficient data storage to process large amounts of market data and execute trades with minimal delay.

Advanced Algorithms: HFT relies on sophisticated algorithms capable of processing vast amounts of market data, identifying patterns, and executing trades in microseconds. These algorithms often incorporate machine learning and statistical modeling techniques.

Risk Management Systems: Effective risk management is crucial in HFT due to the high-speed nature of trading and the potential for significant losses if risk controls are not in place. Risk management systems continuously monitor trades and market conditions to identify and mitigate risks.

Regulatory landscape and challenges associated with HFT:

Market Manipulation and Disruptive Trading: Regulators closely monitor HFT activities to ensure compliance with market integrity rules. HFT firms need to adhere to regulations related to market abuse, spoofing, front-running, and other manipulative practices.

Fairness and Equal Access: Regulators aim to ensure a level playing field for all market participants. HFT firms must comply with regulations that promote fair access to market data and trading opportunities, preventing unfair advantages for certain players.

Systemic Risk: The speed and interconnectedness of HFT can contribute to market volatility and pose systemic risks. Regulators monitor HFT activities to mitigate potential risks to the overall stability of the financial system.

Regulatory Compliance and Oversight: HFT firms must adhere to regulatory requirements, including registration, reporting, and disclosure obligations. Compliance with regulations such as MiFID II in Europe and Regulation Systems Compliance and Integrity (SCI) in the United States is crucial.

Technological Challenges: HFT requires substantial investments in technology infrastructure, data feeds, and connectivity. Firms need to stay ahead in terms of technological advancements and address challenges related to system reliability, cybersecurity, and data protection.

The regulatory landscape for HFT varies across jurisdictions, and regulations continue to evolve as regulators strive to balance market efficiency, fairness, and stability. HFT firms need to have a strong understanding of the regulatory framework and comply with the relevant rules and obligations to operate in the market.

20.8 Considerations for Advanced Trading Strategies:

Capital requirements and liquidity considerations for scalping, arbitrage, and algorithmic trading:

Scalping: Scalping typically involves executing a large number of trades within short timeframes to profit from small price differentials. Scalpers need to consider their capital requirements to maintain sufficient buying power for multiple trades. Since scalping relies on quick trade execution, it is important to have access to highly liquid markets to enter and exit positions efficiently without significant slippage.

Arbitrage: Arbitrage strategies aim to exploit price discrepancies between different markets or instruments. Successful arbitrage requires sufficient capital to take advantage of opportunities and cover transaction costs. Additionally, arbitrageurs need to consider liquidity in the markets they trade, as low liquidity can limit the ability to execute trades at desired prices.

Algorithmic Trading: Algorithmic trading strategies, including high-frequency trading, often require significant capital to support the necessary infrastructure, data feeds, and technology. High-speed connectivity and access to liquidity providers are crucial to execute trades efficiently. Liquidity considerations are particularly important for high-frequency traders to ensure they can enter and exit positions without adversely impacting prices.

Compliance with regulatory requirements and market rules:

All traders, including those involved in scalping, arbitrage, and algorithmic trading, need to comply with relevant regulatory requirements and market rules. It is essential to understand and adhere to regulations related to trade execution, market manipulation, reporting, and risk management. Traders must stay informed about changes in regulations and adapt their strategies and systems accordingly. Non-compliance with regulatory requirements can lead to penalties, legal issues, and reputational damage.

Monitoring and adjusting trading strategies to adapt to changing market conditions:

Traders engaged in scalping, arbitrage, and algorithmic trading must continuously monitor market conditions and adjust their strategies accordingly. Market dynamics, volatility, liquidity, and other factors can change rapidly, requiring traders to adapt their algorithms, risk management parameters, and execution tactics. Regular performance analysis and optimization based on historical data and real-time market feedback are crucial to maintain the effectiveness and profitability of trading strategies.

Market surveillance and risk management systems are essential for identifying anomalies, detecting potential errors or malfunctions, and managing risk exposures. Traders should have mechanisms in place to monitor their trading activities, assess the impact of changing market conditions, and implement necessary adjustments to improve performance and mitigate risks.

In summary, traders engaging in scalping, arbitrage, and algorithmic trading need to carefully consider capital requirements, liquidity conditions, compliance with regulatory requirements, and the ability to adapt strategies to changing market conditions. Proper risk management, technological infrastructure, and a deep understanding of the markets being traded are crucial for success in these trading approaches.

20.9 Risk Management and Controlling Drawdowns:

Implementing robust risk management techniques is essential for advanced trading strategies to protect capital and preserve long-term profitability. Here are some key risk management practices:

Setting appropriate risk-reward ratios: Determine the risk-reward ratio for each trade, which defines the potential loss relative to the potential gain. Establish a minimum acceptable risk-reward ratio that aligns with your trading strategy and risk tolerance. This helps ensure that potential profits outweigh potential losses and that you maintain a positive expectancy in the long run.

Position sizing rules: Determine the appropriate position size for each trade based on your risk tolerance and the specific trade setup. Consider factors such as account size, risk per trade, and stop loss placement. Adhering to consistent position sizing rules helps manage risk across different trades and prevents excessive exposure to any single trade.

Managing drawdowns: Drawdowns refer to the decline in equity from peak to trough during a trading period. Implement risk management techniques to limit drawdowns and preserve capital. For example, you can set a maximum allowable drawdown percentage and reduce position sizes or take a break from trading if the drawdown exceeds that threshold. Regularly review and analyze drawdowns to identify patterns, assess the effectiveness of your risk management techniques, and make necessary adjustments.

Avoiding excessive risk-taking: Maintain discipline and avoid taking on excessive risk, especially during periods of high market volatility or when emotions are running high. Stick to your predefined risk parameters and avoid making impulsive or emotionally-driven trading decisions. Be mindful of overleveraging or trading with position sizes that are too large relative to your account size, as this can amplify both gains and losses.

Diversification: Diversify your trading portfolio across different instruments, markets, or strategies. This helps spread risk and reduces the impact of any single trade or market event. Consider incorporating assets with low or negative correlations to further diversify your portfolio and reduce overall risk.

Regular monitoring and assessment: Continuously monitor your trading performance, assess risk exposure, and adjust risk management techniques as needed. Keep a trading journal to record trades, analyze their outcomes, and identify areas for improvement. Regularly review and evaluate your risk management practices to ensure they remain effective in different market conditions.

Remember, risk management is an ongoing process that requires discipline, self-awareness, and adaptability. By implementing robust risk management techniques, setting appropriate risk-reward ratios, managing drawdowns, and avoiding excessive risk-taking, you can enhance your chances of long-term success in advanced trading strategies.

20.10 Ethical and Legal Considerations:

Adhering to ethical standards and complying with applicable laws and regulations are crucial aspects of engaging in advanced trading strategies. Here are some considerations to keep in mind:

Market manipulation: It is important to avoid engaging in any form of market manipulation, which includes activities that create artificial or misleading market conditions. Manipulative practices such as spoofing, wash trading, or front-running are strictly prohibited and can lead to legal consequences. Maintain integrity in your trading activities by adhering to fair and transparent practices.

Insider trading: Avoid trading on material non-public information, as it is illegal and unethical. Insider trading involves trading securities based on material information that is not available to the general public. Stay informed about insider trading regulations and ensure compliance to maintain the integrity of your trading activities.

Compliance with regulations: Familiarize yourself with the regulatory framework governing advanced trading strategies in your jurisdiction. Regulations may vary depending on factors such as the type of trading, markets involved, and your location. Comply with reporting requirements, licensing obligations, and other legal obligations to operate within the confines of the law.

Market stability: Understand the potential impact of advanced trading strategies on market stability. Some advanced trading strategies, especially high-frequency trading or algorithmic trading, have the potential to generate a large volume of trades within short periods. While these strategies can contribute to market liquidity, they can also introduce volatility and market disruptions if not properly managed. Be mindful of the potential impact of your trading activities and employ risk controls to mitigate adverse effects on market stability.

Self-regulation and professional standards: Consider adhering to self-regulatory standards and professional codes of conduct that govern trading activities. Industry organizations and associations may provide guidelines and best practices to promote ethical behavior and responsible trading practices. Stay informed about evolving standards and engage in ongoing education to ensure your trading activities align with ethical and professional expectations.

By adhering to ethical standards, complying with regulations, and being mindful of the potential impact of advanced trading strategies on market stability, you contribute to maintaining fair and efficient markets while protecting your own reputation and legal standing as a trader.

Don't miss out!

Visit the website below and you can sign up to receive emails whenever Alex Thompson publishes a new book. There's no charge and no obligation.

https://books2read.com/r/B-A-FEPY-RTDKC

Connecting independent readers to independent writers.

Also by Alex Thompson

Side Hustle Success: Unlocking Your Entrepreneurial Potential
Side Hustle Success: The Ultimate Guide to Passive and Financial Freedom
Mastering the Markets: Advanced Trading Strategies for Success and Ethical Trading Practices

About the Author

Alex Thompson is a renowned business professional and trading guru with over 20 years of experience in the financial markets. Known for his expertise in trading strategies and market analysis, Alex has established himself as a trusted advisor and mentor to aspiring traders.

Throughout his career, Alex has successfully navigated the complexities of the financial world and achieved remarkable results. His deep understanding of market dynamics and his ability to identify profitable opportunities have earned him a solid reputation among investors and traders alike.

Alex is passionate about sharing his knowledge and empowering others to achieve their financial goals. He has conducted numerous seminars and workshops, guiding individuals on the path to mastering the market. Through his insightful teachings and practical approach, Alex has inspired countless traders to unlock their potential and achieve consistent profitability.

As an accomplished businessperson, Alex has not only excelled in trading but also made significant contributions to the corporate sector. He has held key executive positions in prominent financial firms, overseeing investment portfolios and driving strategic decision-making.

Beyond his professional achievements, Alex is known for his strong ethical values and commitment to integrity in the financial industry. He believes in fostering a transparent and responsible trading environment, empowering traders to make informed decisions and manage risks effectively.

When he's not analyzing market trends or mentoring traders, Alex enjoys spending time with his family and exploring new investment opportunities. He holds a Bachelor's degree in Finance from a prestigious university and continues to enhance his knowledge through continuous learning and staying updated with the latest market developments.

With his wealth of experience, unwavering dedication, and passion for empowering traders, Alex Thompson is a trusted authority in the world of trading and investing. His book, 'Mastering the Market," is a testament to his expertise and serves as a valuable resource for traders of all levels seeking to navigate the complexities of the financial markets and achieve long-term success.

www.ingramcontent.com/pod-product-compliance
Lightning Source LLC
LaVergne TN
LVHW080037210926
848481LV00011B/3220
9798223053798